ENGLAND'S ELIZABETH

ELIZABETH

ENGLAND'S ELIZABETH

By

MILTON WALDMAN

BOSTON AND NEW YORK

HOUGHTON MIFFLIN COMPANY

The Riverside Press Cambridge

The Riverside Press
CAMBRIDGE · MASSACHUSETTS
PRINTED IN THE U.S.A.

FOR
MARION

The reason people are so difficult to govern is that there is so much policy. The wise ruler will let his people alone and they will let him alone.

LAO-TZE

CONTENTS

FRONTISPIECE PLATE

This portrait, attributed to Marcus Gheeraedts the Younger, is one of the Bowyer Smyth heirlooms and until recently hung at Hill Hall in Essex. The family tradition is that Queen Elizabeth presented it to Sir Thomas Smith, Ambassador to France and her Secretary, for his services. It is now in the National Maritime Museum at Greenwich, to the Trustees of which grateful acknowledgment is made for the right to reproduce.

ENGLAND'S ELIZABETH

Prologue

England was Her Husband

THE death of empires and the fall of great men are the eternally exciting subjects of history as of great literature. No Gibbon has traced with luminous amplitude the mounting line that culminated in the glory of Rome, and even a Motley is more concerned with the rising of the Dutch against a falling Spain than with the rise of the Dutch Republic. Many acute and eloquent pens have recounted the reasons of Napoleon's fall; none has adequately accounted for his presence on the eminence from which he fell. Death, decay, bravely futile struggle, and Nature's revenge on pride exercise a greater fascination upon that melancholy poet man than fortune and success — doubtless because he distrusts their permanence and his own merit. Yet it may sometimes be instructive and not utterly uninspiring to observe the earlier and more cheerful process whereby a thing came to be born and flourished ere its turn came to wither and die. For that purpose nothing in the annals of nations, no contrast even in that age of spectacular contrasts, can compare as an example with the splendid years during which Elizabeth sat on the throne of England.

At the beginning all was darkness and despair. The hopelessness that prevailed in her realm at the new Queen's accession was complete and universal. To all were visible the bankruptcy of the State and the weakness of its arms;
the

the taxes and loans and worthless currency; the poverty of the people, their fear of their enemies abroad, their hatred of the Government and of one another; the inexperience of the Queen and her despised position before the world, a position so low that her very life seemed to depend on obedience to the ambassadorial preceptor whom the ruler of Spain had sent over to direct her first faltering steps. For the country as it then existed the Ambassador de Feria saw no possible hope of recovery, let alone a sustained march to a first place amongst the nations.

Forty-four years later the reign of Elizabeth ended. The throne she vacated by death on March 26, 1603, was beyond all dispute the most powerful on earth. Of England's two enemies the one, France, was clinging to her for help, and the other had been beaten to his knees. Her ships had sailed into all seas and penetrated the forbidden areas of the New World as if Spanish guns had been Indian arrows and Papal edicts parochial sermons. Everywhere abroad as far as Moscow and Constantinople, amongst the pirates of the Barbary Coast and the savages of the Indies, was the greatness of England acknowledged.

At home the transformation was equally striking. England's trade was incomparably the largest in the world, her shippers the most active, her credit the soundest. English money was the one currency worth its face value; elsewhere forty years of war, ruined trade, and desperate borrowing had proved again that figures, though plainly stamped on coin or paper, can lie. One could scarcely ride a dozen miles through the countryside without hearing the sound of saw and hammer cheerily putting together that immense and splendid company of Elizabethan country houses — the infallible sign that a land knows itself to be rich and secure. What remained of party hatreds was expressed in taunts on the floor of the Commons or metrically ingenious insults in the popular broadsheets instead of in guerrilla warfare on
the

the highways and the monotonous cadence of the headsman's axe. Taxes were so low as to excite the astonished envy of visitors, rents had been kept down during an era of rising prices, and unemployment was disappearing as the result of the manufacturing industries which had newly sprung up during the reign.

André Hurault, the Sieur de Maisse, who arrived in London in November, 1597, thirty-nine years almost to a day after de Feria, observed these facts and reported them to his master, King Henry IV of France. He described the 'magnificent sight' he saw on coming from Greenwich to London, 'the number of ships which lie at anchor, insomuch as for two leagues you see nothing but ships that serve as well for traffic as for war.' Five hundred could be assembled if needed, he learned, 'well-armed and well-maintained.' For the rest he looked into the civil state of England, contrasted it with that of the Continent, and reported it was 'more than any realm rich and abounding.'

It hardly seems possible that these two ambassadors can be describing the same country — de Feria, who arrived in 1558 to impart the King of Spain's instructions to Elizabeth, and de Maisse, who came in 1597 to obtain her instructions for Henry. What had happened in the mean time to convert four million frightened, distracted people into a mighty nation, capable of nourishing a civilization which will forever illuminate the map of time and of evoking an Empire which would one day reach to the uttermost spaces of the earth? What, if anything, who, if anyone, was responsible for that transformation?

Some, chiefly the poets, say it was a miracle, or an infinite series of miracles. But that kind of explanation is not acceptable to reason. It is not within the compass of ordinary human faith to believe in the consistent intervention of the divine power in practical worldly affairs. There may have been something miraculous in the wind from the east that scattered on the sturdy soil of the Middle Ages the seeds
                                                              which

which brought forth the exuberant blossoms of the Renaissance. At least it is impossible to explain the process and the results in terms of human knowledge or experience. But it is not beyond the scope of the mind to attempt to discover why, as that wind blew westward, the virile Italian city-states became the despised victims and toadies of the other Latin peoples; why Spain was unable to hold the dazzling heritage of Ferdinand and Isabella; why France could not maintain that proud integrity which made her the first of Western nations; and why England, which in 1558 it was expected 'would be another Savoy' for her neighbours to squabble over, should instead have risen to a place where she not only ruled over a large part of mankind during the ensuing four hundred years, but within the next forty wrote in blood and ink an epic that will survive so long as this planet is tenanted by men.

Others, principally the historians, give the credit for the magnificent structure of state that arose between 1558 and 1603 to the Queen's ministers, to Cecil, Bacon, Walsingham, even Leicester. To support this theory the scholar dives into seas of old paper and emerges with a mutilated sentence which, when decently laid out in the semblance of a fact, proves that the Queen was a liar, a miser, a weakling, and a fool; that she cheated her friends, starved her sailors, could not make up her mind or had no mind to make up. Everything she did was wrong, everything she said crooked, and only the imperturbable wisdom of her honest ministers saved her from disaster. Yet they acknowledge that she was a woman of imperious will, in whose person was concentrated greater power than had ever before or has ever since attached to an English sovereign. Her advisers were appointed and dismissed at her pleasure, and it was as impossible for any of them to venture on a course without her sanction as for an act to become law without her consent. So we are presented with the paradox of an autocrat whose creatures forced upon her a tremendous achievement, each step of which

which was contrived with her knowledge but without her understanding.

It is too fantastic. Machiavelli, who studied the art of government in the council-chamber instead of in libraries, would have exposed the absurdity of it in a sentence: 'Good counsels, whencesoever they come, are born of the wisdom of the prince, and not the wisdom of the prince from good counsels.' Incidentally Elizabeth knew her Machiavelli: 'they call me the Florentine' was one of her boasts. It is a pity that the author of 'The Prince' did not know her — he would have had a satisfactory heroine instead of a second-rate hero for his little masterpiece.

It is true that Elizabeth was borne into power by the group of politicians who supplied her principal ministers. But on the day of her accession, as an inexperienced young woman of twenty-five, she took the reins in her hand, and held them until the weariness and pain of approaching death relaxed her crippled old fingers. No minister was ever indispensable to her, but her death would have meant mortal as well as political extinction to them. Time and again her advisers betrayed her in matters of policy and money, lost their heads in moments of danger, and quarrelled so violently that only her reconciling, dominant presence enabled the Government to be carried on. More than one raised armed rebellion against her, but it was always she who survived, more unassailable than before, to pronounce clemency or doom at her undisputed will.

She knew men far better than any man knew — or ever will know — her. Some she loved, some she trusted, but they were not the same, and no man could ever say that she had yielded him complete trust of either heart or brain. From the isolation of her throne, a cold and lonely pinnacle, she could issue commands but not yield confidences, distribute rewards but never share responsibilities. Her servants bowed before her with news from the shires or from foreign capitals: she heard, discussed, stormed, swore great oaths, ordered,

retracted,

retracted, contradicted herself — but in the end it was her will that was the will of England, on her decision was hazarded England's fate.

Elizabeth has been out of favour with historians and their readers, for a very long time, ever since romantic yearning took the place of common sense as a guide to historical judgment. The romantic age repudiated her because she could not be made to conform to its idea of a heroine. It was easier to tingle the spine with the simple nobility of Sidney's death or the splendid futility of Grenville's. It was possible to forget that Shakespeare quarrelled over money and that Spenser crawled after pensions, for, lost in the music of their verse, one might recover the sweet delusion that man is divine.

But it was Elizabeth's business to live, not to die; to act, not to write. It was her task to provide for her four million subjects so that any of them could die as he chose without danger of the rest, or compose verses if he could without danger to himself. For thirty years of her reign it was in the highest degree probable that if she died the State would collapse. In no part of it could she have indulged in romantic adventure without jeopardizing the welfare of her people. Whatever offences she committed against the immortal canons she may possibly have had to expiate elsewhere: we mortals have the right to judge her only by the measure of six short words — the safety and greatness of England. All else is irrelevant.

Her lies may be granted and, if necessary, deplored. She was admittedly not too scrupulous in the means she used to keep the enemies within from tearing the country limb from limb or the enemies without from trampling it into the sea. But it so happened that even when she told the truth nobody believed her. For when half the royalty of Europe wanted to marry her and she quite dishonestly encouraged them, she warned each in turn that she would never marry, since she was already married and her husband was England. She

was

was telling the truth, but no man who heard her had the wit to see it. One of her subjects might have understood, but he was only an actor-manager who had not the privilege of conversation with princes.

England was her husband. Perhaps the reason she arouses more curiosity than passion is that it is hard to get excited about a successful marriage. She was merely a good wife, whose superlative intellect, feminine suspicion and unscrupulousness, thrifty management and unfaltering courage aided and guided her consort to conspicuous success in the world. She indulged in no heroics — an omission to be thankful for in a helpmate but depressing in a heroine. No man ever killed himself or flung away a kingdom for her sake. She swore too boisterously, laughed too readily, talked too wittily and thought too subtly to inspire Tennyson to a ballad or Swinburne to a drama. But she happened to possess the particular talents required to make England the secure repository of the Elizabethan Age.

Chapter I

The Troubled Inheritance

IN THE early morning of November 17, 1558, Mary Queen of England died and left to her half-sister Elizabeth the shakiest throne in Europe.

It was the unhappiest legacy that ever fell to an English sovereign. The country was prostrate under famine and plague. Four million wretched and sullen people, maddened by a sense of betrayal, were on the verge of taking up arms against one another in the belief, not altogether unsound, that religious factional differences were at the root of their troubles. The great mediæval empire that aforetime extended from the Cheviots to the Pyrenees had in that year shrivelled to its smallest size since the coming of the Conqueror, and the island power that had once thrown its shadow over the whole Continent was itself in the shadow of imminent national extinction.

The immediate cause of the general misery was the war in France, since the previous month suspended under a truce. That war, an especially violent outbreak of the long struggle between Valois and Hapsburg for the domination of Europe, had been none of England's business; most Englishmen disliked it at the beginning and all loathed it before the end. But the Queen of England was married to the Prince of Spain, who in the course of the struggle succeeded his father as Philip II, and her country followed his into the conflict as a matter of course. The greater ally won, the smaller lost; a few months after the overwhelming Spanish victory at Saint Quentin, England miserably handed over Calais, her last Continental possession, to the French. It was the deepest humiliation that English pride had ever suffered, and it cost the government the little that was yet left of the people's faith.
To

To satisfy her husband and ally's demands, Mary had emptied the exchequer, ruined the country's credit, and completed the debasement of the currency, that iniquitous system of governmental cheating so ably exploited by her father and grandfather. Spanish emissaries had come over from Brussels and gone off with money and yet more money until the English themselves marvelled at the ability of these haughty visitors to extract blood from stones. In the five years of Mary's reign public expenditure had multiplied six times, yet the unheard-of taxes imposed to meet it had fallen short by forty per cent, and the Government was frantically offering fourteen per cent abroad for foreign loans to meet its current needs. But taxes had already been so piled on taxes and loans on loans, English money had become such a synonym of contempt, that not even a usurer with a turn for speculation would any longer lend on an English bond.

Unlike most of the country's Continental wars, this one had extended its ravages to the ordinary life of the people. England was still almost entirely agricultural and pastoral, dependent on the export of food and wool for its prosperity; the manufactures which the next generation was to build up for future ages, through a wise though crude system of protection and the misfortunes of its neighbours, had not yet come into being. Devastated markets had thrown England's exportable surplus back on her hands; her mercantile ships, having nothing to carry and being able to count on only the most nominal protection from an inadequate navy when they did venture forth, rotted in the harbours; while the state of the currency and of the nation's credit completed the ruin of its commerce. The countryside was rapidly sinking back into a mediæval landscape of sullen fortresses and filthy hovels. The young men fled from it into the cities, where the only alternative to starvation was robbery. These fugitives were augmented by the soldiers returning from France, and the two together made up that army of 'stalwart rogues' which was the terror of the townsfolk and the insoluble

uble problem of the magistrates. Hunger and hopelessness on the land, hunger and turbulence in the cities, describes in brief the state of England as Mary left it at her death.

No people will put up with such a state of affairs for long unless their spirit be broken or their faith in their institutions seasoned and strong. The English were anything but supine, and there existed for them as yet no institution that commanded their affection or allegiance, not even the State. Least of all, perhaps, the State. It was above all the Government in London that they blamed for their misfortunes, for the extortions and the persecutions, the coins that should have been silver and were lead, the needless war and its humiliating defeats, the subservience to foreign interests and the indifference to England's. They hated the Queen who had delivered their bodies to Spain and tried to deliver their souls, by burning those bodies if necessary, to Rome. They were disgusted with the Parliament whose members, in order to save their private properties as allotted under the settlement of Henry VIII, had acquiesced in the horrible cruelties that sealed the reconciliation with the Holy See.

The sacrifices had all been for nothing. Reconciliation had not brought peace nor the vast expenditure on armament security. The poor who would not accept the official religion had been burnt; the rich had fled into exile abroad or into hiding at home, so depriving the country of many of her wisest and strongest servants when she most needed them. The crushing subsidies for the war had not only not served to save Calais, but had been spent without the smallest regard for the country's own safety. The once proud navy was unfit for sea (as England's impatient ally learned to his disappointment), and the army was contemptible — 'You have neither money, men, armour, practice in war nor good captains,' was the taunt of Philip II's chief agent of extortion, the Count de Feria, to Sir Thomas Challoner, the English ambassador in Brussels, who did not even attempt to contradict him. The all-important Border fortress at Berwick, the

lock

lock on the 'postern gate,' the first defence against a French invasion by way of Scotland, had fallen into such disrepair that a French officer reported that it could be taken by a single company of infantry. In a world where religious hatreds and commercial jealousies were preparing a century of enthusiastic destruction, England, so vital an element to whoever would master the Continent, lay utterly unprotected.

Vital, yet not in herself important. In the political calculations of Europe, England was simply half an island dependent for life on the protection of a friendly neighbour against the hostile neighbour who owned the other half. 'To make a hard comparison,' wrote one of Mary's agents abroad, 'England may be likened to a bone thrown between two dogs.'

The friendly neighbour was the Spanish Empire, an assortment of states, cities, provinces, and colonies sprawled diffusely across the earth and connected by no stronger tie than the reluctant payment of taxes to the same king. In 1491, the year that Elizabeth's father was born, it had consisted of three small Iberian kingdoms lightly knotted together by a marriage service. What one marriage had begun other marriages carried on. The daughter of Ferdinand and Isabella married a Hapsburg, and the Hapsburgs were the most accomplished practitioners of matrimony for profit the world has ever known. A well-disciplined infantry consolidated the gains of those well-planned weddings, and by the middle of the sixteenth century the King in Madrid was the Emperor in Vienna, as well as King in Naples, Duke in Milan, Count-Regent in Brussels, and little less than the Deity to several million red men in America. Though Charles V had resigned the Imperial Crown in 1555, Austria still remained in the family, entitled to support as long as she did not compromise herself too openly with the Lutheran princes of the Rhine. And the year before his abdication Charles had arranged another marriage which made his son Philip King-Consort of England.

The

The hostile neighbour was France, the oldest nation of the West, enlightened, aggressive, and bursting with ambition for which she had insufficient scope. Wherever she turned, to the south in the Pyrenees, to the east in Burgundy, to the north in Flanders and England, to the west in the Americas, she saw the glum face of the Hapsburg sentinel warning her off. She made trouble wherever she could, especially in Italy, where the Popes, none too pleased with the importance of the Church's Eldest Son in Madrid, now and then lent her an unreliable hand, but there was more loss than gain in quarrelling over the mercurial Italians. What France particularly wanted was access to the rich free markets of Northern and Central Europe, for which Antwerp was the chief port and the Rhine the principal highway; but Spain, by virtue of her proprietorship of the Netherlands, effectively barred her from both. On the other hand, since she could prevent communication between Spain and the Low Countries by land, her enemy's richest estate was only useful to him so long as the English Channel was open. One side of it already belonged to France; if she could control the other, the Narrow Seas would be closed to Spanish shipping, the Netherlands isolated, and ultimately the whole of Spanish dominion in Central Europe rolled up like a carpet and tossed over the Pyrenees — with obvious consequences to Castilian empire in Italy and across the Atlantic.

These were elementary and unchanging facts which Charles V and Henry II of France grasped as thoroughly as, in other times and under other conditions, did William III, Marlborough, Louis XIV, Pitt, and Napoleon. Charles showed his appreciation of them by sending the dutiful Philip to answer to his banns in Winchester Cathedral in July of 1554; and Henry had them equally clearly in mind when he supervised the marriage of his heir Francis to Mary Stuart in Notre-Dame de Paris in April of 1558. For Mary was Queen of Scotland, a country which provided the readiest facility for a military expedition into England, and she had a widely recognized

cognized claim to the English Crown which Henry, a devoted father-in-law, intended to enforce as soon as he was free from his present preoccupations. In the mean time he laboured to make the Scots good subjects of the French Crown by bestowing their offices on Frenchmen, filling their garrisons with French troops, and spending their money to pay for these benefits.

Yet, unenviable as was the portion of the little country entangled in the rivalry of the two larger, England was overhung by an even greater danger than the commercial and dynastic jealousies of the Continental giants. There was a force in Europe still mightier than either, and though its material resources were uncertain and its leadership ambiguous, it was capable on occasion of erasing frontiers to procure men and money for its purposes. The Catholic Church had been successfully defied by the Lutheran insurgents during the first half of the century and even amongst the faithful its word was no longer secular law. Yet it still commanded throughout most of Europe a deeper love in the hearts of ordinary men or women than state or dynasty. The great rebellion had run its course, the evils that had instigated it were being purged away, the Counter-Reformation was now poised to sweep heresy out of the world and all Europe once more into the embrace of the Universal Church. For the purposes of this crusade the ambitions of kings and the passions of their people marched together, with the result that England, unless she conformed, might find herself the object of hostile interest, not from France or Spain alone, but from both together with half a dozen other enemies thrown in for good measure.

But if any one thing was sure, it was that England would not continue Catholic without a civil war. Too many Englishmen had suffered from the Marian fury to forgo the first opportunity of change and revenge, and the men that most fiercely clamoured for them were the strongest in the country, the merchants and the ablest of the landed gentry.

Resentment

Resentment had gone deep: though the majority of the
common people still called themselves Catholics, yet, as the
Count de Feria significantly observed, when Calais fell
Englishmen stopped going to church. It could be taken as
certain that when Rome sent in her demand Englishmen
would respond by falling upon one another, and the result
would only be determined after the country had been made
the battlefield of the one kind of war that is ever fought
without pity. It was conceivable that all factions might
unite to repel a secular enemy, but in a religious war neither
Catholics nor Protestants would hesitate to call in their
foreign sympathizers to help persuade their countrymen to
their own way of thinking.

Such was the inheritance and these the prospects of the
young woman who waited for news at Hatfield House,
twenty-five miles from the capital, on that dismal November
morning. She was a Queen, but of a country unlikely to
tolerate any ruler for very long, head of a Government
which the governed hated, possessor of a title which enemies
far stronger than herself denied.

Her very succession was largely a matter of luck. She
had twice been disinherited by a complaisant Parliament,
once in her father's time and once in her sister's. She had
finally come to the throne because to the discontented she
was the symbol of opposition and because to the King of
Spain she was the only available alternative to Mary Stuart,
future Queen of his enemy France. An ironic stroke of luck,
therefore, made her the simultaneous choice of the most
violent Protestants in England and the most powerful
Catholic in the world. Had France and Spain for the moment
been at peace there was every probability that they would
have united to keep her from the succession.

It is true that her people greeted her as if she had been
God's choice unanimously ratified by themselves. When
she entered the capital on the twenty-third of November,
the bells rang and the guns boomed, the crowd on the line
of

of procession cheered itself hoarse and strewed flowers on
her path before going off to get drunk round the bonfires
that roared in the various open spaces of the city. But this
was precisely the greeting they had given five years earlier
to the woman who now lay unmourned in the cold and
scented silence of Saint James's Chapel. It was less the
present than the past that inspired Elizabeth's ovation —
the memory of Henry's reign, now translated by distance into
glory, and the near memory of Mary's, still offensive with
the odours of burning human flesh in Smithfield Market.
More dispassionate observers — diplomats in London on
their country's business, the soothsayers with professional
reputations at stake — united in giving her a short and anything but a merry reign. Just one chance was conceded her:
if she married a strong man, strong both in himself and the
support he could bring from one of her powerful neighbours,
if she had a son to carry on the dynasty and put her subjects
in better hope and humour, she might keep the peace and
her throne. But the chance was regarded even by her well-
wishers as slim.

Of the heiress herself the world knew very little: hitherto
she had been only a name and a minor factor in the political
reckoning. The sharp-eyed diplomats in London had of late,
as Mary's death became certain, mentioned her with
greater frequency in their reports, but their information
was almost entirely at second hand. They had heard that
she was exceptionally well educated, with a gift for languages
and a taste for music, simple in her habits and clothing,
adroit at disengaging herself from anything that might
involve her in trouble. The nobility of England knew little
more; in her relations with them she had preferred the
demure safety of the background. To the populace she was
a pale slender figure whom they cheered on her rare appear-
ances in public in order to show their dislike of her sister.
But of the qualities of mind and character that she brought
to her office no living person could speak with certainty.

What

What she knew of the world was little enough, but that little she had learnt from need and danger. The first third of her life had been as empty of friends as the rest of it was to be. When she was three her father had finished with her mother in his own drastic fashion and until he died took so little notice of her that her guardians were reduced to supplicating his ministers for enough to keep her clothed and fed. At fifteen she had taken the eye of Henry Seymour, Lord High Admiral of England and husband of Henry VIII's widow, Catherine Parr. This first experience of masculine attention cost her her reputation and very nearly her head, for Seymour set in motion an interesting scheme involving the seduction of the young Princess and his own subsequent elevation to the throne as her husband. His ambitions clashed, however, with those of his brother, the Lord Protector Somerset. Since the Protector was the stronger, the Admiral went to the block and the Princess to prison.

A whole battery of lawyers were briefed by the Government to find out how much she knew of Seymour's treason. From Elizabeth they discovered nothing: terrified but haughty the girl fought back, denying, evading, and seizing with extraordinary instinct on the prosecution's weakness. The baffled lawyers turned on her confidential servant, Mrs. Ashley, and extorted a confession which touched Elizabeth's honour, but did not prove her guilt. It was not enough on which to convict an heir-presumptive to the throne and the case was dropped by the prosecutors.

Not so by the defence. The prisoner wrote Somerset a letter in her beautiful Italian hand pointing out that, since he had been unable to convict her, it was his duty to remove all suspicion in the eyes of the world by a proclamation of her innocence. It was a reasonable request — policy forbade the Government to allow an unsupported charge of treason to rest on a possible Queen — and Somerset complied. Whereupon the young woman, or rather child, since her

cheeks

chccks still retained the plumpness of infancy, demanded the release of Mrs. Ashley on the ground that, since she herself as principal had been acquitted, her suspected accomplice must necessarily be innocent as well. The Protector was forced to yield on that point too, and the rout of the forces of State was complete.

Seven years later the performance was repeated. This time it was Wyatt's conspiracy, designed to marry Elizabeth to William Courtenay, Earl of Devon, heir to the White Rose, and set them on the throne in the place of Mary, which brought her to the Tower. Again the lawyers cross-examined, bullied, and threatened; again Elizabeth, white-faced but ˙undaunted, defied them to prove that she had lent any countenance to the plot. There was enough evidence to convict her twice over, according to the rules of the time in cases of treason, had she once flinched or told two inconsistent lies, but her wits and her courage were not less at twenty-two than they had been at fifteen. This time thc Queen's husband, Philip of Spain, interceded, partly out of policy, partly, as was generally thought, out of a more tender regard, to call off her persecutors and not improbably to save her life. Thereafter she spent her time in the politer confinement of country houses, perfecting her languages and keeping free from the various marriages which her exasperated sister was trying to arrange in order to get rid of her.

There was naturally an intense curiosity to see thio mysterious girl of twenty-five whom Fate had so dramatically lifted from obscurity into the glare of a throne. All the polite world in London — peers, bishops, statesmen, diplomats, whoever could claim the privilege by right of rank, place, or fashion — crowded to see hcr first State reception on the night of November 23 at Lord North's house, the old Carthusian monastery 'close by the horse market,' to observe and report under cover of paying their respects.

Through

Through the recorded impressions of that brilliant scene
there runs a unanimity of approval like a murmur of refined
applause. The chrysalis had emerged a full-grown butterfly,
the obscure Princess had stepped forth from her rustic
captivity in all respects a Queen, as different from the
Milady Elizabeth of Woodstock and Hatfield as the prim
grey frocks of her girlhood were from the splendour of
brocade and gems she would wear henceforth to the day
of her death. She stood on the steps of the dais radiant,
alert, and completely mistress of herself. She was 'above
middle height and of well-proportioned figure,' her movements and manner uniting 'stately grace with frank con-
descension.' The pale oval of her face, 'pleasing rather
than beautiful,' was surmounted by 'golden-coloured hair...
more reddish than yellow, curled in appearance naturally.'
Her eyes were light blue, 'of exceptional beauty,' her lips
thin but finely modelled, her nose high and slightly aquiline.
Most particularly was she vain of her long white hands,
which she used with conscious elegance and for which she
exacted, and sincerely received, the tribute of everyone
with whom she spoke. / To the older and more discerning
eyes fixed upon her that night she recalled, in her vitality
and charm, in the glint of gold in her hair as in the gay
humour of her expression, above all in that indefinable
quality of kingliness in her presence, that great King and
all-too-easily-forgiven villain her father.

She gave them also, in the course of this ceremony, a
glimpse of the quality of her mind. Spain's ambassador,
the Count de Feria, was there, a dark proud stalwart man,
one to inspire awe, for it was not improbable that he
would be set by the world's mightiest King to rule over
England as his viceroy when circumstances should have
overwhelmed the heroine of the present occasion. The
ambassador had not meant, as he confessed to his master,
to talk of business on this evening, since it was neither the
time nor the place. But Elizabeth's cordial response to
his

his words of good-will encouraged him to proceed beyond his intention, and to add a gentle hint that she would be well advised to please King Philip by being 'very careful of religious affairs.'

It was an awkward moment: she was being asked to stand and deliver, at the threshold of her reign and on the spur of the moment, a declaration of religious policy. If she answered as the ambassador wished, she would alarm that large body of her subjects who were her chief supporters; if she declined, she would offend her one powerful ally abroad. Whichever answer she made would reverberate with unforeseeable consequences through England and Europe.... Only Elizabeth seemed innocently unaware of her dilemma. Smiling down at the attentive Spaniard, while a thousand ears bent to catch her words, she agreed with him that 'it would indeed be bad of her to forget God, who had always been so good to her.' The tension relaxed, the festivities continued, and the dissatisfied de Feria withdrew to write his master in Brussels that 'this seemed to me rather an equivocal reply,' though only what one might have expected from 'a young lass who, although sharp, is without prudence.'

She would have need of that sharpness, that power of equivocation, if she was to succeed in governing in such a time as the sixteenth century. The Renaissance demanded of rulers qualities such as had not been seen in Europe since Gregory VII organized the political supremacy of the Church nearly five hundred years before. A new world had been born whose outstanding characteristic was the sovereignty of the State, and the monarch who was not prepared to reign in the grand manner could no longer count on habit and the prestige of Rome to keep his country whole and himself on his throne. The feeble decentralized little groups that had lived and quarrelled in hand-to-mouth fashion under the supervision of the Universal Church were coalescing into nations as faith grew weaker and the sense of community of race, language, and interest stronger.

stronger. The consolidation of these units and their battle
for survival against the similar units, expanding in a world
grown suddenly too small, demanded for each a quality
of leadership utterly different from the traditional, almost
nominal, suzerainty of the feudal system that was passing
away.

Habit had fixed the loyalties of mediæval people, the
Church commanded their primary obedience, religion em-
braced their ultimate ambitions. That was all changing
swiftly. The Church had in recent times demonstrated its
unfitness to rule itself, let alone the whole earth. In an age
of restless and energetic expansion it had failed to provide
the ordinary man with the security to himself, his family, and
his chattels which is the first duty of government. As riches
poured in from the East and the New World, the need for
that security grew more imperative and men began to look
elsewhere for it. The Renaissance had pushed back all
horizons and exposed the existence of wealth and of ideas
more immediately desirable than a starved plot of ground
on earth and a shining seat in heaven. And so common
men everywhere, even those who gladly entrusted their
salvation to Christ's Vicar, rallied to the secular princes of
their own blood in the hope of appropriating for themselves
the material and spiritual advantages that could only be
obtained by fierce competition with the greedy subjects
of other princes.

Thus there fell on the ruler a heavy and unfamiliar
responsibility. He was now expected to do the work that
the defiant and practically independent barons had hitherto
done for him. Though the old tradition and authority had
become useless, there had not yet grown up a system of
parliamentary cabinets to divide the responsibility with
him or take it off his shoulders altogether. Parliaments
were still embryonic, their powers limited and their prestige
(except at certain times in England) small. In their enthusiasm over their new national States, people were disposed
                                                          to

to throw all power into the hands of the visible Prince, with the sole proviso that he use it for their benefit, and even that proviso was largely cancelled by the theory of the divine right of kings which sprang out of the reaction against rule from Rome. The political doctrine of the sixteenth century pretty well defined ruler and State, the Prince's wish and the public law, in synonymous terms.

So the same process that gave the sovereign such high responsibility also made him almost totally irresponsible. Unless a long-suffering people called him to account, he initiated, decided, and compelled according to his temperament and capacity, made and enforced laws, concluded treaties and fought wars with no restraint except the advice of such ministers as he voluntarily kept round his person. This at least was the theory. The ministers might in practice be strong and crafty enough to wield the sceptre themselves, but it was from their master that they derived their being, and if he was a tool instead of an autocrat it was by his own wish or through his own weakness.

To satisfy within reason the desires of several million people while keeping them moderately in order is under any circumstances the most exacting task that a human being can undertake, but at no time in history could it have been more difficult than in the sixteenth century. By the standards of the twentieth century, with its organized morality, timorous scepticism, and slow-moving mass action, nearly every sixteenth-century man or woman of sufficient importance to have left a record of his existence seems more or less mad. What else is there to make of people who could apply the most tortuous cunning to the daily affairs of business or State, and remain unaware as children of the effect of their acts on tomorrow? Who could challenge the truths sanctified by a thousand years of belief and dumbly accept the nostrums of quacks for their ailments and the advice of astrologers as revelation? Who could sacrifice all they held dear for a religious belief and cheat their neigh-

bours

bours by most sacred oaths in God's name? Who would retreat in terror from a sensible action because a flock of crows flew the wrong way and assault with delight an enemy ten times their number on the mere rumour of fantastic gain? Hard as it is to govern the sluggish, half-educated masses of modern democracy by any process of reason, it was infinitely harder to apply any rules of logic to those wild, treacherous, superstitious, crafty, ungovernable individualists who filled the markets, armies, ships, and offices of the high Renaissance.

Their gusto, their casuistry, their inconsistencies, are beyond understanding; they can only be allowed for. One reads that those excellent Catholic Kings, Charles V and Philip II, spent their lives and Spain's fortune in attempting to restore Europe to Papistry, yet both made war against the Pope and stood under sentence of excommunication. Charles assaulted Rome, captured the Pope and held him in strict confinement for a heavy ransom — then sent to all his loyal subjects throughout the broad provinces of the Empire a command that they should adjourn to their places of worship and pray for the release of the Holy Father! One can comprehend the fact that, although all Christendom execrated the Moslems, Catholic France and Protestant England yet made alliances with them against Spain. That is called statecraft. But what is one to make of a report sent by Elizabeth's envoy to Morocco, in which that sturdy islander reported to his superior, Sir Francis Walsingham, that he had conversed with the black Emperor and found him a most excellent Protestant? The ruler who based his policy on the actions of people like these, whether enemies, friends, or subjects, had to have more than good sense — he could scarcely do without a clairvoyant instinct that could make reason out of unreason, logic out of bedlam.

Two other characteristics of the time made that instinct indispensable: its political morality and the quality of its available information. Minds changed quickly, news travelled

travelled slowly. On the average, eight days was required for an answer to a letter sent from London to Brussels, a fortnight for Paris, six weeks for Madrid or Vienna. Reports from agents in those countries were therefore often out of date by the time of their arrival — and even when they were up to date they were only too likely to have taken on colour from their writers' religious prejudices or susceptibility to the universally prevalent bribery. Yet on the strength of what those dispatches contained it was necessary to decide on a course of action towards people capable of changing their minds half a dozen times over in the interval. Since the ruler was irresponsible and the opinion of his subjects on most matters either unimportant or impossible to obtain, one's ally might become an enemy within the week, might be attacking one's troops on the same field on which by previous tidings he had been fighting at their side against the common enemy.

Expediency, very short-sighted expediency, was the general rule of sixteenth-century conduct, and probably the wisest where nothing was certain except violent and unexpected change. The truth of today might be the lie of tomorrow, and the easiest way of meeting a new situation was by inventing another lie. Machiavelli, the keenest and most honest student of his century, wrote, 'Our experience has been that those princes who have done great things have held good faith of little account, and have known how to circumvent the intellect of men by craft, and in the end have overcome those who have relied upon their word.' The Duke of Alba, as conspicuous in Spain's counsels as on her battlefields, laid it down as a principle that 'convenience is the measure of obligation even between Christian States, far more therefore between a Christian and a heretic.' The matter under discussion was the assassination of Queen Elizabeth.

In a game played under such rules suspicion could never rest and credulity was a cardinal vice. One could trust
one's

one's dearest friend only in so far as his sudden desertion had already been allowed for; one dared not assume him to be unselfish, loyal, or honest unless one was also to believe him a fool. No doubt these are considerations that no statecraft can entirely ignore, but at least in modern practice, with news moving swiftly and opinion forming slowly, the statesman can proceed with reasonable reliance on his facts. But in the sixteenth century he had to guess, and how well he guessed depended on the stuff of which his brains were made.

No wonder then that the world doubted whether Elizabeth's young lifetime of classical studies in the country had sufficiently equipped her for survival against hardened adversaries whose experience and resources so greatly exceeded hers.

Chapter II

The Heiress Takes Over

THE writing of history and the making of it are so different. In the history book a sovereign or a statesman comes into power in a new chapter, is confronted with a set of problems, solves them well or badly according to his talents, and passes on leaving his successor to take up the next set in the following chapter. But in no department of life are these tidy methods of the schoolroom less applicable than in politics.

To the statesman the fresh start is unknown. He cannot scrape colours off his canvas, erase words or notes from paper, stop his ship to make repairs, or halt production to reorganize his factory. He must take hold of a vast, complicated, and living society composed of millions of men and women whose habits, traditions, affections, and means of livelihood make them the enemies of experiment and even suspicious of change. If conditions are so bad that the majority believe reform to be necessary, the individual or the class prefers it to be conducted elsewhere — few consider themselves so badly off that they will welcome disturbance in their own particular routine. The statesman must take hold so gently that the State will feel no more ill effects than seasick passengers when the wheel of the ship passes to another hand, and insinuate his reforms so unobtrusively that they will seem to be renovation rather than innovation. Unless in time of serious national danger the consequence of drastic change is discontent, resistance, economic disaster, and civil insurrection. This principle, sufficiently binding on the official elected to carry out specific promises, is a very law of nature to the hereditary ruler who succeeds at the whim of death instead of by the
explicit

explicit mandate of a majority in the State. For him continuity is everything, the whole reason for his being — 'The King is dead, Long live the King.'

That much at least Elizabeth seems to have derived from her study of the Greek poets and the Christian Fathers; that and an appreciation of time as the sleeping but dominant partner in human affairs. Perhaps the knowledge had to some extent been fortified by her small experience. Never, even in the darkest moments of her unhappy youth, had she doubted that she would one day be a Queen. Twice had she been offered short cuts by way of plots, and both times had she refused to consider them; twice, nevertheless, had she been put in danger of her life and twice disinherited, yet time, which modifies circumstances and memories with equal ease, had seen her through. She had learnt that to act prematurely was to hustle time and so forfeit the help it could give. It was a lesson whose application was to cost her much of her credit, but at least she applied it with her eyes open: 'I have let time pass,' she would one day write in explanation of her remarkable success, 'which I generally find helps more than reasoning.'

She took hold of affairs with a gentle and steady hand, ignoring alike the drastic expedients demanded by the partisans of the one side and the panicky prophecies of those of the other. The ambassador of Spain came to dictate to her on the strength of his master's help when her succession was in doubt: she replied with firm courtesy that she acknowledged no obligation for her throne except to God and the will of her people. The Protestant leaders exhorted her to cleanse the realm at once of Papistry, while their followers began the familiar smashing of Roman relics in the churches: her answer was a proclamation that for the present the old observances were to be continued and no man was to be molested for his faith; within a few days the disturbances had died down. When she published the names of the Privy Council, the body of ministers through whom

whom she would govern, it was found that eleven of Mary's advisers had been retained and that to them had been added seven of the ablest from amongst the former opposition. It was not an ideal cabinet: but what it lost in vigour through division was more than compensated for by its reassuring balance, and time would cure its principal defects. Some of the old majority conveniently died or dropped out as a sign of disapproval, rising men were given places, and in the end the Queen had an instrument more suited to her purposes.

The chief minister, the first to be sworn into office, was a perfect expression of the spirit of compromise as well as a warning to the astute, which none of them mistook, of the policy of English self-sufficiency which his mistress intended henceforth to follow. William Cecil had been a conspicuous public servant under Henry VIII and Edward VI, yet he had managed — no mean feat — to keep his life and his very considerable property under Mary. Although sharing his countrymen's dislike of foreigners, he had been able to restrain his feelings in deference to Spanish sensibilities; although bred a Protestant, he had conformed to the old religion with just sufficient display of conviction to keep him out of trouble and not enough to disqualify him when the reaction set in.

Commerce and the Reformation had made his family's fortunes; he wanted the one expanded and the other restored, but without upsetting the order of things, for order was at least as important to a new fortune as to an old one. He firmly believed that omelettes could be made without breaking eggs, in politics if not in cookery; and up to a point he was right. Recklessness and extremes appeared to him the diseases of weak minds; caution was his armour and the golden mean his end. He had already been of great service to Elizabeth, standing at her elbow to advise her in the last critical days of Mary's illness, to control opinion in the right quarters, to organize her party in Parliament and

at

at Court. On the morning of November 17 the Lords and Commons had little to do but ratify the proclamation already drawn up by Cecil and adjourn; the new ministers, amongst whom his friends and relatives were not inconspicuous, had already been approved and received their orders to report to their mistress at Hatfield.

From then on until his death Cecil continued to stand at his Queen's elbow. Often she pushed him away with impatience, whereupon he would take to his bed, an old and successful practice of his when things grew uncomfortable, and send her a message that he was ill and would have to resign; then, after a reasonable interval, they would make it up and go on as before. Rivals tried to supplant and even assassinate him; Elizabeth would listen to them, and word would go out that Cecil had at last fallen, but in a short time the rivals would again be growling at a distance and Cecil once more be seen at respectful attention on the right of the throne. He never took a chance, never encouraged a gamble, considered adventure a career for fools and glory the goal of madmen. As he truly said of himself, while he was first minister Epimetheus had more to do than Prometheus. So he survived for forty years, the perfect servant of a woman who preferred not to let her right hand know what her left was doing, and died the founder of a great family with all his dreams satisfied. Of neither Shakespeare, Drake, nor Elizabeth herself can as much be said.

Quietly, without ostentation, the new Queen and her ministers got down to business. The immediate need was money, and it was at once apparent that Elizabeth had inherited from her grandfather, Henry VII, a talent for finance that had skipped his intervening descendants. Perhaps it lighted again on her because of the thrifty aldermanic blood transmitted by her mother. Increased taxes, foreign borrowings, debased currency, all the traditional Tudor devices for raising money, were abhorrent to her, while

while economy was even more of a passion than an expedient. It was the first of a long series of happy coincidences between her people's necessities and her own temperament.

A spendthrift age gaped as economy swept into the most privileged corners. Somnolent officials in court and country suddenly found themselves without jobs, tax-collectors were peremptorily summoned to make good discrepancies in their accounts, the Spanish ally was informed that henceforth he must get along as best he could without English subsidies. Soon English currency, whose value had been going down for nearly three quarters of a century, was shrewdly restored to its face value with an actual profit to the Exchequer, and in a short time it was selling at a premium.

The result was that in the first six months of her reign Elizabeth achieved a reduction of sixty per cent in expenditure compared with the last six months of Mary's. Funds were then remitted to Sir Thomas Gresham, whom Elizabeth had sent to Antwerp on the fifth day of her reign, to pay off a large part of Mary's debts as promised at her accession; and within eighteen months that celebrated financier was joyfully writing home that his Queen's credit was above that of all other princes. Never again till the coming of the Stuarts was England in desperate need of money. When war threatened, as it was soon to do, when arms and ships were wanted, when foreign help had to be bought, the money was always at hand or could be borrowed at low rates — even from the subjects of an enemy State whose ruler could not borrow at all. A great deal of the glitter that surrounds the Elizabethan Age is due to the gold stolen from Spanish treasure ships or vainly hunted in Eldorado — yet that gold bears the same relation in the national economy to the money saved by hard work and good management as the Casino at Monte Carlo does to the Bank of England.

In addition to her debts, Mary had left a war to be liquidated,

dated, a matter that could not unfortunately be dealt
with by close saving and strict auditing. It had been a
typical sixteenth-century conflict, begun for no particular
reason, fought for no definite object, and ended when everybody had grown tired of it. At the beginning the quarrel
had been between the Pope and Spain over Italy; by the
end the dispute between France and England over Calais
was the sole obstacle to peace. Spain, having penetrated
deeply into France, had without doubt won; England,
having been driven off the Continent, had certainly lost;
and the opponent France, having both won and lost, was
willing to give way to the victor but not to the vanquished.
Thus matters stood in October. As Mary's death approached, it was agreed to prolong the truce and adjourn
the peace conference, then sitting at Cambrai, to Cateau-
Cambrésis in February in order to see what the change of
sceptre in England would bring forth.

It was Elizabeth's first test in foreign affairs, and a harder
one could scarcely have been invented for her. There was
no hope of getting the lost town back, for Philip, oppressed
by debt and heresy, obstinately refused to go on with a
struggle from which he had nothing more to gain. Yet to
surrender was to arouse a dangerous bitterness at home:
even Mary, devoted as she was to her husband, had not
dared to obey him in this, for her consent might have cost
her her throne. So she died murmuring that 'her lost jewel
of Calais' would be found graven on her still heart, and
escaped from the predicament by bequeathing it to her
sister.

Whatever solution of the problem Elizabeth expected to
achieve — and there is no evidence that any presented
itself to her mind during the two crowded months that
followed — she did the only thing possible at the beginning,
which was to issue a sonorous announcement that never
for a moment would she consider waiving her people's
claim to their ancient possession. It was sheer bluster, of
                                                    course,

course, as every informed person knew, but whether she
was aware of the fact herself it was impossible to discover.
If she really meant what she said there could be no peace.
Spain might, of course, conclude a separate treaty with
France, and King Philip, weary with overwork and of other
people's perversities, now and then peered down this allur-
ing avenue of escape from his embarrassments. Once a
peace was signed, he could disband the armies that were
eating away his substance and making him afraid to look
his bankers in the face, he could return home to Spain
where he would find the rest he craved and mete out to his
heretics the punishment they required. But if he succumbed
to the temptation it was only too likely that his sister-in-
law would turn about and, for her own safety, enter into
that alliance with the slippery Valois which was the perpetual nightmare of all good Spanish imperialists. There
was nothing for him to do but go on in the hope of ultimately
convincing his sister-in-law that her interests and his peace
of mind came to the same thing.

The actual labour of convincing her he delegated to the
Count of Feria: the importance of the task was in fact his
chief reason for naming this tried confidential minister to
the English embassy. The joy of the Catholics and the
gloom of their opponents at the appointment appeared to
justify Philip's belief that if anyone could manage the new
Queen it would be this adroit and resourceful nobleman.

De Feria accepted his assignment without enthusiasm.
He had already had some experience of the English the
previous summer, when he had come over to collect their
money for the war, and had found them in every way un-
sympathetic. They had given grudgingly, displayed most
inadequate appreciation of Spain's interest in their welfare
and a deplorable tendency to both heterodoxy and disorder:
'they had matter but wanted form' was his terse verdict,
which his contemporaries repeated with admiration. The
only notable exception to his dislike was Jane Dormer, the
young

young lady of sixteen whom he was engaged to marry. His reluctance to reappear at the Court of Saint James's was aggravated by an inner distrust of his King. There could be no more doubt about Philip's devotion to his country than of his orthodoxy, but the ambassador scarcely took the trouble to conceal his conviction that his master went much too far in his toleration of opposition. Shortly after de Feria's arrival he heard that a boatload of heretics were on their way from Flanders to preach in England, and promptly wrote to the King, 'I have decided... to try and seize them... and throw them in the river. I must do it so dexterously and secretly as to give no ground for complaint to the Queen or her people.' But Philip, fearful that even de Feria's dexterity would be insufficient to the occasion, vetoed the suggestion. The ambassador himself would never have allowed Elizabeth to come to the throne in the first place, considering her badly brought up and her friends an ill-chosen assortment of 'young folks, heretics and traitors.' Had he had his way Philip would either have taken the country for himself or made a composition with France in favour of Mary Stuart.

Nevertheless, he threw himself into his task with all his considerable powers. Holding the Queen to be of small account, 'a mere lass,' he attempted to win over the Council by secret bribes. It was a form of persuasion that had always succeeded in the past, indeed did not seem to admit of failure. Nevertheless, the ambassador at once discovered in the ministers a sudden shy reluctance to take his money. The principal ones 'avoid me as if I were the devil,' he wrote irritably, and he was at a loss to understand why. He was soon to learn. Lord William Howard, an old pensioner of Spain, had been appointed chief delegate to the peace conference, and the ambassador, naturally eager to discover the nature of his instructions, hurried to offer a renewal of past favours with the promise of additional favours to come. But Howard hemmed and hawed. At
first

first he accepted with almost excessive gratitude, then declined with evasive explanations. In the end he yielded, telling his benefactor the reason of the delay. He had, he confessed, been uncertain how his Queen would look at a transaction, the whole essence of which was that she was to know nothing about it. So he had screwed up his courage to ask her consent, which she had graciously given. Despite his rage with the servant's scruples, the Spaniard could not but be impressed with the mistress who inspired them: 'she is far more feared,' he reported, 'than her sister ever was.'

To the Queen, therefore, he now addressed himself, but without perceptible success. He offered her jewels, having found that 'she is very fond of having things given her,' but received in return only prettily worded thanks. He tried threats, painting in terrifying colours a picture of what the French would do to her if her contumacy compelled Philip to cut her adrift; she answered haughtily that 'she knew her own resources and her subjects were not so poor that money and arms could not be got.' This was either ignorance or stupidity, the ambassador neither knew nor cared which. In any event there seemed to be no use in arguing with her; in fact, he had already observed that she was too fond of argument for its own sake rather than for the practical conclusions to be arrived at. The only remaining hope, de Feria decided, was to marry her to somebody who would know how to make her obey him.

He gave much thought to this matter, and discussed extensively with his King the merits of various possible husbands. His own choice at length fell on that same King, the one man whom, the Spaniard believed, Elizabeth would not dare treat with her feminine inconsequence. He wrote a tremendously long letter to Brussels inciting Philip to propose. Philip, after four weeks of communion with his conscience and his ministers, replied in mid-January authorizing the royal heart and hand to be laid before the Queen.

She

She acknowledged their offer in terms of unmeasured gratitude and affection, but could not bring herself to accept them; not for a while, at any rate. Marriage was a very serious step, she had not yet made up her mind to it in the abstract, she must have time to think it over. She could only promise that if she took any man to be her lord, her brother-in-law should be preferred over all. It was a form that, with the name left blank, she might have had printed for future use. De Feria dared not press the matter further at the moment: to have insinuated that the marriage was in any way contingent upon her political complaisance would, he recognized, be an uncouth insult to the lady and probably destroy all hope of its consummation. He left the proposal with her and took nothing away that could be construed as a sign that she would relent over Calais.

If de Feria had been privileged to read the instructions he had tried vainly to purchase from Howard, his heart would have been lighter. They make it clear that Elizabeth was playing with him, and not improbable that she had been doing so during the latter part, at least, of his anxious manœuvres. For she had already decided to part with Calais, as Cecil knew and her commissioners were shortly to be informed. But the plans for the religious settlement were now taking shape, and it was imperative to keep Philip worried about Calais lest he worry her about this new and far more dangerous cause of dispute. From the vantage-point of those secret instructions one is privileged to appreciate this her first essay in diplomacy as the poor perplexed Spanish ambassador was not. To him it seemed quite senseless to harry Philip with reproaches for his old promise not to make peace unless Calais were restored, since he had not made peace and Calais could not be restored. There was no apparent meaning in her entering into secret negotiations with the King of France, since she herself kept him informed of their progress. Out of her friendly correspondence with Henry II she derived only some jewels,
which

which she kept, and some remarkable propositions, which she discussed to shreds. Amongst these propositions was one to the effect that Henry should hold Calais only as trustee for the benefit of Elizabeth's grandson and Mary Stuart's granddaughter when these infants should have emerged from the womb of the future and married. Henry himself derived nothing except an insight into Elizabeth's ready command of the French language.

The significance of her reproaches and the negotiations, and of her hundred other devices for delay, was unwittingly supplied by de Feria himself. In March, Philip, frantic at the threatened reformation in England and smarting under the Queen's failure even to answer his proposal of marriage, suggested to the ambassador that she be brought to account for both these injuries. De Feria was even more wroth than his King: yet he strongly advised that Elizabeth should be let alone for the present for fear of antagonizing her and so further postponing the peace. In the following month the Church of England came into being: then only did Elizabeth agree to surrender Calais on the promise of an indemnity of five hundred thousand crowns to be paid in eight years. In May, de Feria, who had come expressly to obtain that agreement, resigned his office with the candid acknowledgment that his mission had been a failure. Spain had her treaty, but England had regained her unity and peace, and the ambassador departed lamenting, 'We have lost a kingdom body and soul.' Before he left he also learned from Elizabeth that she would never marry Philip.

It is impossible to know how much there was of necessity and how much of policy in Elizabeth's final surrender of Calais. All motives of State are mixed and all futures inscrutable. Yet during the next forty years were laid at her feet far greater Continental possessions than Calais, all of which she returned to their bereaved owners over the ravings of her admirals because it did not suit her purpose or her policy to keep them. In those secret colloquies of
early

early 1559 with her ministers is discernible the germ of the instinct which was to become her great policy — and not only hers, but her country's for hundreds of years after she was dead — that the future of England lay away from the Continent of Europe in the distant and yet unexplored spaces of the earth.

In the language of statecraft forever is merely a long time, and an age only the interval between two dramatic events. What chiefly remains of an historical epoch is the residuum it leaves in the imagination of mankind: its political institutions, devised to meet current needs, survive at best as picturesque but uninhabitable ruins. The Elizabethan institutions, like the rest, served their purpose and gave way to others — it cost a revolution and a king's head to remove the Tudor doctrine of royal supremacy from active usage to the quiet dust of the historical archives. But the ecclesiastical edifice that Elizabeth built proved spacious and strong enough to shelter her people against the murderous tempest of religious war which swept down on Europe during the next hundred years, and to stand for unknown hundreds more while empires, dynasties, constitutions, and systems grew up and perished.

Elizabeth herself had no wish to found a new Church. On the contrary, her inclinations, so far as she had any religious feelings at all, were towards a traditional dogmatic creed and the rich beauty of the old ritual. All her life she showed a nostalgic preference for the vestments, candles, music, and incense of the Church she abolished, and it was due to her that they were so largely preserved in the Church for which she was responsible. She was by nature conservative, and the very circumstances which imposed on her the need for change made her the stronger champion of continuity. It seemed to her ridiculous that Christians should slaughter one another over disputed interpretations of their Master's words, and that pig-headed mistrust should prevent
the

the Church and its rebels from healing their murderous schism. 'If there were two Princes in Christendom,' she still maintained long years after the triumph of her own insurgency, 'who had good-will and courage, it would be easy to reconcile the differences in religion, for there was only one Jesus Christ and one faith, and all the rest they disputed about but trifles.'

But she had no choice in the matter. The Roman statesmen, whose contemporary record of imbecility was already sufficiently brilliant, outdid themselves in their treatment of Anne Boleyn's daughter. She was the natural heir in the eyes of the English people, the only surviving daughter of their late lawful King. Yet the Church first fought against recognition of her legitimacy with all its strength, then opposed her accession with the awful threats of interdict and excommunication. Charles V and his son Philip, taking the facts as they were, had interceded for her in vain; the same spirit that had prevented the entry of moderation and good sense into the first Council of Trent, despite the sincere wish of thousands of good churchmen for a reconciliation with Luther's erring flock, guided the dictators of Roman policy throughout in their dealings with the English Princess. When they had done, she could only acknowledge their authority if she was willing to confess herself a bastard and a usurper.

Her subjects were no more inclined than she to any such admissions. What the priestly politicians refused to realize, after several hundred years of warning, was that the people of England were English first and Catholic afterwards, that in a quarrel between their sovereign and the Pope the Holy Father was a foreign prince to be regarded like any other enemy. It took many years of plot and punishment, all those miserable attempts to assassinate Elizabeth and all the horrible reprisals on the gallows, to drive into the heads of the Papal advisers that the fact of being a good Catholic did not excuse a man, even to himself, from being
a good

a good Englishman. Truly Mother Church proved her immortality by the way in which she survived the good offices of her friends.

The Queen and her subjects were agreed in general that the breach with Rome must come, but there the concord ended. What form was the new Church to take? The Catholic peers and bishops who were in the majority in the House of Lords would have made the change as perfunctory, the newly elected Commons as sweeping, as possible. The nobility, conservative by temper as always, jealous of any encroachment on their rights, were naturally hostile to change; many of them were long-standing pensioners of the Catholic Powers. The prelates, who derived their wealth and dignity from Rome, could not but be uneasy at the prospect of another authority distributing place and patronage. The newly elected Commons, on the other hand, swooped down on Westminster in January determined to avenge all the offences and cure all the abuses of the previous reign without further ado. Most of them had suffered discomfort and many persecution under Mary; not a few were returning from exile almost incandescent with Calvinist electricity.

Between these two extremes stood the Queen. She could accept no less than a complete rupture with her enemy in Saint Peter's. Yet no more would she yield an inch to the truculent zealots who would have stripped her of ecclesiastical power as thoroughly as, and imposed their will on the country with far greater fury than, their opponents. She meant to have a truly national Church, untrammelled alike by the dogmas of Geneva or the discipline of Rome, containing sufficient room for all those millions of ordinary Englishmen who profoundly desired to be rid of the conflict between loyalty to their country and the service of their God.

She may have been wrong: she suffered vituperation from both sides then, and has suffered it since, for her indifference to theological niceties. But she was wrong only if politics is a department

department of religion and a nation subordinate to a system of divine worship. Her business on earth was not to expound ultimate truths, but to deal with transitory facts as they affected her people; and the one unforgivable offence to any God of whom she could have conceived would have been a failure in her duty towards them. She expressed their desires when she relieved them of dictation from the Italian Prince who was also the Bishop of Rome, and when she expelled 'those lazy poltroons,' the bishops whom he had set over them and by whom 'so much money was taken out of the country for the Pope every year that she must put an end to it.' She shared their feelings when she retained, against outraged Puritan protests, the familiar Catholic symbols; for she knew — and she was astonishingly alone in the knowledge — that the little parish churches of the land would seem less strange to their congregations if prayers were said amidst the sights, sounds, and smells to which they had always been used.

Her own religious sentiments were not perhaps very strong, yet she had a faith which she upheld with as pure a conviction as any mediæval priest. In that age of intolerance and inquisition, when all authority believed that its life depended on stripping the mask off men's thoughts, of reading their minds even if one had to bore into their brains with hot irons, she dared to believe that his conscience was each man's private affair. So long as people were loyal to England and obedient to the laws, she declined to interfere between them and their Maker. 'The law touches no man's conscience,' she proudly informed the Holy Roman Emperor, 'so as public order be not violated by external act or teaching.' When bigots screamed at her that she would ruin herself by her indulgence, she smiled and answered that 'she made no windows into men's souls.' When Parliament passed acts born of fanaticism and fear, she vetoed them; and if expediency compelled her to sanction them, she neglected their enforcement. So long as she lived she remained the sole obstacle to
bigotry

bigotry and persecution, over and over forgiving even attempts made on her life in the name of religion. But the breadth of her vision never penetrated the law-makers' minds, and for forty years she had to fight with them for tolerance — a battle in which she could only be victorious so long as the people trusted her more than they did the legislators. When her successors forfeited that trust, an unpopular creed became the defender of the popular liberties and civil war raged in England.

The Church that she eventually built was her own handiwork. It was not so much designed as improvised, rearranged, and pulled about until it was best suited to the ground it was to occupy. It expresses, no doubt, her spirit of compromise, but it also expresses her spirit of toleration and her instinct for practical reality. One might say of it what she said of herself, that it was 'mere English.'

The opposition she had to overcome or beguile before the Church took the shape she proposed for it seemed at first insuperable. The horror of sixteenth-century Catholics for the Reformation was like that of eighteenth-century monarchists for the French Revolution or twentieth-century democrats for the Russian; even greater, because the Reformation was not only a threat to order and property, but an insult to God. Elizabeth's one friend in Europe, the King of Spain, was particularly perturbed by it, since heresy in England was only too likely to encourage heresy and ultimate rebellion in his Netherlands, as in fact it did. She parried his interference in the manner already described, and momentarily placated him by refusing the title of Supreme Head of the Church that the Commons offered her, taking instead that of Governor, which the Kings of England bear to this day. By the time Philip was fully aware of the depths of her iniquity, his first and best opportunity for interference had passed.

It was a still harder matter to gain the substantial accord of Parliament. Feeling in both houses was bitter as it was diverse, and neither side was yet disposed to place unlimited confidence

confidence in the new Queen. Nor had she herself as yet any experience of complicated negotiation with selfish and determined men. But she was a born Parliamentary tactician, and was soon to prove herself as consummate a one as her father. Some of the leading peers she gained over by holding out hopes of marriage with herself, and they in turn worked upon their fellows. Others she convinced by a judicious distribution of offices. The bishops resisted to the end, but were outvoted, and their clergy, with comparatively few exceptions, conformed. The conduct of the uproarious battle in the Commons she entrusted to her chief subordinates, Cecil and Nicholas Bacon, who as sound Protestants had the confidence of the majority. One cannot help thinking how much happier the half-century after Elizabeth's death would have been if her successors had followed her example of entrusting to their most intelligent ministers the leadership of the Lower House.

The Crown's spokesmen, adroit, and tireless, met threat with threat and logic with logic. They dilated in public on the worse that would befall unless there were a speedy religious peace, and conferred with their opponents in private upon helpful matters of patronage. The Queen herself never took her finger off the pulse of the struggle. She let it be known that Philip had proposed to her, and confronted her critics with the horrible alternative of another Spanish marriage if they pressed her too far. She strengthened her ministers' hands at critical moments with messages that are living documents to this day. After three months of heated debate, the victory was won and the Church of England had been called into being by law.

This was at the end of April, 1559. In the five months since Elizabeth's accession the finances had been started on their way towards a restoration that would soon make England the envy of the world, a peace had been concluded which would presently enable her for many years to wield the balance of power in Europe, the danger of a civil war of religion

gion successfully averted. Those five months, void of a single great battle or a solitary execution, are scarcely more familiar than the first half-year of Charlemagne's reign; they are a mere prelude to the shadowy tract of time that lies between the bonfires of Smithfield and the explosion of Bothwell's gunpowder in Kirk o' Field. Yet they contain as solid achievement as any period of similar length in history can show, and it was they, with the event that was immediately to follow, that made England capable of becoming guardian of the Renaissance and 'a bulwark for the cause of men.'

Chapter III

The Unfriendly Neighbour

WHEN the attempted invasion of England took place, as it was certain to do, the assault would come from one of two directions. Either Spain would cross from the Netherlands and disembark her armies on the east coast, or France would descend from Scotland. The first danger was averted for thirty years through a lingering tradition of friendship and England's growing power at sea, but the second was immediate, since France had both the motive and the means for acting swiftly. She had need of the island in her Continental schemes, and a claimant to the throne in Mary Stuart, whom one half of Europe already acknowledged. She held the Scottish border, 'the postern gate into England'; on the southern side of that border lived the solid group of Catholics who hated Elizabeth and were ready as the French to put a rival in her place.

The rulers of France made no secret of their intention. The dominant party at Court were Mary Stuart's uncles, the princes and prelates of the House of Guise, whose avowed objects in life were the enrichment of their family and the extermination of heresy in France. Both would be considerably advanced if they succeeded in putting their niece on the neighbouring throne. Their influence had so far prevailed on the King as to make him quite docile towards Spain at Cateau-Cambrésis, in the hope that that power would not interfere with his English enterprise. As an additional precaution Henry II, catching Philip on the rebound after his recent rejection by the Queen of England, secured his consent to a marriage with his own daughter, Elizabeth of Valois.

That was the situation when the commissioners for France, Spain, and England set their hands to the treaty which, like all similar treaties, undertook to bring perpetual
peace

peace to the world. The plain course before Elizabeth was to send an army over the frontier to expel the potential invader before he could move against her, which she would no doubt have done with as easy a conscience as she expelled the Papal troops from Ireland twenty years later — had she only been able to. But her people were still weak, divided and exceedingly weary of war; the Scots might take as unkindly to an English invasion as they had invariably done in the past; and there was no means of knowing whether Spain would be friendly, hostile, or neutral.

What might not be accomplished by force might nevertheless be achieved with cunning. The Scots, proverbially thrifty and by temper if not in fact Protestant, had come to detest the foreign Papists who simultaneously emptied their pockets and ridiculed their religion. The nobles, not so sensitive on the score of worship, were no less resentful of outsiders in monopoly of the places of profit and power. Here were all the ingredients of a rebellion in the name of liberty, if only assistance could be found somewhere to give it a reasonable chance of success.

That assistance was now to be supplied by Scotland's oldest and bitterest enemy, her southern neighbour. John Knox, who had been expelled as a result of a rebellion a few years earlier, was plucked forth from his hiding-place on the Continent and brought home. The effect of his turgid eloquence on the Scottish masses was as electrical as ever: in an instant they rose to cast the idolatrous images out of the churches and the idolaters themselves out of the land. The nobles, finding that they had followers, again constituted themselves leaders, under their old name of Lords of the Congregation, and were at once in deep conference with the English agents at Berwick, by whom they were promised help as soon as the rising was decently flourishing. The Queen knew, of course, what was going on, but took no open part. It was desirable for the present that she should be able if challenged to hold up a clean pair of hands.

To

To the Scots, however, and those of her people who considered a war with Catholics equivalent to an onslaught upon the Devil, her attitude of detachment was unsatisfactory. They put their heads together, and out of their consultations re-emerged the project that had once been so dear to Henry VIII. The Duke of Châtelherault, the head of the great clan of Hamilton, whom Mary Stuart's mother had after the earlier rebellion replaced as Regent, had a claim on the Scottish throne. The plan was that the fatuous old duke should surrender the claim to his son, James, Earl of Arran, who would then marry Elizabeth and join the two countries into a single nation to be called Great Britain.

The conspirators sounded Elizabeth out, gingerly, since she had never spoken of the young man except in terms of most incurable dislike. They were therefore all the more gratified when told that she had grown deeply interested in him and was willing to have him brought to England for an interview with a view to matrimony before sending off to make himself useful in Scotland.

Arran, formerly a favourite in Paris and captain of the King's Scots Guard, had been proscribed because of the unrest in Scotland and was in hiding. Elizabeth dispatched Sir Thomas Randolph to France to find him. With the help of Sir Nicholas Throckmorton, the English ambassador in Paris, Randolph ran him to earth at the end of May and smuggled him across the frontier into Switzerland. Randolph then returned, and on July 6, Arran, travelling with a false passport under the name of M. de Beaufort, set out for England to claim a kingdom and a bride.

The coincidence of the outbreak in Scotland and the disappearance of Arran threw the courts of Europe into bewildered alarm. Philip II, slow to anger and slower to act, was particularly upset by the dilemma in which he was being placed: if Elizabeth married Arran and challenged France by invading Scotland, she would either succeed and convert the whole island to heresy, or she would fail and deliver it bodily

to

to France; either outcome portended a war for Spain. The Catholic King instructed his ambassador to spy out the land and threaten Elizabeth with unpleasant consequences to herself if she was caught disturbing the peace.

The new ambassador, Alvarez de Quadra, Bishop of the diocese of Aquila in the Kingdom of Naples, had inherited de Feria's principles together with his post. Less experienced than his predecessor, less flexible, inferior in intelligence and personality, he was if anything a more uncompromising enemy of Elizabeth and her chief counsellors. De Feria had been and still was convinced that what Philip required in London was a viceroy rather than a legate; de Quadra, not so confident of himself, was content to intrigue since he could not command, but he was unfortunately more apt to be detected in that dangerous occupation than was his discreet predecessor.

In the effort to protect his master's interests the Bishop at once set spies to follow Cecil, hoping to trace him to Arran's hiding-place. The effort was vain: partly because Arran was still in Switzerland, and partly, as de Quadra sadly admitted, because the moment the elusive Secretary left his house he seemed to vanish into thin air. He tried Randolph, who had just come back from his business with Arran on the Continent, and who might therefore be expected to know how matters stood. He learned little except that Elizabeth had been so annoyed to hear that Mary Stuart was publicly wearing the royal arms of England that she had sworn to 'take a husband who would give the King of France a headache.' That could only mean one thing: her marriage with the missing pretender and a joint attempt on the Scottish throne.

Convinced that his worst forebodings were justified, the Spaniard hastened to see Elizabeth herself. He issued from his audience with but the dark suspicion that she was laughing at him. When he tried to talk of Arran 'she smiled and looked archly.' Then in an apparent burst of confidence she admitted that the King of France thought that the Earl was in England

land (which was of course no news, since everybody else thought the same), 'but she believed he was mistaken, or at least if he was there she did not know it' — a specimen of her ability to tell the exact truth so that it would sound like a convenient lie. The Bishop saw nothing to laugh at and gave his opinion that 'if what she says...be a joke, nothing more can be said than that this woman has not much sense.' It was hard to tell whether she was joking or not and the Bishop quite properly declined to lean too heavily on his own sense of humour. Only one thing could he report of her with confidence, that 'she is very difficult to negotiate with, having learnt shifty speech from the Italian heretic friars who brought her up. For with her all is falsehood and vanity.' But he had discovered nothing which would justify Spain in taking decisive action, and Philip remained quiescent.

Elizabeth's threat to give the King of France a headache was empty as soon as uttered, for on the same day Henry had suffered a mortal wound from the chance thrust of a spear in the eye. That stroke was one of the most ironic ever dealt by Fate. When Henry received it he was taking part in a tournament to celebrate the marriage that would make him master of Europe. For when he had put his new son-in-law to sleep with matrimony, as a waggish diplomat expressed it, he would be free to acquire England for his daughter-in-law without danger of opposition from Spain. Whether or no he reckoned accurately, he was never to discover. For eight days, from June 22, the date of the wedding by proxy in Paris, to June 30, the day he was wounded, he could look out over the fair earth with visions of an Alexander. Ten days later he died in agony. On July 10, Francis II and Mary Stuart were crowned King and Queen in Notre-Dame.

The situation had materially altered by the end of July. With Henry's death the Guises were to all intents and purposes complete masters of France, and the invasion was by so much nearer. The first impulse of the Scottish rebellion had exhausted itself and the French were nearly free to advance

vance over the border into England without danger from their
rear. On the other hand, Philip was less likely to take France's
part than he would have been when his father-in-law was
alive. It seemed safer, as it was certainly more urgent, than
it had been in May for Elizabeth to move against her enemy.

Still reluctant to be seen in the open, she instructed Sir
Ralph Sadler, on August 7, to proceed to Scotland with
secret offers of help to the rebel lords and three thousand
pounds in gold for distribution in bribes. 'Such discretion
and secrecy is to be used,' she directed, 'as no part of your
doings may impair the treaty of peace lately concluded with
France.' On the same day she wrote personally to the Queen
Regent of Scotland, who had been complaining of the secret
meetings between the English officers at Berwick and the
Scots leaders, 'We cannot but find it very strange that any of
our subjects, and much more that persons of public trust
should, of their own accord and regardless of our displeasure,
have sought means to meddle with any such people,' and
promised chastisement to any who were caught so offending.

It was not a performance of the first order. When the
Queen's smooth cheeks grew hard and lined, when she had
tricked every king and statesman in Europe a dozen times,
she would have to do better. The lion-hearted invalid who
ruled Edinburgh for her daughter was not deceived. Totally
unimpressed with Elizabeth's disclaimer, she directed de
Noailles, the French ambassador in London, to give the
Queen her very affectionate greetings and demand an honest
answer to a simple question: Did Elizabeth intend to continue meddling with the Scottish rebels or not? She had certain knowledge that her good cousin and sister was offering
help to the Scottish lords and that they were boasting about
it.

De Noailles tried to see Elizabeth, but she put him off on
the plea of illness. Other and very pressing business was
claiming her attention. Arran, chaperoned by Randolph, had
reached London and was hidden in Cecil's house. Elizabeth
saw

saw him several times, there and at Hampton Court. He was a dark, sallow young man of twenty-two, clumsy and nervous in manner. He had his father's empty conceit and symptoms of a more sinister inheritance which was soon to make him an incurable imbecile. Her earlier prejudice was strengthened, but she spoke to him sweetly, listened to his vapourings as if they were wisdom, and sent him off to Scotland to make himself King if he could. So deftly was his transit through England arranged that the French, whose spies were looking for him everywhere, were completely in the dark as to his movements.

When Messrs. Beaufort and Barnable, *alias* Arran and Randolph, had started north, Elizabeth felt herself sufficiently recovered to see de Noailles. She heard the Regent's 'remonstrances' with surprise. She admitted that 'it was likely that some of her ministers had been foolish enough to meddle with evil practices among the Scots,' but she had ordered an inquiry to be made as she had promised in her communication of August 7. In fact she 'had sent a man expressly to set matters in order.' She neglected to say that the man's name was Sadler and that he carried three thousand pounds in bribes. If the Scots boasted that she was helping them, they were merely talking through their hats. 'Her signature was easily recognized; let it be produced if it could be found. She well knew that there were men who spread wicked lies in order to cause trouble.' To clinch the matter she led the ambassador to the portrait gallery at Hampton Court, showed him that Mary of Guise's likeness occupied a place of honour on the walls, and reverently hung a verbal wreath to her 'goodness, honesty, and virtue' on its frame.

De Noailles was convinced: five days later, on September 6, he hurried to tell her that he had news from his agents of Arran's escape and to request her to turn him over to the French police if he landed in England. Elizabeth showed surprise, but only a detached interest. She had heard nothing of Arran, it seemed, but promised to do as the ambassador asked

if

if the exile showed his face in England: 'she was not the person to say one thing and do another.'

The Regent remained unaffected by the ambassador's masculine credulity, and went ahead in utter disbelief of her neighbour's good intentions. She opened parleys with the Scots, who, discouraged by their meagre success and the lack of visible help from England, seemed to be weakening; and the Lords of the Congregation, an aristocracy that changed its coat oftener than its linen, responded amiably to her overtures. Money for bribes was sent from France in liberal quantities and two thousand troops, while twenty thousand more were prepared for early embarkation under the Marquis d'Elbœuf, the Regent's brother. Philip II was approached by the Guises, and it was presently rumoured that Spain was now wavering in her neutrality, that the fleet Philip was preparing to carry him home would be used for the suppression of his sister-in-law in the interests of the *status quo*. By the beginning of September, Elizabeth's bolt seemed to be shot, and for nothing. De Quadra and de Feria wrote one another congratulatory missives on the retribution that would swiftly follow.

The first French reinforcements landed in Scotland early in September. That same week de Quadra communicated to Elizabeth his master's displeasure at her conduct in general and her reported engagement to Arran in particular. A day or two later, Lord Robert Dudley, who enjoyed the reputation of being the Queen's lover, and his sister, Lady Sidney, one of Elizabeth's few women friends, visited the Spanish ambassador and confided to him, under an oath of deep secrecy, that the Queen would marry Philip's cousin, the Archduke Charles, son of the Holy Roman Emperor, if she were suitably approached. Oppressed by her difficulties and her inability as a woman to cope with them alone, she was, vowed the brother and sister, ready to yield.

De Quadra believed the story — coming from such an unimpeachable source he could scarcely do otherwise. He tried to to obtain the Queen's confirmation, but neither quite succeeded nor altogether failed. As woman to man she put it to him that a lady could not be so brazen as to inaugurate a wooing. If the Archduke came on his own to court her...she hoped he would come...she had been told he was very handsome...till then she could say nothing. Meantime the Bishop must not believe everything he heard. She was not actually engaged to Arran....Nor was she a heretic, as unkind people maintained. Crosses and candles appeared in her chapel. 'Enough of that,' she roared to a preacher who spouted too raw a doctrine in her presence, and walked out in the middle of his sermon. Even Cecil received a stinging public rebuke for trying to involve her with his Scottish 'Brothers in Christ.'

Soon embassies, messengers, and drafts of marriage contracts were passing one another between Brussels, Vienna, and London. The Catholic King, again pleased with his sister-in-law, reserved his displeasure for the Guises and induced the Pope to withhold the bull they were begging him to issue against Elizabeth, because 'it would do much damage both before and after the marriage with the Archduke.' During the next few weeks Philip was on the high seas bound for Spain and out of touch with events.

The French, frightened by his defection, hastily looked round for a rival to Hapsburg and Hamilton instead of hurrying d'Elbœuf to Leith with all possible speed. They dangled several for Elizabeth's inspection: the Duke of Nevers, who, it was temptingly suggested, might possibly bring her back Calais as part of his dowry; and Eric, heir-apparent of Sweden, who had been her suitor since childhood. The Swede was the more serious, since he was rich and a Protestant; the only thing that could be fairly urged against him was that he was even madder than Arran. More negotiations were begun, and the Swedish embassy, assisted by the French ambassador, reported progress to Paris while de Quadra wrote wrathful letters to de Feria in Brussels deprecating

ing Elizabeth's encouragement of the newcomers, although he recorded more than a suspicion that she was laughing at the lot of them.

So September passed, and in October the Scots, heartened by Arran's appearance and a fresh supply of English money, came together again and struck the first blow, a hard one, at the enemy. They demanded of the Regent that the fortifications which her new French troops were building at Leith should be demolished and the troops themselves sent home. She retorted from her sick-bed with a haughty refusal and ordered the rebels to disperse. The Covenanters thereupon took the field, drove the outlying French soldiers into Leith and posted a resolution in the market-place of Edinburgh deposing the Regent from her authority. The proclamation, issued in the name of Francis II and Mary Stuart as sovereign lord and lady of Scotland, was drawn up under Elizabeth's influence. It was not part of her policy to be caught fighting against legitimacy — it would have been too dangerous a precedent for the discontented amongst her own subjects — and for that reason she had prevented the extremer Scots from deposing Mary in favour of Arran.

Once within the walls of Leith the French merely laughed at the attempts of the ragged and mutinous natives to dislodge them. The English officials at Berwick, who were anxiously watching the siege, wrote pessimistically to Cecil, 'You know that the Scots will climb no walls.' The Regent's experienced infantry broke through at will and soon retook Edinburgh. The answer of the Lords of the Congregation was, as usual, to beg Elizabeth for more money.

She responded promptly with a further three thousand pounds. The bearer, the Laird of Ormistoun, left Berwick for Edinburgh on October 31. Next day he was waylaid by a young Border free-lance, Patrick Hepburn, Earl of Bothwell, for whom Mary Stuart was to lose the kingdom her mother was now so gallantly defending for her. Bothwell was nominally in the service of the Regent, though (also nominally)

ally) a Protestant, but his principal motive in stealing the
money was a personal dislike of the bearer. He carried both
off to his stronghold at Crichton, whither Lord James Stuart,
Mary's bastard half-brother and the active leader of the rebellion, pursued him with a troop of cavalry. But he escaped
to Edinburgh with his prize, and at last the Regent had in her
hands the means of exposing Elizabeth's villainy.

. She ordered de Noailles in London to confront her with the
damning evidence of English money intercepted *en route* to
the Scots leaders. 'If you look her straight in the face,' de
Noailles was told, 'she can hardly help blushing, whatever assurance she may possess.' The ambassador was not so sure.
He had by now lost faith in Elizabeth's power to blush, but
acquired a deep respect for her diplomacy. 'Few people living,' he wrote to Francis II, 'can play that game as well as
she.' He did as he was told, however, only to be informed
that Elizabeth had never heard of the three thousand pounds:
it must have represented some private transaction between
Sadler and Croft at Berwick and Lord James Stuart. Those
three gentlemen with their hands on their hearts vowed in
chorus that it was even so.

It would no doubt have satisfied Elizabeth to go on indefinitely making war in this fashion. It was amusing, it was
comparatively safe, and it was considerably cheaper than the
more violent forms of the art. But its great drawback was
that it failed to accomplish its principal object, which was to
get the French out of Scotland. Diplomacy and the Scots together having proved unequal to that task, it appeared that
war, much as she loathed its expense and bloodshed, was un-
avoidable. She called her ministers together and asked them
to draw up a memorandum of advice for the conduct of hostilities.

The word vacillation has been firmly riveted to Elizabeth
by her critics; and one of the principal articles in support of
that indictment is her delay in challenging the second power
in Europe at the beginning of her reign. But if the Queen was
cautious,

cautious, the Council was prostrate. The ministers quarrelled, flung epithets at one another, looked about in fright for some escape from the terrible necessity of decision. A few were for marching headlong into war under the banner of Protestant-ism or Perish, regardless of the people's disinclination for either. The majority favoured peace, compromise, anything that would relieve them of the dreaded uncertainty of an appeal to arms. Finally, by a vote of eleven to nine they hammered out a resolution advising the Queen to refrain from hostile action unless English soil was actually invaded, to borrow a hundred thousand pounds in Antwerp for more bribes to the Congregation, and to make alliance with Spain and the German Protestants. It was not a helpful document. Bribing the Scots was throwing money down a bottomless well, purely defensive warfare violated every principle of strategy, and the Spaniards and Germans were as likely to enter into simultaneous alliances with her as were the Sultan and the Pope. What the counsellors principally hoped, and advised, was that she would get married, though how that would have helped they did not explain. She threw the paper aside — it still exists, endorsed in Cecil's hand, 'Opinion of the Council, *not allowed by the Queen's Majesty*' — and abandoned forever the idea of waging war by committee. 'What we have feared so long,' wrote de Quadra to the Duke of Alba, 'has at last come to pass.' And he added, 'It is the Queen's act....'

The harassed ambassador tried to check her in her course by telling her that the Archduke was already on the way. It was what she had insisted on in September; now she merely shrugged her shoulders. She would be glad, she said, to see him and make his acquaintance; it might be useful if she ever felt inclined to marry. Otherwise she was not interested. She requested him to announce to his King that a state of hostilities would shortly exist between her and the French unless their troops were promptly removed from her border. The French ambassador, coming to inform her that a powerful army would be sent at once to punish her unless she de-
                                                                                                          sisted,

sisted, was told 'abruptly that it was very reasonable that this provision should be made, but it must not be thought very strange if she on her side were also to arm herself.'

She instructed Gresham in Antwerp to raise two hundred thousand pounds for war supplies, twice the amount recommended by the Council. Incidentally it was only a tenth of what the Archduke's relations were prepared to contribute towards the expense of his English courtship. Gresham succeeded with ease — so much difference had one year of good government made. She ordered the musters to be prepared and offered the command of her forces to the Duke of Norfolk, not for his soldierly qualities but, because, as first peer of the realm, he would be helpful in winning the support of the Conservatives. Having received word that d'Elbœuf was about to leave Dieppe for the relief of Leith, she assembled fourteen men-of-war and sent them to sea under the command of Sir William Winter, the first of her great sailors, with instructions to sink any French vessel that attempted to enter or leave the Firth of Forth. Christmas of 1559 found the two fleets converging on Scotland with all Europe waiting breathless for England's first hazard of her destiny by sea.

And, as so often happened later, the elements, her immemorial friends, came to her aid. While Winter and d'Elbœuf raced for the Firth, a great gale came out of the north and flung itself upon them. Superb seamanship brought the English squadron in safety to Lowestoft, but the French was torn asunder and dashed to pieces on the coasts of Holland and East Anglia. D'Elbœuf himself got back to Dieppe, and one of his lieutenants arrived at Leith with a hundred men, but these were the only survivors of the Guise Armada.

Winter, all unknowing, resumed his course on January 21 and two days later sailed into the Firth. He carried no flag, and when the garrison at Leith demanded the nature of his business he declined to answer. The French naturally fired, the fire was returned, and Winter proceeded up the bay to take up his station. From this position he was able to intercept

cept all shipping going in or coming out, and shortly drove two French vessels loaded with munitions and stores ashore, where the Scots sacked them. The Regent sent a trumpeter to demand by whose authority he was acting. He coolly replied 'his own.' That was literally true: the very instructions which commanded Winter to blockade Leith and 'do some effectual enterprise upon the French navy' also contained the significant clause, 'We will that ye shall as of your own courage attempt these things.' He had, he explained, come on a peaceful errand to Berwick, the weather had driven him out of his course, and before he could retire he had been assaulted without excuse. Being the aggrieved party he now intended to remain.

The Regent dashed off furious protests to Elizabeth, denying Winter's stories of the weather and the order of firing. She reminded the Queen of England that God avenged unjust dealing and demanded of her again whether she wished to be a friend or no.

Elizabeth replied that she did not like the tone of the exasperated Regent's letter and 'would be friendly or otherwise with the French according as they gave her excuse to be.' As to Winter she would institute inquiries. Her report from her Admiral, she told de Noailles, had differed from his mistress's in important respects. In any event, he was not acting under her orders. It was the dodge that was later to be used with such devastating results while Drake, Hawkins, and their kind were draining the blood out of the Spanish Empire at the risk of being hanged as pirates in order to keep the country out of war. / If Elizabeth's theories of government were not heroic, they were at least favourable to the incubation of heroes.

The spirit of her sailors was in her, and from her it was communicated to her people. The Spanish ambassador, hostile but reluctantly admiring, wrote to his friend de Feria in February that 'the Queen rides out every day into the country on a Neapolitan courser or a jennet to exercise for this war, seated

seated on one of the saddles they use here. She makes a brave show and bears herself gallantly.' Of her subjects who, eighteen months before, had been so sick and tired of war, he added, 'the people here are full of warfare and armament.'

The French, dismayed at the unexpected martial ardour of England, the disaster to their fleet, and the strength of Winter's blockade, now tried to seduce the Queen with offers of peace. De Noailles was replaced by Michel de Sèvres, who was more friendly to the English Protestants, and a special commissioner, the Bishop of Valence, sent over to open negotiations. But the negotiators were insincere and their terms unsatisfactory. They insisted on leaving the nucleus of an army, keeping the fortresses, and merely submitting the 'arms and style question,' which involved Elizabeth's whole claim to her throne, to a mixed tribunal. Elizabeth rejected their offers with a sharp rejoinder that her right to her crown was not a matter for arbitration, and despite the plea of Philip to stay her hand until he could send over a special commission to argue with her, she signed the Treaty of Berwick with the Scots, committing both peoples to a fight to a finish, on February 27. On March 29 she ordered her army over the border.

At the same time she issued the reasons for her step, in a proclamation ostensibly addressed to her own people, but actually to the French. It was a powerful, eloquent, and disingenuous document. She declared that she had no quarrel with the French people, that her object was merely to protect herself against the overweening ambition of the Guises, who had obtained unlawful control of the French King and Queen, and bade her subjects continue their friendly and profitable dealings with their neighbours. The proclamation aimed at and succeeded in driving a wedge between the Huguenots and the ruling party in France, and had not a little to do with the civil insurrection, known as the Tumult of Amboise, which shortly broke out across the Channel. It was more than suspected that her dispatch of 'a noted heretic named

named Tremayne with a message for the Huguenots' on March 7 also had something to do with her enemies' domestic difficulties. They tried to answer with a strong protest against 'the proclamation which she had printed and which contains no semblance whatever of right,' but in a war of words they were no match for the young woman who, even in her youth, possessed the talent native only to the greatest politicians of distilling complicated arguments into a single, simple, and overwhelming appeal. Her response was one of the grandest defiances ever uttered by a sovereign, a defence of her conduct in words that must have thrilled the hearts of the highest and lowest of her subjects:

You complain of the fleet and army which we have sent to Scotland. What were we to do?... You challenge our crown; you deny our right to be Queen. You snatch the pretext of a rebellion to collect your armies on our Border; and you expect us to sit still like children? You complain that we sent our fleet to intercept your re-inforcements. It is true we did so; and the fleet had done its work; and what then?

Those cannon, those arms, those stores which you sent to Leith were not meant only or chiefly for Scotland; they were meant for us. You tell us we are maintaining your rebels — we hate rebels, but the Scots are none. These men whom you call rebels are the same who fought against England at Pinkie Cleugh. It is you who are in fault — you who stole the rule of their country from them, overthrew their laws and sought to govern them with foreign garrisons. You have seized their fortresses, you have corrupted their money, you have filled their offices of trust with greedy Frenchmen, to rob and pillage them; and they endured all this till they saw their sovereign, the childless Queen of a foreign prince — herself an absentee — and their country, should she die, about to become a province of France.

With these facts before us we are not to be blinded with specious words. We know what was intended for ourselves — some of your own statesmen have given us warning of it. Your Queen claims our crown; and you think that we shall be satisfied with words. You say you recalled d'Elbœuf. The winds and the waves recalled him, and our fleet in the Forth frightened him from a second trial. You have given us promises upon promises; yet our style is still filched from us and your garrisons are still in Leith.

Leith. We have forborne long enough. We mean nothing against your mistress's lawful rights: but events must now take their course.

They were brave words, but she had sought judgment by battle, and no words, however brave, could do more than act as a tonic to her people and a plea for the good opinion of the world. Her fate now hung on the war she had provoked: if her army were beaten, she had nothing to hope from her exasperated people or the victorious French.

There were few even amongst her friends who conceded her much chance. Philip, alarmed for her as for himself, sent over his special agent, the Fleming de Glajon, to beg her not to send her 'untrained labourers and country fellows' against France's experienced infantry and to make it clear that he could not protect her from the consequences of defeat. But the expeditionary force had already been sent — it was believed that she had hastened its departure to avoid giving a flat negative to her brother-in-law's emissary — and she firmly refused to recall it at de Glajon's demand. In fact she declined to discuss the matter at all and sent him to air his grievances to the Council, where he privately told Cecil that however his King might bluster he would not dare act against her for fear of provoking his Dutch subjects.

Yet events in the field turned out as badly as even the gloomiest prophets could have hoped. During the first four weeks of the siege of Leith, the French veterans had the best of every sally and skirmish, for the English recruits and the undisciplined Scots habitually threw down their arms and ran away. Norfolk, who disapproved of the war, sulked in Newcastle amongst the disaffected nobles of the North, and his subordinate Grey, upon whom fell the burden of command, laboured under the moral disadvantage of his defeat at Calais two years earlier. The Elizabethan Age had inherited no soldiers — Norris, Williams, and Vere were yet to be bred. The contractors responsible for the muster and supply of the army were as dishonest as the commanders

were

were inefficient. Sir James Croft at Berwick profited enormously by falsifying his returns, with the result that the troops were short of their reputed strength, underfed and underarmed. At the same time Scottish steadfastness was being undermined by every sort of French temptation.

After a month of this costly stalemate, the English commanders, afraid that if Leith were not soon reduced it would be relieved by the fleet which was rumoured to be on its way, determined to take it by storm. The assault began on May 7 at dawn, and by noon had ended in a disastrous repulse. The French, warned by a traitor, were ready on the walls before sunrise with cauldrons of boiling tar. The Newcastle miners, brought for the purpose, made two breaches in the walls, but they were too small. When the storming parties advanced to the attack, they discovered that they had been provided with scaling ladders seven feet too short; after standing up to a devastating fire from above, they broke and ran away.

The defeat was serious enough, but the form in which it reached London magnified it into a catastrophe. For it was reported that fifteen hundred men, or about a third of the English troops, had been killed. Grey himself estimated his losses at over a thousand. Not until weeks later was it learned that the dead numbered only a hundred and twenty, of whom a third were Scots. The rest existed only on Croft's pay-rolls until the battle gave him the chance to conceal his dishonesty by converting them into casualties.

The news threw the Queen into a fine rage, not with her army, but with the politicians whom she suspected of bad management and corruption. She sent her cousin, Sir Peter Carew, to investigate the causes of the defeat, and meantime vented her anger on the comely head of her chief minister. 'I have had such a torment herein with the Queen's Majesty,' he wrote to his friend Throckmorton, 'as an ague hath in five fits not so much abated.' He had no leisure, however, for his usual defence of taking to his bed.

Elizabeth

Elizabeth neither wrung her hands nor cried over spilt milk. 'Order hath been given,' Cecil wrote in the same letter, 'to send both men, money, and articles with all possible speed.' On May 11, the day after the arrival of Grey's dispatch in London, the Queen wrote in person to Norfolk, 'We be sorry to see that the success was no better, but considering the importance of the matter, will neither suffer delay, nor retire, but that the enterprise must needs be achieved for the honour and safety of our realm....' She promised him four thousand more men at once, and bade him 'recomfort our army in Scotland with the assurance of a speedy re-inforcement': she would let them 'lack nothing that may accomplish the enterprise....' She blamed nobody amongst her soldiers, even Grey: 'As it seemeth, the place was not assaultable.' She approved his decision not to venture another assault with his present numbers, but to keep the field and maintain the siege. It was the sort of letter to make commander and army think their ruler worth fighting for — not a common sentiment in the breasts of soldiers reading a communication from the Government at home after a defeat.

In the first days after the failure at Leith, it was believed that England had suffered irreparable disaster. But that opinion was short-lived: the Queen's high resolution dissipated fear and united her people in the determination to see the war through to the end; after a momentary exaltation it also broke the spirit of her adversaries. The Guises were faced with a civil war of whose instigation Elizabeth's agents were by no means guiltless. The reinforcements they had hoped to send to Scotland under still another of the brothers, the Grand Prior of Lorraine, were travelling north from the Mediterranean as if on a pleasure cruise, with stops for entertainment at every port on the way. 'No one was vexed at the delay,' wrote Brantôme, the diarist, who was of the company, 'for we all found mistresses as well as our commander.' The English fleet, whose blockade had become impenetrable,

penetrable, at this time intercepted a letter from Paris to
Edinburgh admitting that no help could now be looked for
before the end of August. On top of all the Regent, the
very soul of the resistance, was within measurable hours of
death. The rulers of France saw that they had lost — at the
end of May they sent over Charles de la Rochefoucauld,
Comte de Randan, to sue for peace.

The subsequent conference opened in Edinburgh on June
17, having moved from Newcastle out of consideration for
the dying Regent. The English delegates were Cecil and
Nicholas Wotton, the only man ever to hold the deaneries
of Canterbury and York at the same time. The French,
though victors in every land engagement of the war, acknowledged themselves thoroughly beaten, and the death of Mary
of Guise a few days later seemed to dispirit them altogether.
All was apparently plain sailing and Cecil in so cheerful a
mood at the prospect that he ventured one of the few jokes
to be found in the mass of his surviving papers: 'This afternoon Mr. Wotton and I should have heard the French and
Scots artillery, I should say the articles of their treaty [the
literal-minded Secretary obviously did not trust the Queen
to see the point], but they be so long in planting that I think
it will be tomorrow in the morning before the battery will
shoot off.' But his optimism lasted only a short time. The
French were quite willing to remove their starving troops
from Leith, but refused to waive their Queen's claim to
Elizabeth's throne or to recognize the English protectorship
of their Scottish dependants.

On these two questions the negotiations were deadlocked.
Unless the French gave over their pretensions to Elizabeth's
title, it was certain that they would in their own time return
to Scotland; and unless England were made the guarantor
of their undertakings to the Scots, there was no way in which
she could prevent them from doing so. Cecil and Wotton,
two very capable bargainers, wrestled for weeks with both
questions, but in vain. The Secretary at last wrote to his
mistress

mistress that it would not be prudent to press the matter further, else the whole treaty would be lost.

By way of answer he received a vigorous scolding because he had been asking so little and an instruction to increase his demands forthwith. The poor Secretary was convinced that the Queen was either being worked upon by his enemies at home or had lost all sense of proportion. Nevertheless, he dared not disobey her orders; with small hope he tried again. He then found that Elizabeth in London had a better grasp of the situation than himself on the spot, for when the French were convinced that English determination was stronger than their own they capitulated.

The Treaty of Edinburgh was a triumph for England as complete as it had been unexpected. It removed the enemy from Scotland and restored the Government to the Scots; it disowned the Catholic thesis that Mary Stuart was rightful Queen of England; and it acknowledged Elizabeth as 'trustee and next friend' to compel Mary to keep her word to her own subjects. The implications of the documents ranged far, so far that the young King and Queen of France disavowed the action of their own plenipotentiaries and refused to sign it. Such a breach of faith was too cynical even for that age and was to cost the young Queen of Scots dear. For the provisions of the treaty were executed in spite of her disavowal, while she remained to her subjects and to the English Queen during the tragic conflict soon to come a woman whose word was not to be trusted. Nor did Elizabeth hesitate to remind her of the fact.

The treaty also marked the end of the long unhappy story that reached beyond distant Bannockburn. For once Englishmen and Scotsmen had fought side by side in a common cause. English blood had been spilt in liberating the smaller neighbour from a foreign yoke, yet not a yard of territory nor the allegiance of a single Scot had been required by way of recompense. The Scottish people saw that the rapacity of Edward I and Henry VIII had not been transmitted to the

woman

woman who now sat in their seat, and though there might yet be many quarrels and recriminations in the future, the cornerstone had been laid for that understanding which was to result in a united kingdom.

Chapter IV

The Stubborn Virgin

BY MIDSUMMER of 1560, when Elizabeth's transports deposited the beaten French troops on their native shores, she had become the most celebrated woman alive. Statesmen argued heatedly whether she was a prodigy or a lucky adventuress, while ordinary men, content to leave such judgments to their betters, were already asking those tantalizing questions, exchanging those scandalous rumours, which have never been answered or allayed. The world burned with curiosity to know what impulses and feelings were hidden behind that glittering exterior, what her likes and dislikes were, what her occupations when she was not in the public sight. In short, what manner of woman she was.

It was natural to ask the questions, but unfortunately no one could pretend to supply the answers. Even now, with all the testimony taken and sifted, the student ruffles the documents in perplexity and puts them aside in despair. Everywhere are obscurities and contradictions. If he strikes an illuminated patch, it goes mockingly dark before his eyes; if he tries to glean in a promising area, he soon discovers that it has been deliberately ploughed into the ground. In the end he finds that Elizabeth herself has defeated his inquiries in the same sly way as she thwarted those of his contemporaries, by holding the monarch up on every side as screen for the woman.

One sure impression only remains, so strong, so persistent that in the receding dim-lit galleries which are called history it may be taken for truth. From the moment she ascended the throne she meant to be Queen, only that and so far as possible nothing else. From first to last there surrounds her a sense of dedication to her office which is amongst the rarest
properties

properties of kings. In her intercourse with individuals she was often frivolous and untrustworthy, and her language boisterous or coarse. But when she put away courtiers and politicians and rose to communicate her thoughts direct to her people, all those extravagances of manner dropped from her and she expressed herself straightforwardly in syllables of simple beauty. It is impossible then to mistake the authentic note of majesty. 'I marvel that ye have forgotten,' was her rebuke to Parliament at the beginning of her reign when it pressed her to marry, 'the pledge of this my wedlock and marriage with my kingdom.' And therewith she withdrew the ring from her finger and showed it, wherewith at her coronation she had in a set form of words solemnly given herself in marriage to her kingdom. Here, having made a pause, she added, 'And do not... upbraid me with a miserable lack of children; for every one of you and as many as are Englishmen, are children and kinsmen to me; of whom if God deprive me not (which God forbid) I cannot without injury be accounted barren.' As an old woman rising to make her last speech from the throne, clutching its arms to steady her swaying body, she reaffirmed with undimmed fire the creed by which she had lived: 'The glory of the name of a King may deceive those princes who know not how to rule, as gilded pills may deceive a sick patient, but I am none of those Princes, for I know that the Commonwealth is to be governed to the good and advantage of them that are entrusted to me, who will have to give an account one day to a Higher Prince of my stewardship....' And throughout the forty intervening years there issued from her lips at great moments the restatement of that theme in phrases that have remained amongst the treasures of the English language.

One can no more be consistently insincere throughout a lifetime than uniformly lucky; nor has anyone yet succeeded in lighting the glow of noble sentiment at a cold and empty heart. With Elizabeth the style was indisputably the woman. Anyone familiar with her language recognizes instantly the difference

difference between the elaborate phrases she used to deceive
and the simple felicity of those that were inspired by the
spirit of her dedication.

It was an essential condition of this high and conscious
dedication to her sovereignty that she might never give herself away. 'We Princes are all set as it were upon stages, in
sight and view of all the world.' For her there could be no
retirement to the peace of friendship, where one may con-
fide those perplexities and wants which occupy the greater
part of ordinary people's lives. There was no one she dared
sufficiently trust, no one so unselfish that he would refrain
from exploiting such confidence for the benefit of his own
pocket or policy. Of other female rulers much is revealed
by their intimate loves and sorrows, their conduct as wife,
mistress, mother, or daughter. But Elizabeth was an
orphan without husband or child; while bitter experience had
taught her to mask affection and grief under her characteristic grimaces. The more the world wondered about her, the
more she tried to convince the world that the Elizabeth she
allowed it to see was all the Elizabeth there was.

But no one can hold a pose forever; either it becomes part
of him or he relaxes from it under stress. Elizabeth made the
woman so thoroughly the Queen that the Queen became more
than she was aware an expression of the woman: the mask
was moulded so like that it revealed the lines of the face
beneath. At certain intervals she would give way to temper
or to fear, show too keenly her craving for admiration and
popularity, or her resentment when they were withheld.
Then for a moment she would forget that she was on a dais
sitting for a portrait she herself was painting and unthink-
ingly expose the living heart whose very existence she was at
such pains to deny.

To see her at her best both as Queen and woman, one should
take up a post of observation in the crowded chambers
through which for a quarter of a century her suitors had to
pass. It is a strange court, they are strange courtships. The
sovereign

sovereign will be seen deftly extracting from the stronger sex advantages for her country while exacting for herself the flatteries which are her substitute for the affection she must distrustfully forgo. At one moment she is stern, shrewd, suspicious, the next she is posturing and coquetting like a rather light-headed heiress who insists on being loved for herself alone. And the dispassionate bystander observes that no suitor, however coldly calculating his desires, is allowed to offer himself except as a lover, and no lover, even the foremost, may escape the solid and sordid uses of a suitor.

The number of men with whom Elizabeth's name was linked defeats all calculation. She was not yet four when her father tried to engage her to a Prince of France, and she was nearly seventy when a death-warrant signed by her own hand ended her last masculine attachment. She could barely speak when she first announced her preference for permanent virginity, yet at fourteen opinion awarded her the first of a dozen or so of reputed lovers. On her accession she declared in loud tones that she would never marry, while simultaneously it was whispered all over Europe that she could never have children: yet during the next thirty years scores of kings, princes, dukes, and others were to beg for the privilege of fathering the next King of England. Her boasted virginity was a principal instrument of policy as well as a pass-key to her character. Before half her reign was over, it had become one of the most venerable of insular institutions, vying in age and importance with the Royal Navy and the Church of England.

She herself provided almost the sole feminine element in that astonishing concourse of men. Amidst the bewildering maze of waving plumes, perfumed beards, jewelled swords, and gaudy-coloured hose that throngs her presence chamber, and even the bedchamber, one rarely catches a glimpse of farthingale or petticoat — and most of these adorned that chorus of ladies-in-waiting who stood round to clap their hands

hands when the Queen was pleased, to wail when she was unhappy, to be slapped when she was irritated. Unlike the Queen of Scots with her four attendant Marys, Elizabeth did well enough without female companionship. She was apparently fond of Mrs. Ashley, the governess who betrayed her out of fright and whom she saved by her resolution, and of the Marchioness of Northampton, with whom she was friendly in the early years of her reign. But the members of her sex with whom as Queen she had chiefly to do, Mary Stuart and Catherine de Médicis, she never met, and the more conspicuous of those she knew she hated — such women as the famous shrew, Bess of Hardwick, who entertained Mary Stuart's captivity with lewd stories of Elizabeth's sexual humiliations, and Lettice Knollys, 'that she-wolf' whom her darling Leicester seduced and secretly married.

During those first two years at least fifteen gentlemen proposed to her either in person or through their relatives and friends. Some of them were old suitors, some new. They included in their nationalities Spanish, Austrian, German, French, Swedish, Danish, Scotch, and English. Two of them were kings, two hereditary princes, seven dukes, two earls, one a lord by courtesy, and one a knight from amongst her own subjects. Some were rank outsiders, others could lay a family crown or the hope of one at her feet. Their respective chances of success could not always be estimated by their worldly place or expectations. It was widely agreed that when the Queen came to marry she would be guided by her own inclinations — in which as in other things opinion wronged her. Even the betting, usually so reliable a forecast of events in England, proved utterly inaccurate; for the Austrian Archduke, whom she considered more seriously than any other of her early suitors, was quoted at ten to one by the City sportsmen, whereas Sir William Pickering, who cheerfully admitted that he never had a chance, was offered at four to one. The bookmakers must have made a fortune out of their Queen's invincible spinsterhood and the public's
persistent

persistent belief, fathered by its wish, that she would surely marry.

The majority of the suitors were as faithful as Penelope's. They seemed able to sustain their affections for years on the meagrest crumbs, which was all the more remarkable when one remembers how many of them never even set eyes on the object of their desire. Nothing seemed to put them off, even Elizabeth's monotonous asseverations that she wanted none of them. That was too incredible: 'it is inconceivable that she should wish to remain a maid and never marry,' wrote the Austrian ambassador to the Holy Roman Emperor, the father of two of the suitors. They drew encouragement from the fact that she seemed not to know her own mind, which was not unnatural in her sex; time and again she swore that she would marry no man she had not first seen, which of course implied that she might marry a man whom she had seen and approved of. Numbers therefore overcame their fear of a refusal and presented themselves for inspection. Although they were never accepted, they were rarely pained by a flat rejection. The Queen liked having them about and went so far in inducing them to come that her ministers were regularly terrified by the risk she ran in subjecting the sons of great kings to the gratuitous insult of refusal — even Cecil, her daily companion and matrimonial agent-in-chief, wailed in bewilderment, 'This sing hath many parts and I am skilled only in plain song.' But their doleful warnings could not cure her: she like being courted too much to forgo the enjoyment because of its risks; she also like the risks. Probably she was not unaware that her unconcealed pleasure in receiving proposals kept sharp that useful weapon, the world's belief in her ultimate intention to marry.

It is hard to understand now why the disillusioned princes of Europe did not wash their hands of her. Courting Elizabeth was like groping through one of those Halls of Mirth in which the floor gives way under foot, the walls reflect a leering distortion of one's own face and the echoes jeer at one's whispers.

whispers. The mighty King of Spain had to undergo the embarrassment of reading her comments on his fussiness and the unromantic caution of his proposal; when finally he gave up and took the French Princess, Elizabeth in a mingling of sighs and laughter denounced him to his own ambassador as a poor sort of lover who could not wait four months for a lady to make up her mind. The indispensable archdukes roused her mirth, the one for his middle-class piety, the other for the exaggerated size of his head. The Duke of Holstein was so enraged by her jokes at his expense that he challenged the Austrian ambassador to a duel for repeating them; yet he rushed off to Denmark to raise an army for her use in Scotland. One after another carried her through peril to success with no greater reward than the sound of her strident laugh and the sight of those bizarre effects in costume and coiffure. Yet for nearly thirty years they continued to come, to serve, to be laughed at — on the last of them all, by whose use she saved the lives of thousands of Englishmen and perhaps England itself, she lavished her highest spirits, her most sardonic wit. Certainly no one would ever have put up with all that ridicule and frustration had she not possessed that singular charm — so irresistible in life, so utterly unrecapturable in print — and a profound knowledge of how far a woman may safely trade on the inexhaustible vanity and ambition of men.

To posterity, a dispassionate spectator of the comedy, her reasons for playing it are simple. So long as many men wanted to marry her she could play one against the other, use his country or party against another country or party. But once she took a husband that weapon was destroyed, and in the place of helpers she would have raised adversaries — not the least of them the successful suitor, to whom would have inevitably been drawn the elements of opposition.

To Lord Robert Dudley alone out of those scores of men did she ever give her heart; if at any time she seriously dreamed of marriage he was the only one she would of her

own

own choice have taken for husband. From the spring of 1559, when the first rumour of scandal floated down the back-stairs of Whitehall, until the autumn of 1588, when he died while the bells were pealing the nation's joy at the greatest moment in its history, she loved him with all the passion that her nature and her position allowed. Yet even he was denied entrance to the secret chambers of her brain where she worked out her designs in solitude, and like all the rest he had to sub-mit to her arbitrary rules of courtship. She heaped upon him more favours than upon any half-dozen of the rest combined, but also greater humiliations. She made him rich, nursed him devotedly through illness, shielded him from his enemies and forgave his injuries to herself; but she bullied and teased him, made him jealous by her flirtations, cursed him out of her presence when her mood or his conduct so impelled her. What he most wanted, a share in the sovereign power, she never gave; and her utmost fondness as a woman did not relieve him of his strict duty to her as Queen.

At least as much curiosity has been expended on Elizabeth's affair with Dudley as on her statesmanship, but no one has ever discovered the exact truth and no one ever will. Neither of them was inclined to go into details, and the stories of her physical abnormality are irresponsible tittle-tattle of her own day or ingenious inferences of a later time. If the stories were true, they could only be confirmed by medical evidence, of which there is none; nor were the contemporary practitioners competent to form conclusions of any scientific value. She may have been malformed, as the tavern pathologists averred, or sterile, as better authority with less confidence conjectured. The guessing will continue, and no one will ever find the answer.

That she was his mistress in the sense that a sexual rela-tionship existed between them seems beyond dispute. If words and actions mean anything, theirs was the conduct of lovers, especially on her part. Those sudden accesses of tenderness, those outbursts of stormy jealousy; her anxious

vigils

vigils by his sick-bed, oblivious of herself, of his misconduct to her or of what the world would think; the familiarities and fondlings and whispered teasings. His own consistent admissions and those of his relatives and partisans that she was his mistress may perhaps be discounted, for he and they wanted the world to believe in his ascendancy over her. She herself protested, when she thought she was dying of smallpox in October, 1562, 'that although she loved and had always loved Lord Robert dearly, as God was her witness, nothing improper had ever passed between them.' Yet when she was better she gave a pension of five hundred to the groom who slept in his chamber, lest he be tempted to discuss with outsiders Lord Robert's nocturnal comings and goings. She tried to shake de Quadra's belief in the scandal by showing him that the arrangement of Dudley's apartments and her own made secret access difficult: a month later Robert went into a temper over something she had denied him, which 'ended in giving him an apartment upstairs adjoining her own,' with the explanation that it was 'healthier than that which he had downstairs.' The Bishop made no redundant comment, merely adding, 'He is delighted.' And when she drew de Quadra to her, murmuring that she would 'like to make him her father-confessor,' that 'she was no angel ... she did not deny that she had some affection for Lord Robert,' what else could she have meant to imply but that she was Dudley's mistress? Her confessions and denials cancel out — it is safe to assume that they were the usual properties of her own peculiar comedy of diplomacy — but her actions reveal as unmistakably as actions could that she and Lord Robert were lovers.

In spite of the mystery that people made of the affair there was nothing mysterious in its origins. Dudley was acknowledged, even by those who hated him, to be a dashing young fellow who knew how to wear his gay silks or bright armour with an air, to turn a pretty phrase or to resent an insult with equal facility: a man of mark in the ballroom, the bou-
doir,

doir, the tiltyard, and the hunting field. Many a fine lady besides the Queen found his handsome face, supple body, and bold tongue too much for her virtue.

There was nothing unnatural in Elizabeth satisfying her heart's needs on the man who pleased her beyond any of her acquaintance; it would have been more unnatural if she had not. To her, as to all other human beings, love in some form was indispensable if life was to be borne at all. To her perhaps more than to most — for of all characters in history except the rare few who sustained themselves on love of God or hatred of man she was the loneliest. She had never known, even as a child, the love of parent or kin that all people of whatever degree take for granted. In the dazzling concourse that ever surrounded her there were none who looked upon her with the kind eyes of disinterested affection. It is little wonder that she took her handsome courtier, to whom she was bound at least by a common tie of age and youthful association, to help her through the weary eternity of her populous solitude.

Yet she knew — and had known since Seymour's brutal attempt at seduction when she was fourteen — that any masculine love she could afford must be but a second best. The surrender which for most women is the fulfilment of love was forever forbidden to her, unless she was prepared to subordinate the State, whose care was hers alone, to the demands of her sex. The same alternative confronted other queens, some of whom chose differently.

Being what she was she took Lord Robert for what he was, gave him what she could, and made herself content with the result. But if ever he reached for more, she repulsed him with the cold dispassion of the monarch who judged all men's pretensions, his equally with the rest: 'God's death, my Lord, I have wisht you well,' was her outburst when he attempted to humble one of the lesser courtiers, 'but my favour is not so lockt up for you that others shall not partake thereof; for I have many servants, to whom I have, and will at my pleasure

ure bequeath my favour, and likewise reserve the same, and if you think to rule here, I will take a course to see you forthcoming. I will have here but one Mistress and no Master....' It was not the sort of speech Cleopatra would have made to Antony or Mary Stuart to Bothwell, but it was Elizabeth, and of its kind it too was great.

The association stretched far back into their early youth. Dudley's father, the Duke of Northumberland, had been the leader of the rebellion which brought his daughter-in-law, poor little Lady Jane Grey, to the throne and both of them to the block. Young Robert was sent to the Tower, a prison of grim reputation but mild confinement, where he found as companion a young woman of his own age and many similar tastes. Four years later the young woman was Queen and Robert, now married, hastened to be amongst the first to offer his services in return for her favourable notice.

Probably neither she nor Dudley dreamed at the beginning that the affair would become the great scandal that it did. For that Robert's insatiable ambition was chiefly responsible and Elizabeth's indulgence. Her people were no more critical of their Queen's carnal lapses than of her drinking and swearing, which in fact they greatly admired; what they principally took exception to was Robert's rapacity, for which they had to pay. Nor was the ruling caste on the whole greatly upset by the immorality of the proceedings except in so far as Elizabeth's blemished reputation might diminish her value in the marriage market. What first excited the hatred of Dudley's peers was jealousy of his success in obtaining such things of value as they happened to want themselves. To this grievance was presently added the fear that he would induce the Queen to marry him and set him above them as master. Many of the bitterest intrigues at Court and much of the effort expended towards getting Elizabeth married rose from the widespread desire to end the good fortune of the too lucky favourite.

It cannot be denied that she enriched him beyond his
                                                        deserts,

deserts, but it is not so easy to say what his exact deserts were. In addition to being the Queen's lover he was the servant of the State — Master of the Horse, a member of the Council, a soldier, a high official of the Court. His reward may have been out of all proportion, but the whole system of payment in that age was peculiar. There was no public treasury out of which public employees could be paid, so all disbursements came out of the Queen's purse, which was replenished by Parliamentary grants (in theory free-will gifts of the subject to the Crown), the revenues of the Crown lands, and various miscellaneous royal perquisites. At no time was Parliament excessively generous, nor did it ever suit Elizabeth to make herself beholden to it by demanding more than was barely necessary to pay the expenses of Government. Her principal servants she reimbursed according to custom, that is, by distributing amongst them various of her monopolies and privileges, or the lands that accrued to the Crown through the rare windfalls of escheats and attainders. Thus Walsingham and Raleigh were given licences to export certain types of cloths, Dudley to import specified wines — and Ben Jonson the exclusive right to levy a duty on toothpicks. These were the accepted ways of paying for conspicuous public service, but they were also the means in many cases of regulating imports and exports in the interests of English manufacturers. Only after the Revolution were Treasury and fiscal policy transferred from the monarch to a responsible cabinet, and it took even longer for an honest and efficient civil service to be evolved. In Elizabeth's reign the ancient practices still prevailed, though in the course of it they were considerably altered and purified. Yet even while the purification was going on, the beneficiaries of the system made no such profit out of it as the statistics would seem to show, for what they drew from the State they had to pay back to the State. Out of their gains they found the cost of armies, diplomatic missions, and of ships for defence, exploration, and the founding of colonies. That, too, was the custom and it was

as

as rigorously enforced by the Queen as the other by her servants. From nothing or little Dudley, Hatton, Walsingham, Raleigh, and the rest became rich, but every last one of them died poor while their countrymen were prospering. Cecil alone, who for forty years grumbled at the favourites' revenues and his own expenses, left an estate not seriously impaired by his tenure of office.

Vain, selfish, and greedy Dudley certainly was, though it is not without importance that the accusations against him flowed from the busy venomous pens of those who hated and envied him; he himself was not addicted to composition. But if all they said was true, he differed from them only in degree, not in kind. Men far more honest and capable than himself entered the Queen's service for what they could get out of it, and naturally resented a competitor whose principal recommendations seemed to them merely his more regular features and his more plausible tongue.

But there was more to him than his enemies allowed: with all his faults he was a true Elizabethan, bold, reckless, and enterprising, a lover of art and of war. He valued money too highly and cared little how he got it, yet he spent it right and left on objects that benefited his country more than himself. He was Chancellor of Oxford and many a young man had his generosity to thank for an education. None of the Queen's subjects was readier than he to contribute capital to the seafaring venturers, whether to Drake in quest of golden galleons or Frobisher in search of the North West Passage. Though he invested for gain, he rarely got even his capital back, yet no amount of loss seemed to dampen his enthusiasm. It was gamblers of his stamp, successful or unlucky, who created both the colonial empire and the naval power that made that empire possible.

Selfish as were his ambitions, he was nearer the true spirit of Elizabethan England than better men, than even Cecil himself. For when the kingdom became peaceful and prosperous, the great Secretary implored the Queen to rest on
her

her laurels and do no more than protect what she had got. It was Leicester's party whose dreams reached out to yet untravelled horizons, who demanded that Spanish dominion in the West be assailed and broken because it stood in the way of England's expansion. It was Leicester who led the army to battle for Holland's freedom (not very well, it must be granted) and paid a good part of the expense out of his own pocket. Round the Queen's favourite were to gather all the gifted, impetuous young men whose exuberant enterprise led to the destruction of the Armada and the penetration of the New World — Walsingham, Raleigh, Francis Bacon, Essex, Sir Philip Sidney — and though he was not the greatest of them they acknowledged him as their political leader. There was more than mere avarice or fatuity in the man who commanded the allegiance of those splendid young spirits.

But that was still in the future. In the summer of 1560 Robert was merely the unscrupulous upstart whose intention to marry the Queen was interrupting the slumbers of statesmen and inspiring the most baleful metaphors of the preachers. There seemed only too good ground to believe that he would succeed. The Queen had rebuffed Philip, was obviously finished with Arran now that he had served his purpose, was keeping the Archduke and Eric of Sweden dangling ungracefully in mid-air. One did not offend great princes and friendly peoples for nothing... the suspicion was widespread that she was merely biding her time until she could have the husband of her heart's selection.

Robert's enemies challenged him to his face with obscure and disloyal designs, and only the Queen's high-handed interference saved him from the hazards of a duel. The Austrian ambassador demanded whether there was no man in England with enough spirit to run a poniard into him. The gentle voice of Cecil himself was heard to murmur that it would be better if Lord Robert were in paradise. Sinister rumours were collecting round his wife, then living, a secluded guest, at Cumnor Hall near Oxford. Dudley was said to to be spreading a report that she had cancer, so as to prepare opinion for her sudden death; de Quadra had heard, he wrote to Philip, 'from a person who is accustomed to give me veracious news, that Lord Robert has sent poison to his wife. Certainly all the Queen has done with us and the Swede, and will do with the rest in the matter of the marriage, is only keeping Lord Robert's enemies and the country engaged until this wicked deed of killing his wife is consummated.'

Elizabeth's behaviour that summer was anything but reassuring. The many keen eyes fixed upon her saw disturbing and inexplicable symptoms. It was noted that 'she is not so gay as usual': the sparkle seemed to have gone out of her; she was snappish where she had formerly been suave. She complained frequently of small illnesses and neglected the violent sports which ordinarily she so greatly enjoyed. To the uneasy observers she had suddenly become a mere woman burdened with too great cares and without the will to conceal her disappointment at being deprived of what she most wanted. The enthusiasm that one might have expected from her after her resounding triumph in Scotland was strangely lacking, and when Cecil laid the victorious treaty before her on his return from Edinburgh in August, she greeted him with querulous indifference.

With that the gossip boiled over. Her displeasure with her first minister at this moment could only be construed as an intention to dismiss him because of his unconcealed opposition to her marriage with his enemy. The Secretary himself tearfully prepared to hand over the seals of office, and ran up the public temperature by pouring his misgivings into the ears of friend and foe alike. All that the Court and the watching diplomats now waited to hear was how the marriage was to be contrived and when.

In an atmosphere as dark as that which hovered over Edinburgh during the fatal winter of 1567, the Queen, accompanied by Dudley, went on progress to Hampshire, ending up at Windsor as was her custom, in the beginning of of September. A week later, on the ninth of that month, a courier rode in from Oxfordshire to the Castle with the news that Lady Dudley had fallen down the stairs of Cumnor Hall the previous day and died instantly from a broken neck.

As the news spread with unbelievable swiftness across England and Europe, there arose a confused cry of horror in many tongues; for a terrible instant Elizabeth and her good name trembled together over the abyss. The country stood momentarily dumbfounded, not knowing what to think. Englishmen abroad bowed their heads in shame as they heard their Queen's name coupled with the epithets of harlot and murderess. The Continent waited tensely for word that her subjects had thrown her and her paramour into prison, deposed her, executed them both.

These expectations were not altogether fantastic. One has only to recall the feeling of the Scots towards Mary Stuart after Darnley's murder — and Bothwell's friends far outnumbered Dudley's. Elizabeth's popularity was great, but her people's experience of her was too short for their affection to be proof against such a shock as Amy Robsart's death. If the Queen was guilty, she had besmirched the whole nation, and for no better reason than to gratify the most hated man in it. Elizabeth's position was further complicated by the events imminent on the Continent: the second Council of Trent was soon to meet and England to be formally summoned to renew her allegiance to Rome. The Queen would have need of all the prestige she could command to meet that challenge. If she refused the Papal invitation there was certain to be trouble with her Catholic subjects: if the rest of the people in their disgust joined with them, then the prayer of every good Papist, that Heaven would overturn the heretic Queen and reconcile England because of her abominations, would be answered.

Any such hopes were quickly dashed. Elizabeth shook off her lethargy and mastered the situation before it could

master

master her. Exhibiting neither bravado nor anxiety she encountered the world's accusing eye with royal indifference and set about laying bare the truth of the tragedy, not as an interested party but as the sovereign fount of justice. She alone remained calm in the midst of that hysteria, and even recovered her sense of humour. The ambassador in Paris, Sir Nicholas Throckmorton, aghast at what was being said of her in the French Court, sent his secretary to beg her not to give substance to those innuendoes by marrying Dudley. Young Jones breathlessly delivered his message. Elizabeth had had the same arguments dinned into her ears for weeks, but the young man's zeal amused more than it annoyed her — 'she laughed and forthwith turned herself to one side and to the other and set her hand upon her face.' Jones's conviction as he returned to Paris, that he had come on a fool's errand, was a fair reflection of the tranquillizing effect her presence exercised on suspicion and doubt.

Dudley himself signed the order for the inquiry into Amy's death, then withdrew from Court at the Queen's command. The inquest revealed that the unhappy neglected wife had sent her servants out of the house and was alone at the time of the accident. That fact and her state of mind might have justified a verdict of suicide, but the coroner's jury chose, quite properly on the evidence before them, to record a verdict of misadventure. Dudley's enemies muttered accusations of perjury and corruption; another, quite independent inquiry was held and with the same result. Suspicion even then persisted, but it rested on no foundation, and far sounder charges of corruption could, in fact, have been brought against the favourite's accusers than against himself. Public opinion was in general soon satisfied that he and, by the same token, the Queen were innocent of any connection with the tragedy — an interesting contrast to the popular fury that followed Bothwell's 'cleansing' after the murder of Darnley.

By the end of November the storm had blown over and
Dudley

Dudley was back at Court nagging Elizabeth more busily than ever to marry him. But she remained non-committal and he presently grew aware that he was no nearer his goal now that he was a widower than when he had been married. The Queen even refused him the earldom she had previously promised, with the curt remark, as she ran a knife through the patent, that 'the Dudleys had been traitors for three generations.' The lover brooded over his wrongs. He was free to marry, free also of that terrible accusation in men's eyes. His friends swore that he had but to persist in order to win, and various influential persons began to accept him as the inevitable consort, including the Earl of Sussex, who declared with a soldierly oath that he cared not whom the Queen married, even Robert, if he were capable of producing children by her. Yet, in spite of all this encouragement, the young man knew himself impotent, as things were, to turn Elizabeth's no into a yes. He was sure that she would have him if she dared, but he recognized that his lack of support in the country made her afraid of braving the opposition of his enemies. If only some powerful friend would sponsor him and guarantee her against the immediate consequences, he would, he affirmed with conviction, be King within a year.

On the basis of this conclusion he sent his faithful brother-in-law, Sir Henry Sidney, to see the Spanish ambassador and lay before him the following proposal: if the King of Spain would take his part with Elizabeth and prevail on her to marry him, he would repay the favour by leading England again into the Roman fold.

No more astonishing offer was ever made by an English politician to a foreign ruler. It meant no less than a reversal of the whole current of English history, the sale of his country body and soul to Spain if Spain would allow him thereafter to hold it of her as a fief. It sounds incredible — and yet it did not seem impracticable to some of the shrewdest statesmen in Europe. For England was not yet by any means unanimously

unanimously reconciled to the Elizabethan settlement, and if the Queen herself could be won over through her love for Dudley the prospects for its repeal were distinctly promising.

De Quadra gave the proposal his immediate and serious attention. His first response, however, was necessarily cautious; he had already suffered one disillusionment as a result of listening to the Sidney family, when Elizabeth had let him down so badly over the Archduke business, and this time he wanted to be sure that Sir Henry was speaking the Queen's mind as well as his own. He had also to find out how Philip would look on the suggestion: it had until now been the King's fixed idea that Elizabeth must not be allowed to marry a subject, which might make her too independent of him. Moreover, the Bishop had over and over particularly warned His Majesty against the particular subject in question — 'He is the worst young fellow I have ever encountered; heartless, spiritless, treacherous, and false.' The best that de Quadra could say for him was that he was a suitable consort for the woman to whom he familiarly referred as 'this Jezebel.' Sidney was told that the matter would have the ambassadorial consideration, but that the offer could not be laid before Philip until Elizabeth herself was a party to it. The marriage and religion could, of course, have nothing to do with one another — the Church could not, the Bishop was careful to explain, sanction a political bargain involving one of its sacraments. Yet — if the Queen asked him to — he would feel it his duty to write to Madrid for instructions. Alas, for the temptations of holy men in worldly office — the moment Sidney had departed the Bishop sat down at his desk and wrote his master a full account of the visit, recommending His Majesty to give the marriage his blessing.

This was at the end of January, 1561. A few weeks later a formal demand was served on Elizabeth for the admission of the Papal Nuncio, the Abbé Martinengo, then waiting in Brussels,

Brussels, who carried not only the summons to the Council, but his own appointment as permanent legate to England. For the first time the issue was clearly joined between the new English Government and the Catholic Powers. The terms of the invitation left no room for compromise: the Council would be under the authority of the Pope, even in disputed matters to which he was a party. There could be no appeal from its decisions; and Elizabeth was permitted to send as delegates only the Marián bishops now shut up in the Tower, her own bishops being ineligible for lack of Papal consecration. To have consented to receive the Nuncio on these conditions would have been a virtual abdication of sovereignty; Mary Tudor herself had never ventured on so complete a submission. If Elizabeth yielded, half of England would resist with the sword; if she refused, she would be confronted with a coalition between a substantial portion of the other half and the King of Spain. Blood was already running hot: the Catholics of the North were arming, while ugly scenes were taking place in London, where Papists had to run for their lives from the infuriated mobs. There was no help in the ministers, who were as torn and frightened as the country.

Elizabeth turned to France for aid. Francis II had died the previous December. The new King, his brother Charles IX, was a child of ten, and his mother, Catherine de Médicis, Henry II's widow, that sad-faced woman with a serpent's heart, was in control of affairs. Catherine hated the Guises, who had contemptuously elbowed her out of the way during her eldest son's reign, and she distrusted the Holy See, whom the Guises represented in France. Her dominant purpose was so to hold the balance between the various factions as to make the Crown supreme — very much Elizabeth's own. The English Queen, therefore, instructed the Earl of Bedford, who had been sent to Paris with the usual condolences on Francis's death, to discuss an arrangement with the Queen-Mother whereby England and France should join

in

in demanding an impartial Council or, if that were refused, in resisting any attempt at coercion by the Catholic Powers. The alliance had its attractions for Catherine, but its dangers outweighed them, since a league with the English heretic would have raised the whole of Catholic France against her. So she declined, and Elizabeth was left to meet the Roman challenge alone, with the additional possibility that Catherine might in the end be compelled to join her enemies.

The Spanish ambassador contemplated her difficulties with a pious satisfaction which required only two things to complete it — Philip's affirmative answer to his letter and a definite assurance that Dudley's proposal had originated with Elizabeth. For the former he would have to wait on Philip's creaking administrative machinery and a courier service dependent on the winter winds; for the Queen's state of mind he had only the expansive daily bulletins of her lover. De Quadra was no gullible novice: he kept at the back of his mind the possibility that Dudley and Sidney had been talking without their book. If that were so, it was not worth treating with them any further. At the end of February, Philip's answer not yet having arrived, he determined to find out from the Queen herself how the land lay.

The audience was very friendly; the ambassador told Elizabeth how delighted Philip would be to see her married and how much pleasure the rumour that she was seriously thinking of it had given him. If she wanted Philip's opinion he would be glad to ask for it; he omitted to mention that he had already done so. When Dudley's name came up — it was then that she made the confession that she was no angel — de Quadra told her that Philip would approve of him, for he 'well knew the high character which was borne by Lord Robert.' So the Bishop made amends to 'the worst young man in the world.' That was all for the time being; de Quadra had the impression that Elizabeth wanted to hear more, 'but I refrained for fear of making a mistake and because she is — what we know her to be. As there was danger,
                                                                however,

however, that, carried away by her passion as she is, she may fly into some opposite extravagance, I would not leave her without hope.'

The ambassador had reason to be satisfied with the interview. Elizabeth had been interested, even intimate; she had wanted to go on and would have done so had he been in a position to encourage her further confidences. He had even better reason when shortly thereafter Dudley appeared bringing in tow no less a person than Cecil himself, who proceeded at once to take the matter in hand. This indeed looked like business. If the Secretary, 'the man who rules all,' favoured the marriage, then surely nothing remained but to publish the banns. His appearance could only mean that the Queen had converted him by threats or promises or both to her own wish. It was also a good omen that the Secretary and the lover now appeared everywhere together as bosom friends and spoke enthusiastically of each other's virtues. What was more, Cecil, the renowned heretic, was willing to discuss quite reasonably the terms of England's entrance into the Council — though he warned the Spaniard that Elizabeth would be offended unless the Pope addressed his communications to her as Defender of the Faith. The Bishop quite revised his opinion of the man — 'he is neither foolish nor false,' he wrote Philip of the once 'pestilent rogue.' Pleased with himself and the general outlook, he allowed himself to talk to his Catholic friends in England somewhat more indiscreetly than was his habit. When Philip's letter approving the marriage arrived a few days later, there seemed little need for further secrecy.

Then came the shattering news that the Government had flatly refused to admit the Nuncio. De Quadra, unable to believe his ears, staggered forth in search of information. Dudley was as dazed as himself, knew nothing, talked Byronically of going off to the wars to forget his disappointment. Cecil held himself for a while invisible, and when caught merely broke into a two hours' dissertation on the
practical,

practical, historical, and theoretical objections to Church Councils. Of the marriage he had barely heard and was both too busy and too uninformed to be interviewed about it.

Bursting with rage and bafflement the Spaniard requested an audience of the Queen herself and got it. With difficulty remembering his diplomatic manners he asked her to set forth in writing her reasons for excluding the Nuncio. She declined. Nor would she discuss the matter with him: if he wanted her reasons he could apply to her ministers, who would no doubt be pleased to supply them; she owed no explanation either to him or his King.

But why, demanded the ambassador desperately, had she sent Dudley to broach the marriage on conditions perfectly understood on both sides? It was on that understanding alone that he had written for Philip's approval of their arrangement.

Elizabeth opened her eyes in amazement: she had given Dudley no authority to apply for Philip's approval and was at a loss to imagine how the ambassador had ever got the idea that she had. De Quadra firmly reminded her of their previous conversation. She as firmly denied that she had in any way asked him to move in the matter: Robert was a free agent and she could not stop him from discussing his propositions with other people, but what he said in no way committed her. And she recalled to the Bishop his own unqualified statement that the marriage and religion had nothing whatever to do with each other.

There was no more to be said. The Bishop could only console himself with the thought of the revenge soon to fall upon those who had tricked him. Philip must be written to, the Catholics roused.... Heaven just then obliged with a sign of its disfavour — a bolt of lightning that shattered the steeple of Saint Paul's. De Quadra was comforted.

But the omen proved unreliable. The Catholics refused to rise and de Quadra's own friends, to whom he had lent or from whom he had borrowed money, coldly explained why.
They

They were sore at the Nuncio's rejection, no less disgusted than ever with Elizabeth's heresy, but they were even more furious with Philip and his ambassador. They might rebel for their faith or in their own interest, but they would not risk treason in partnership with a Catholic King who could underhandedly connive to put Lord Robert Dudley over them. Philip himself they would follow, but Philip as the protector of the detested favourite, never. Even Elizabeth and Cecil were better than that. In short, de Quadra had talked too soon and too much. Unfortunately for him the Government also discovered at that time that the Papal Nuncio in Ireland was instigating the Irish to rebel. It made an effective bit of domestic propaganda to illustrate the danger of admitting Papal envoys, and together with the Dudley episode united Catholic and Protestant at this critical moment.

As the ambassador brooded over the fiasco he saw his mistakes in their proper proportion. He had been suspicious all along, but of the wrong thing. Robert had been merely the Queen's innocent decoy. He had begun negotiations with Spain in a genuine belief that she would marry him if he had sufficiently strong endorsement. She had allowed him to think so and to convince the ambassador, not a difficult matter since the whole world had already awarded her to Robert. As a crowning touch to give reality to the affair, she had sent her chief minister, Dudley's most dangerous enemy, to arrange the marriage for her. And as a result Spain instead of herself had been manoeuvred into the position of Dudley's sponsor, to the wrath of every Papist in England. So she had deliberately given her lover, as she would have given any ordinary suitor, to be sacrificed on the altar of State, with Cecil as high priest, and thereby postponed the great Catholic rebellion in England for nine invaluable years. Nothing in her life was more typical of her character.

The lover remained, the prospective husband faded into the populous limbo of Elizabeth's suitors. For years yet he and

and other men pulled wires on his behalf, but during that time he was also pulling wires on behalf of others. His best chance had gone: within six months of Amy Robsart's death he knew in his heart, as his mistress knew in hers, that she would never have him and that he must hew out his career in some other capacity than as her consort. Time was soon to show how wise she was, for if she had married him her story might only too easily have been as unhappy as that of the young cousin whose destiny was now converging upon her own.

Chapter V

The Lovely Cousin

ORPHANED at the age of one week by her father's death, a fugitive at five from the English armies come to betroth her by force to little Edward VI, married at sixteen and a widow three days before her eighteenth birthday — this was Mary Stuart's biography in brief at the moment she was making ready to return to Scotland in the spring of 1561. From the day she was born she was a personage of the highest importance: seven days after her appearance in the world she was Queen of Scotland; her girlhood was passed in preparation for the day when she would be Queen of France; and at seventeen she possessed, in the eyes of most of Europe, a contingent right if not an actual present title to the throne of England. Her father, James V, was the son of Henry VIII's elder sister Margaret by her first marriage with James IV of Scotland, and though Henry had disinherited the Stuart line few now considered the will binding; even many Englishmen, who would have resisted to the death any effort to substitute Mary for Elizabeth on the ground of their Queen's bastardy, granted that Mary had the best claim to rule over them if Elizabeth died childless.

Yet despite her importance Mary was almost as unknown a quantity as Elizabeth had been at her accession. Though she had lived constantly in the glare of courts, no responsibility had ever been allowed to fall on her. Henry II and her powerful uncles had adored her and done their best to spoil her, apparently without success. Nature had been as generous to her in personal as in worldly gifts — had given her a lovely face, a strong body, sparkling wit, a vivacious yet docile spirit — but no one could say, even after her seventeen months as Queen of France, what she was capable of doing with

with all that rich endowment or what life and the world would be able to do with her.

Grief-stricken and gravely ill the young widow retired into seclusion to consult with her relatives about the future which her husband's death had so suddenly darkened. The Queen-Mother hated the whole tribe of Guise, but most of all she hated their niece, whose references to herself had been more amusing than tactful. It seemed impossible for Mary's mischievous tongue to restrain such phrases as 'la grossa Caterina' or 'the daughter of a Florentine pawnbroker' when she spoke of her Médicis mother-in-law. The Florentine never forgave: Mary's uncles could do no more for her than she for them so long as Catherine was Regent of France. For all their sakes the family conclave concluded that she must return to Scotland.

But return under what conditions? She had been brought up in the most reactionary Catholic tradition, while her subjects had not yet found a Protestantism extreme enough for them; after casting out her religion they had formed a league with England to forcibly resist its reintroduction. The Highland Catholics sent John Leslie, who as Bishop of Ross was to defend her so bravely and betray her so sorely, to win her to their side, offering to meet her on the west coast of Scotland with an army and conduct her in triumph to Edinburgh. From the other side came her bastard half-brother, Lord James Stuart, now Earl of Moray, an unscrupulous man but an incorruptible politician, to offer her the allegiance of the Congregation if she would refrain from interference with the Presbyterian Kirk and govern as a constitutional monarch. Ambition and reality, temperament and policy, clashed: she would have been happiest to lead the wild Highland legions down on her capital and ascend the throne as champion of her Church and Divine Right. But if she failed — and the Catholics had been defeated the year before with the French to help them — she might find herself ascending instead the rickety steps of a scaffold.

Laying

Laying aside the temptation to a spectacular martyrdom, she came to terms with the ruling party.

That was, however, by no means the whole of the matter. There was still England to reckon with. Elizabeth had, at considerable trouble and expense, removed the foreigner from Scotland; she could not possibly sanction any arrangement by which the Scots might repudiate that bargain or Mary ignore it. In March of 1561 the English Queen sent Randolph once more to Edinburgh to remind the Congregation of its bond, and instructed Sir Nicholas Throckmorton in Paris to secure Mary's ratification of the Treaty of Edinburgh before her return.

Randolph's reception was far from cordial. The Scots had not yet forgiven Elizabeth her cavalier refusal of Arran, and their leaders were disgruntled by her careful watch over the pensions they drew from her treasury. On the other hand, Mary, the stranger and widow, had suddenly become an object of compassionate curiosity. They did not suggest deserting the alliance, nor was there any immediate danger that they would — their ascendancy at home and their incomes were too dependent on Elizabeth for that — but they made it only too obvious that gratitude had grown cold. It was all the more important, therefore, that Mary should be bound as tightly as possible to sustain the treaty before the hand of welcome was held out to her.

Throckmorton was unable to obtain his interview until June. During the entire winter and spring Mary remained away from Paris, staying with relatives at Rheims and Nancy. The reports that drifted to London of her feelings towards England were not encouraging. Moray after his return from Rheims told Throckmorton that she was 'not glad of the kindness between England and Scotland... but covets to dissolve the league made betwixt them.' It was an open secret that she was treating from her seclusion for a second marriage, and the character of her suitors made it plain that she was seeking a husband who would render her
independent

independent both of her people and of England. It was a very sceptical English ambassador to whom she agreed to give an audience after her return to Paris on the tenth of June.

Throckmorton was a doughty Puritan, one of the direct forbears of that grim band who were to lead Mary's grandson to the scaffold. He distrusted her and all that she stood for, yet even he was touched by the pallor and weariness of the tall, graceful figure in her widow's black and white. The marks of many months of illness and sorrow were upon her. Within the year she had lost her husband and her mother; a short time before the darling of the Court, she was now an outcast from it. Her pride was great, her capacity for love amounted to genius, and both endowed her with an uncommon power of suffering.

Unintimidated by the Englishman's hostile scrutiny she quietly took the conversation into her own hands. Without requiring either his opinion or his recommendation she informed him that she had sent her mother's old minister, d'Oysel, to ask Elizabeth for a safe-conduct in case she had to make a forced landing in England during her voyage home. When Throckmorton demanded that she sign the treaty, she refused to discuss it until she had consulted with the States of her realm. He protested, quite reasonably, that the States had already ratified it. She retorted that they might now perhaps be induced to change their minds, and added a gentle but unmistakable hint that she could manage her own affairs perfectly well without Elizabeth's help.

Throckmorton decided that it would be better on the whole to have her in Scotland than in France, since amongst the Scots she would be more dependent on the English Queen than amongst the French. He therefore recommended to Cecil that he give d'Oysel a cordial welcome, though keeping a wary eye on him, and grant him the safe-conduct. On receipt of the letter Elizabeth again ordered Randolph to to obtain an assurance from the Lords that they would hold Mary to the treaty on her homecoming. D'Oysel was kept waiting in London till she had her answer.

But the Scots were evasive, excused themselves on the plea that Parliament was not in session, and were obviously minded to bargain with Mary before renewing their promises to England. Elizabeth thereupon sent for d'Oysel and publicly declined, in an irritated outburst, to issue the safe-conduct until he could give the required promise on Mary's behalf. His request for permission to go to Scotland was likewise refused, the Queen intimating that the sooner he returned to France the better. She instructed Throckmorton on July 1 to convey her decision to Mary and tell her 'that her manner of dealing is plain and friendly with her friends and with others as they used her.' There was no other answer she could give; it was impossible for her to extend the hospitality of her shores to a person who openly entertained designs against the peace of her throne. De Sèvres, the French ambassador in London, privately admitted to Cecil that it was exactly what he had expected her to do.

On the afternoon of July 20 Throckmorton repaired to Saint Germain to transmit his mistress's answer to Mary. The substance of it she already knew, for when he entered the room she was talking to d'Oysel. She rose from her chair when she saw the Englishman, who told her in a set speech that the safe-conduct had been refused, because of her 'unamicable and indirect dealing,' but that he had been commanded to say that if she changed her mind and would ratify the treaty his Queen would be happy not only to give her free passage through her realm, but to meet and embrace her in person.

Mary commanded everyone except Throckmorton to retire, seated herself and bade him sit down by her, explaining that she was not yet very strong and was not sure how far she could control her temper: if she lost it, she added with pointed sarcasm, 'she liked not to have so many witnesses

nesses of her passions as his mistress had when she talked with d'Oysel.'

When they were alone her proud and sensitive spirit poured itself out in a torrent. She bitterly deplored having so forgotten herself as to require from Elizabeth a favour she need not have asked. She could pass home to her own realm without her cousin's licence just as easily as she had been able to come to France twelve years earlier despite all English efforts to stop her. She meant no evil to Elizabeth, quite the contrary. She preferred her friendship above all others, but if Elizabeth persisted in this strange animosity towards her she had friends in France and elsewhere 'who would be glad and willing to employ their forces to aid her.' The belief was sincere enough, but the future was soon to expose its hollowness. There were many who loved Mary as a person: as a sovereign the only friend of importance she ever had was the Queen of England.

Her concluding speech to Throckmorton was moving and charged with a portent of which she could not have dreamed:

> Monsieur l'Ambassadeur, if my preparations were not so much advanced as they are, peradventure the Queen your mistress's unkindness might stay my voyage. But now I am determined to adventure the matter, whatsoever come of it. I trust that the wind will be so favourable that I shall not need to come on the coast of England; for if I do the Queen your mistress shall have me in her hands to do her will of me; and if she be so hard-hearted as to desire my end she may do her pleasure and make sacrifice of me. Peradventure that casualty might be better for me than to live.

A few days later she left for Calais and on August 14 embarked for Leith in her two great ships and two galleys, the one red, the other all white, her own vessel carrying the white flag with the arms of France aloft and another glistening like silver in the stern. A hush of suspense settled over France and Britain as the little fleet disappeared into the North Sea. It was fully believed by the conventional minds of diplomacy that she would never reach home, that the
English

English Navy was waiting to pounce upon her and bring her a prisoner into an English port. Catherine de Médicis and de Quadra both prophesied it; Mary herself was prepared for it and thought herself in great danger. Throckmorton angrily urged her capture on Cecil after the refusal of the passport. William Maitland of Lethington, the most talented of Scottish politicians, who was to serve Mary so ably, betray her so desperately, and die in her cause to spite his enemies, wrote in his own cynical vein to Cecil, 'If the galleys may quietly pass I wish the passport had been liberally granted. To what purpose should you open your pack and sell none of your wares?...'

But all the anxiety, prayers, and malice that followed the royal vessels on their journey were alike meaningless. Only one person could raise a finger to intercept them, the Queen of England, and she, despite much earnest advice, never for a moment thought of doing so. She would not grant the safe-conduct until Mary had complied with what she considered that the safety of England required of her, but neither would she put herself in the wrong by arresting a fellow sovereign embarked on a lawful voyage. It was said that her fleet had searched for Mary and missed her in the fog, but her own answer, written direct to the Queen of Scots, contains the whole story: 'For the report that we have sent our admiral and navy to impeach your passage: your servants know its falseness and that we have only two or three barques at sea, to apprehend certain Scottish pirates haunting our waters under pretence of letters of marque: whereto we were almost compelled at the complaint of the Spanish ambassador.' This was true: de Quadra knew it, and so did Lethington. If Elizabeth could blockade the Firth of Forth against the whole naval strength of France, it would not have been difficult to lie in wait for and capture four ships furnished for comfort rather than war. With no more serious adventure than a slight delay due to the fog, Mary rode to anchor in Leith harbour on August 19.

A struggle

A struggle to the death between the two cousins was ultimately inevitable. They had been brought up in the traditional hatreds of Protestant and Catholic, English and French, English and Scotch. Mary's whole life from the day of her birth had been overshadowed by England's enmity. Elizabeth's life and her throne as well were under constant threat from the forces that Mary represented. Even if both with the best of good-will were disposed to accept the state of affairs as they existed on Mary's return, there would have remained a fundamental cause of antagonism in the succession to the English throne. Mary believed herself to possess an indefeasible right direct from God; Elizabeth could tolerate no acknowledged successor for the reason she gave in a hundred different ways and at a hundred different times, that all the hostile elements in the country she was trying to unite would fly to the heir with their treasons, as her sister's enemies had flown to her when she was Princess; certainly she could acknowledge no heir whose policy, temperament, and religion must necessarily signify the destruction of all that she had accomplished. Therein lay the core of the conflict and nothing on earth could have prevented it; nor, given the characters and brains of the two protagonists, could anything have altered the result.

During the first year or so after Mary's return there was a distinct attempt at reasonableness on both sides. The elder cousin, in an effort to find a basis of compromise, opened a friendly correspondence — 'When princesses treat by open assembly of ambassadors,' she wrote, 'the world, especially the subjects of both, judge the amity not sound but shaken or crazed which we would no wise be conceived of ours' — to which Mary responded with every sign of agreement and affection. Neither abated her claims, but each, outwardly at least, gave the other credit for good intentions. Mary employed her surplus energies in riding after stags, dancing, and exchanging religious polemics with the truculent John Knox.

The

The good feeling was materially assisted by Elizabeth's treatment of Mary's principal rivals for the succession. Foremost of these was Katharine Grey, sister of Lady Jane Grey, on whom Protestant hopes were fastened as firmly as Catholic on Mary. Katharine was the granddaughter of Henry VIII's younger sister Mary; if that monarch's will, cutting off the line of the Stuarts, was valid, she stood in precisely the same relation to the throne as did Mary herself if the will were ignored. De Feria and de Quadra, elastic in politics as they were rigid in religion, had for a time contemplated taking Katharine under their wing and setting her up as a rival to Elizabeth, but Philip, fonder of his sister-in-law than were his ambassadors and more concerned to avoid trouble, had frowned on the plan. The Protestant leaders, however, anxious to provide an heir of their own selection if Elizabeth died without issue, adopted the young woman's claims. In December, 1560, they married her secretly to one of their party, Edward Seymour, Earl of Hertford, a son of the Lord Protector Somerset and hence a nephew by marriage of Henry VIII.

But Nature made an unexpected irruption into politics. The young couple fell in love and by the summer of 1561 it became impossible to maintain both Katharine's reputation and the legend of her spinsterhood. Cecil, who was by this time thoroughly frightened at his part in the proceedings, wrote to the Earl of Sussex on August 12: 'The tenth of this month at Ipswich was a great mishap. The Lady Katharine is certainly known to be big with child, as she saith by the Earl of Hertford. Thus is God displeased with us.... The Queen's Majesty doth well, thank be God, although not well quieted with this mishap of the Lady Katharine.' The Secretary's dismay at this fruit of an achievement for which he was in large part responsible is somewhat surprising, but no doubt he was what he always claimed to be, a very simple man.

'Unquiet' scarcely does justice to Elizabeth's feelings. In

GENEALOGICAL TABLE OF DESCENDANTS OF HENRY VII

(showing only those mentioned in text)

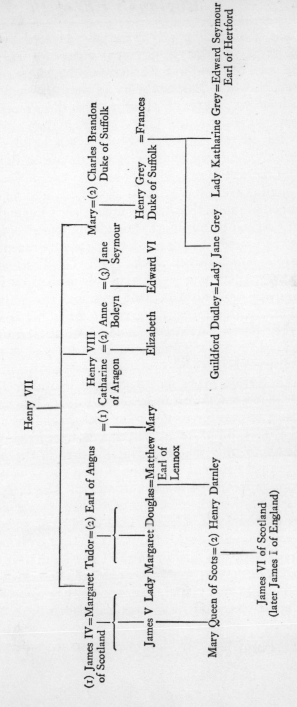

In general she disapproved of people marrying and having children, for reasons which have been variously explained, but it requires no psycho-analyst to interpret her rage at the news of Katharine's pregnancy. The secret marriage looked like a sinister plot to force a successor upon her whether she liked it or not, and she instantly set about showing the busy-bodies who had arranged it that they should not have their way. On the day after Cecil's letter the young bride was lodged in the Tower, where her husband, peremptorily summoned home from France, was sent to join her. On September 24 their son was born. Cecil was directed to institute inquiries into the matter to find out who had arranged the iniquitous union, but for once the astute Secretary professed himself completely stumped: so far as he could discover, the only people who knew anything whatever about the marriage were anonymous 'maids or women going for maidens.' The witnesses dared not come forward for fear of the Queen's anger, and the unfortunate young couple loyally held their tongues rather than expose their friends to it.

Instead of being furious at this conspiracy of silence, the Queen was quick to turn it to her own purpose. If there were no witnesses there had been no legal marriage.... She put the question to an ecclesiastical commission, presided over by the Archbishop of Canterbury; after solemn deliberation it proclaimed the infant in the Tower illegitimate and lopped him off the genealogical tree. The matter was then dropped, since Elizabeth had a very shrewd suspicion that further inquiry would only serve to compromise some of her most useful servants.

The young family was kept in the Tower until the following year, when they were sent to the country at the time of the plague in London. For the rest of her life Katharine was kept in captivity, though of so mild a nature that her second son was born fourteen months after the first. It would hardly have done to let her go free — too many scheming politicians were prowling about to take advantage of her innocence.

cence. The treatment she received from Elizabeth was harsh, considering that her sole offence was her royal blood, but under almost any other monarch of the time she would have come to the same end as her gentle sister Lady Jane.

Before the year was out, Katharine was joined in the Tower by another pretender. Lady Margaret Douglas was a daughter of Margaret Tudor, Henry VIII's elder sister, who had contracted a second marriage, after James IV's death, with the Earl of Angus. Lady Margaret herself was married to Matthew Stuart, Earl of Lennox, who was descended from both the Scottish royal lines of Stuart and Hamilton. Her elder son, Henry Stuart, Lord Darnley, had therefore through her a contingent claim on the English and through his father on the Scottish throne. His English rights were of course subject to the same qualification as his cousin Mary Stuart's, since their common Tudor grandmother's seed had been barred from the succession under Henry VIII's will; in both lines, Tudor and Stuart, he stood second to the Queen of Scots so long as she remained childless. Lady Margaret Douglas had once entertained hopes of herself superseding Elizabeth, but she had now put them by and was conducting a vigorous campaign amongst the Northern Catholics on behalf of her son. The young man himself was in France at the time, trying to convince Mary Stuart's uncles that it would be an excellent idea if he and the young widow were to marry and unite in their joint person his claim and hers to the English throne. It might have been thought that he had little to offer since his title was subordinate to hers, but he was an English subject and she a foreigner, which gave him a stronger claim to English consideration.

Cecil's spies proved more apt at ferreting out the Countess's activities than Katharine's witnesses. Elizabeth commanded Lady Margaret to report in London, where she was placed in custody, while Lennox was sent to the Tower to meditate on the disadvantages of a too illustrious

descent

descent and an over-ambitious wife. Darnley, unlike Hertford, remained safely in France.

Elizabeth then recalled that her Aunt Margaret had been unhappy in her marriage with the Earl of Angus and had successfully petitioned the Pope to have it annulled. The refusal of a similar petition to Henry VIII when he wanted to marry Elizabeth's mother caused the English Reformation; but its grant to Margaret could also be turned to account. For once the Defender of the Faith found the Pope as useful as her own Primate. The annulment proved, if one chose to look at it that way, that her aunt had never been properly married to Angus, and if that were true, Lady Margaret was just as much illegitimate as the new-born babe in the Tower. Bastardy was not an irremediable stigma in the sixteenth century, especially in royal circles — Elizabeth had worn it twice with no permanent effects — but it served at that moment to hush Darnley's advocates in the country and to reassure the Queen of Scotland that her rivals were not faring any better than herself.

The peace between the two royal ladies grew positively idyllic as the months wore on. They even wrote on disputed business matters in terms of endearment. Mary sent Elizabeth a 'ring with a diamond fashioned like a heart,' and the thrifty Elizabeth reciprocated with the diamond 'like a rock,' which Mary was to construe as a promise of asylum in the most dangerous emergency of her life. Mary wished that Elizabeth were a man so they two might marry; later she told Randolph that 'she will have none to her husband but the Queen of England,' which the puzzled Englishman explained to Cecil was doubtlessly 'spoken in her merry mood.' He himself, after having been very nearly thrown out of Scotland on Mary's first arrival, was subsequently tempted with a pension and a pretty Scotswoman to wife, but sturdily refused both.

The Queens at length became so fondly curious about each other that both vowed they could remain apart no
longer,

longer, and arranged to meet during the following summer. The project roused their subjects to frantic alarm. The Catholics in both countries were convinced that Elizabeth's blandishments would win Mary away from her faith; the Protestants were equally certain that Elizabeth would yield to Mary's and promise her the succession. The sovereigns remained deaf to pleas and imprecations; the time was fixed for late August, the place somewhere, preferably Nottingham, in the Midlands. But the round of dalliance, the long intimate conversations in a sunlit garden, were never to take place outside the pleasant realms of historical fantasy. Before the appointed season rolled round, the meeting had been indefinitely postponed by massacre, rebellion, and war.

The first of the long series of religious wars that made France a shambles for over thirty years broke out that summer. Its signal was the massacre of Vassy, where, on Sunday, March 1, the Duke of Guise's retainers surrounded the little Reformed church and set it on fire while the congregation was at prayer. The Huguenots, who had long been expecting their enemies' onslaught, flew to arms, while their leader, the Prince of Condé, at once sent an envoy to remind Elizabeth of the help they had given her during her troubles with the Guises in Scotland and to request her aid now that the Protestant cause in France was threatened with extermination.

It was the second grave decision that Elizabeth had to make in foreign affairs, and quite as momentous as the first. In Scotland she had fought for her immediate safety on the side of the native majority; in France she would be assisting a minority to avert a more distant but perhaps even greater danger. If the Guises eliminated the Huguenot faction they would regain control of French policy and direct it towards a pan-Catholic league for the recovery of England. Elizabeth's subjects, inflamed by the massacre of their co-religionists, were shrieking for blood. Frenchmen in London were driven

driven to seek refuge in their embassy and only the stern intervention of the authorities kept the mob from burning it down with all its inmates.

The Queen shared the popular feeling to the full. Her proclamation against the Guise atrocities might have been written in the hottest Calvinist blood. But she loathed war, then as always, with a statesman's distrust of its uncertainty and a woman's hatred of its bloodshed and expense. The majority of the Council were for keeping hands off. She hesitated and was as usual cursed by everybody. Sir Henry Sidney was sent to find out from the Queen-Mother whether the differences between the parties could not be patched up, but found her utterly helpless; things had already gone too far. The Guises, convinced that they had their enemies on the hip, spurned all talk of compromise and seized Calais while the conversations were going on. This was the last straw: if they succeeded in dragging Philip in on their side, as they expected shortly to do, Antwerp as well as Calais would be shut, and English merchants deprived of any available port for their Continental trade. Overriding the Council with even more vigour than in 1559, the Queen declared for war on her own responsibility. In September the Treaty of Hampton Court was signed, whereby she bound herself to help the Huguenots with men and money, while they promised to restore Calais to her, giving her Havre as a pledge until the victory was won. Before the signatures were affixed, her troops were being embarked for France. Elizabeth announced, according to custom, that she had no quarrel with the French Crown, merely with the faction that was trying to usurp its powers; in this case at least the explanation was more than a pretext.

Her interference in France was the worst blunder she ever made. Had she held aloof she would have compelled the moderate party in France, headed by the Queen-Mother, to defend the Huguenots in order to prevent the Catholic extremists from gaining control of the country. But the sight of

of an English army, recalling unappeased enmities older than
the Hundred Years' War, drove the vast majority of Frenchmen into such a fury of patriotism that they were ready to
accept even the help of Spain against the invader. It was
lucky for Elizabeth that the sluggish Philip did not respond
to the invitation of the Guises and thus convert a domestic
quarrel into a European conflagration.

In the opening engagements, at sea, the allies were uniformly successful. The hardiest deep-water sailors in France
were Huguenots, just as the best English seamen came from
the staunchly Protestant counties of Devon and Cornwall.
The two navies virtually swept French commerce off the
ocean, but they did not stop there: it often happened that
when the prizes were examined at La Rochelle or Plymouth
various neutrals had somehow got mixed up with them.
The Spaniards were especially prone to this misfortune, and
de Quadra indignantly wrote to Philip that the Queen was
'determined to make herself Mistress of the Seas'— a first
use of the title which her sailors and poets between them
were to affix to her name forever.

On land, however, the Huguenots were beaten on every
battlefield, driven out of one town after another. The loss of
Rouen on October 25 shattered them politically, and the
battle of Dreux on December 19, when the Prince of Condé
was taken prisoner, ended their military effort. In February
they fired their last shot on behalf of the allied cause, an
assassin's bullet into the Duke of Guise's back. Satisfied
with this achievement they came to terms with the Duke's
followers and joined in the investment of Havre, whither
the English forces under the Earl of Warwick had retreated
after the Huguenot *débâcle*. .

Elizabeth, convalescing from an attack of smallpox which
had all but carried her off, worked with feverish energy to
save her army. She prepared to reinforce Havre and meantime sent Warwick one of those incomparable messages of
cheer and confidence which were worth a legion in raising the
spirits

spirits of her soldiers. She lashed out at 'the false Condé' with such scorn that he cringed behind Catherine de Médicis' skirts. It was now Elizabeth's turn, however, to suffer the irony with which she had so expertly plied others: the Queen-Mother reminded her of her own proclamation that she was fighting only to protect the King from the Guises; that danger was now happily past, so the King thanked her for her help and begged that she would be pleased to withdraw her troops, since he had no further need of their services. With a great many hundreds of thousands of pounds invested in the war, Elizabeth was neither disposed to relish the sarcasm nor to surrender Havre without repayment. She attempted a diversion on the French coast to relieve the pressure on Warwick, but it failed for lack of a proper landing-place. She then gathered every man and every ship available, and dispatched them to Havre under the command of Lord Admiral Clinton. But the relief arrived too late. The beleaguered army, starving and disease-ridden, ignorant of the approaching reinforcements, had just capitulated with the honours of war. As Clinton hove in sight, Warwick was being courteously assisted by the French to evacuate his forces. The fleet's only employment was to transport the pitiful survivors home and with them the plague that ravaged England that summer.

The defeat stopped short of disaster. The coast of England had never been threatened, thanks to Philip's tepidity and her own naval strength. The Scottish alliance, surviving the test, had kept the Postern Gate secure. Indeed it was the general English opinion, very characteristic of the time, that the country had not, legally speaking, been at war at all. Elizabeth entered upon the negotiations which led to the Peace of Troyes with prestige and claims undiminished, with the result that the French treasury agreed to refund a large part of her loans to the Huguenots. The principal loss, apart from the cost in lives, was her contingent title to Calais, due to come up for final settlement in four years. But

But the principal gain far outweighed it — Elizabeth had learned the valuable lesson never to interfere in the affairs of other States against the wishes of the majority. She was wise enough never to forget it.

Not the least of Elizabeth's luck was the friendly truce between her and Mary during her conflict with the Queen of Scotland's relatives. Mary burst into tears on the news of the massacre at Vassy and, though she could not openly join in her subjects' execration of the act, made haste to dissociate herself from it. During the autumn of 1562, while the combined English-Huguenot forces were being harried across northern France, she not only showed herself sympathetic to her cousin's troubles, but led a punitive expedition against the same rebellious Highlanders who had earlier tempted her with visions of a Catholic descent upon Edinburgh. The campaign was more to her taste than the patient subtleties of politics or the weary routine of administration — exultantly 'she wished that she was a man to know what life it was to lie all night in the fields or to walk on a causeway with a jack and a knapsack, a Glasgow buckler and a broadsword.'

But the 'kindness' between the neighbouring Queens could not last. Mary, her distaste for the petty round in Scotland aggravated by martial activity, was growing restive. For a year and a half she had been told that nothing could be done in the matter of the succession until Parliament met; apart from gentle though steady reminders she had waited with praiseworthy patience. The session, the second of Elizabeth's reign, began in January of 1563, and the Queen of Scots at once resolved to force the full acknowledgment of her title. She likewise determined for a twofold reason to bring her widowhood to an end. In part she was moved by the normal woman's preference for a mate: her deep grief for the young husband that was dead and her future history both prove the truth of her candid admission to Randolph, 'Not to marry,

marry, you know it cannot be for me.' Chiefly, however, she yearned for a marriage that would bring her back to the larger stage of European affairs. At the end of February her Secretary, Lethington, was sent to London to put both matters in train. The life-and-death struggle between the two Queens was at last joined.

Elizabeth had now been on the throne a little over four years, Mary back in Scotland somewhat less than two. Already the wide difference in their characters as sovereigns was plainly to be seen. It was a difference not only of method — the one's disposition to delay, the other's to headlong action (for Elizabeth could at times be forward and Mary cautious) — but of the fundamental outlook upon which the respective conduct of each was founded.

From the time that she could think, Elizabeth's whole thought had been of England. She loved it, and her proudest boast was the purity of her English blood. 'She would not leave England,' she informed her suitor, the Prince of Sweden, 'for half the kingdoms of the earth.' Every progress through its countryside was a renewal of her strength; never in her life did she go abroad or wish to do so. Despite her cosmopolitan education, the customs, manners, traditions, and language of her own people pleased her best. She understood them and they her, nor cared how much others disliked her so long as she was sure of their love. She felt at one with them and by her gracious candour made them feel one with her: 'Come hither, little Recorder,' she addressed that official at Warwick, after he had nervously bade her welcome in an interminable harangue, 'I was told that you would be afraid to look on me or speak boldly; but you were not so afraid of me as I was of you, and I now thank you for putting me in mind of my duty.' The secret of her own happiness and England's adoration lay in her manner of marching into a cottage, praising its cleanliness or damning its cooking, and marching out again leaving behind her a radiance of something at once utterly human and utterly royal.

Mary,

Mary, only half Scottish in blood, and altogether foreign by upbringing and temperament, was never at home in her own country. She learned its language late and never fluently. She turned from its poverty and parochialism with distaste; her people's religion, habits, their very food, were odious to her. She found the manners of her aristocracy boorish and sought whenever she could the company of foreigners. What could it signify to one who had been Queen of France, the first lady and the best beloved of the wittiest and and most cultured circle on earth, to chaffer like a shopkeeper with greedy barons, to sit for hours listening to discordant hymns and endless turgid sermons, to review armies dressed in 'ane mantle, with ane shirt fashioned after the Irisch manner, going bair-legged to the knie.' If she could have the world she would consider Scotland well lost.

The man whom Mary sent to obtain the acknowledgment of her claim and to find her a husband was the most accomplished in her service, if not in all her kingdom. The ordinary Scot of the Reformation was distinguished for religious zeal and moral earnestness, the ruling caste for bad manners, contempt of learning, brutish greed and violence. William Maitland of Lethington was a cynic who believed that God was 'ane bogle of the nurserie.' He was delicately bred, finely cultivated — Elizabeth called him 'the flower of the wits of Scotland' — a diplomat to his finger-tips, flexible, suave, and guileful, the only true Renaissance man and politician his country could boast. He distrusted his Queen and she him, but he recognized her value as a means of uniting Scotland, and was prepared to serve her, faithfully and unscrupulously, in her interests as well as his own.

The first part of his errand failed. Parliament came down on Westminster resolved on forcing the Queen to fix the succession. Elizabeth at once clapped a lid on their demands and sat on it firmly until the boiling in the Commons had subsided. She did not intend, she explained, that her enemies should run after her heir as her sister's 'had run after her when

when she was Princess.' To name a successor at this time
would be 'simply to prepare her own winding sheet and make
her grave ready.' When the Lords tried to intercede, she told
them sharply that she did not relish the thought of her death
being held always before her: 'the marks they saw on her face
were not wrinkles but pits of smallpox, and although she might
be old, God could send her children as he did to Saint Elizabeth, and they had better consider well what they were asking, as if she declared a successor it would cost much blood
to England.'

Actually she was doing Mary the best service in her power.
If Parliament had been free to name an heir the last person
they would have chosen would have been the Queen of Scots;
in the previous autumn, when Elizabeth was thought to be
dying of smallpox, scarcely a voice had been raised in her favour. The legislators believed with de Quadra that, 'if she
[Elizabeth] were to nominate the Queen of Scotland, as she
says she desires to do, it would manifestly lead to a rising of
the Catholics in the country and to rebellion and the re-intro-
duction of the Catholic religion by force.' There is no reason
to doubt that Cecil was sincerely speaking her mind when he
told Lethington 'that if they could find a way by which the
Queen of England might be secured for her life without danger and for religion remaining as it is at present, this Queen
would not be sorry to nominate the Queen of Scots for heir at
once.' Had Elizabeth's sole object been to lay obstacles in her
cousin's way to the throne, all she had to do was to give the
Commons their head.

But Mary could only conceive of monarchy as unlimited;
to her dying day she failed to grasp the limitations imposed
on the Crown by the constitution and popular feeling. It was
Elizabeth's understanding of both that enabled her in the end
to become the autocrat by her own genius that Mary thought
herself to be by act of God. Moreover, Mary's information,
derived from prejudiced sources, was about as misleading as
it could well be. Those who favoured her, the Northern
Catholics

Catholics in particular, gave her to understand that they represented the dominant sentiment of the country, just as Philip's ambassadors led him into the fatal error of thinking that what they wanted England wanted also. It is a common failing of the politically dissatisfied to exaggerate the extent of the sympathy they command. Lethington reported that the case was hopeless and the English Council putting him off with smooth words. His mistress, furious with Elizabeth, pressed forward her plan to marry the heir of Spain.

De Quadra and Lethington, the bishop and the atheist, went into conference together and after wary debate agreed on a proposal to put before Philip II. The occasion was propitious: the King was still irritated with his sister-in-law's crimes against his religion, the whole of Spain seething with wrath at English treatment of Spanish ships, de Quadra at such odds with his hosts that he had barely escaped the indignity of expulsion. On March 18 the ambassador hopefully recommended to his King a marriage between the 'Queen who was in prudence, chastity, and beauty equalled by few in the world,' and Philip's insane hunchbacked son Don Carlos, the most repulsive Prince in Christendom.

Lethington rubbed his hands in satisfaction at the success of this second step in his mission. If Philip consented, well and good; if not, there were still Charles IX of France and Elizabeth's suitor the Austrian Archduke Charles as second strings to his bows. He could now go to France and inform the Queen-Mother that unless she consented to her son's marriage with the Queen of Scots the King of Spain would get in ahead of her, which would make things very ticklish for France. After that Philip might be subjected to the same process if he proved coy, or else might be induced to support the Archduke. There seemed no flaw in the Scot's careful, subtly interwoven designs.

Meantime neither Elizabeth nor her agents were asleep. She knew exactly what 'the Fox' was up to and did not approve of it. If Mary married any one of the trio she had in
mind,

mind, she would eventually bring both Catholicism and a foreign power back into Scotland; if it was Don Carlos she would one day also be Queen of the Netherlands, the gravest danger that could conceivably confront England. Elizabeth intimated to Lethington that it was high time he went about his business — he had come on the pretext of passing into France as peacemaker — but he glibly evaded the hint. She then informed him outright that if his mistress married any one of the three Charleses she would construe it as an unfriendly act. Lethington, deep in a scheme which would put Mary beyond the reach of Elizabeth's threats, refused to be intimidated and continued his dealings with the Spanish ambassador until their agreement was reached.

Suddenly Elizabeth altered her tone. Lethington, presenting himself for a farewell audience, found her blithe, chatty, quizzical. She questioned him lightly about Mary's marriage and seemed inclined to make a joke of the whole matter. The Scot eyed her with amused suspicion, wondering what she could be up to. At length she casually remarked that she herself had in mind a husband for Mary who would make her both safe and happy, a man 'in whom Nature had implanted so many graces that if she [Elizabeth] wished to marry she would prefer him to all the princes of the world.' The man's name was Robert Dudley.

The Scot, as he admitted to his friend de Quadra in reporting the conversation, was staggered. No one enjoyed more than he Elizabeth's unfailing power of surprise, but this time she had outdone herself. He had no idea whether she was serious or not — that question is still under heated debate — but it was important to find out. If she was not, this was a transparent device to put Mary off her Spanish Prince; if she was, what were the conditions of her offer? If a promise of the succession went with it, it might be worth considering — provided his own Queen could bring herself to take her cousin's leavings.

It was gratifying, Lethington replied with urbane disbelief,

belief, to learn how much Her Majesty loved his mistress, for she must love her very dearly if she was willing to give her the man she herself so greatly prized. But he was certain that Mary, even if she had loved Lord Robert as much as did Elizabeth, would never dream of depriving her cousin of all the joy and solace she received from his companionship.

Elizabeth appreciated the sentiment, but refused to accept it as an answer. Lethington, puzzled and uneasy, afraid for his mistress's sake to decline outright an offer that might have much in it, uncertain of what Mary herself would say to it, suggested to Elizabeth an expedient 'which he knew would shut her mouth directly.' His Queen was very young yet: why did not Elizabeth marry Lord Robert herself and have children by him, which was so important for the welfare of the country; then, when it should please God to call her to Himself, she could leave both kingdom and her husband to her cousin? In that way, since it was improbable that Lord Robert should fail to have children by one or the other of them, she would have ensured his becoming father of the Kings of Britain. Elizabeth, amused at his adroitness, laughed. The Scot echoed the laugh, but nervously, and made his escape.

The third part of his errand took him to France, where he had no luck whatever. Catherine would not hear of Mary Stuart as a daughter-in-law for the second time; all hope, therefore, of exerting pressure on Philip through the threat of a French marriage was at an end. Catherine also made it plain that all her considerable influence would be used to prevent a union between Mary and Carlos. Nor was that all: Lethington now discovered one of the reasons of Elizabeth's laughter at their parting. She herself was in treaty for the hand of the young Charles IX, and vastly more favoured by the rulers of France than his own mistress. The disappointed Scot returned to England, only to find that Philip, despite his difficulties with his sister-in-law, was not yet inclined to antagonize her; his answer to the proposal for

Mary's

Mary's marriage with Don Carlos, while not wholly discouraging, was no more than lukewarm. Lethington began to meditate whether it would not be better after all for Mary to accept a husband from the Queen of England's hands.

Mary at first declared passionately that she would not hear of it. She would marry no Protestant, least of all one of Elizabeth's cast-offs. But a few months' reflection caused her to change her mind. Elizabeth had shut the door on her Continental hopes, and there was now an unpleasant rumour abroad that she was about to name Darnley her successor. Mary, oppressed by the sense that all her plans were going awry, sent James Melville to London with the intimation that she was not averse after all to considering Dudley as a husband. Privately she instructed Melville to get in touch with the Countess of Lennox and discuss the conditions of a marriage with Darnley. If that could be arranged, she would be able to unite both claims to the succession and be in a position to defy Elizabeth, perhaps even turn her off the throne. Such a union would require Elizabeth's co-operation — for Darnley was in England — but what a master-stroke if it could be contrived with her consent, using the Dudley marriage as a screen.

Elizabeth entertained Melville with conversation and music, and let the matter simmer for a while. There was no pressing hurry: Mary could not marry either Carlos or Charles IX at the moment, and she had heard on good authority that the Scots would not have the Archduke because he had no money. She idly renewed her own flirtation with the Austrian and slowed down the pace of her negotiations with Charles IX; when the French pointed out that she was taking a longer time to make up her mind than God had taken to make the world, she merely retorted that God was a greater artist than herself. To prevent any recurrence of the Carlos project she set herself to re-establish her old friendship with Spain.

In

In this she was materially assisted by the death of de Quadra and the character of his successor. The poor Bishop, struck down by the plague in the summer of 1563, died just after learning that his great scheme for destroying Elizabeth through the marriage of Mary and Carlos had been indefinitely deferred, and passed away murmuring, 'I can do no more.' Suspected and badgered by his hosts, who arrested his servants, opened his correspondence,. and twice nearly expelled him because of his intrigues, defeated in his aims by Philip's cautious timidity and fettered by His Majesty's parsimony — the ambassador's body remained in the hands of his creditors for a year until his friends privately redeemed it — de Quadra, acting according to his Jesuitical lights, had merely created friction with England without doing his country any good. His successor, Don Guzman de Silva, was of another stamp. He was also a churchman, the Dean of Toledo, but broad-minded, cultivated, a thorough man of the world. He realized certain truths that his predecessor had declined to face, notably that England would not again become Catholic so long as her chief commercial friends were the Protestants of the Netherlands. He appreciated Cecil, though he disagreed with him, and his relations with Elizabeth were cordial from the first. She chose him as a frequent companion of her leisure, joked with him over the allegorical thrusts at her spinsterhood which formed the burden of the topical masques she made him sit through with her. She laughingly burst in upon a private dinner at the Marchioness of Northampton's where she knew he would be present, walked home alone with him through Saint James's Park to discuss her marriage with the Archduke, which de Silva of course favoured, and dismissed him with the unilluminating information 'that a fool was about who had advised her never to marry a German as they were bad men.' She assured him that she had always been a Catholic at heart and nearly convinced him: at Cambridge he accompanied her to a comedy in which the Catholic faith was burlesqued somewhat obscenely,

scenely, whereupon the Queen, 'using strong language,' made
an angry exit, taking the torchbearers with her so as to leave
'the thoughtless and scandalous representation' in darkness
— it was a pendant-piece to her angry exclamation to the
Roman priests who bore candles at her coronation, 'Away
with those torches! We can see well enough.' The vexed
question of the seized Spanish merchantmen was amicably arranged between them and the two countries put on a better
footing than they had been for some years past or were to be
for a generation after de Silva's departure.

Almost the first result of this renewed friendliness was
Philip's definitive refusal of his son to Mary Stuart. The reason he gave was that his cousin, the Holy Roman Emperor,
was already counting on Mary for the Archduke, but this
was merely the forgetfulness of a great and busy brain: when
de Quadra had made the original suggestion the previous
year, Philip had answered that 'the less His Apostolic Majesty knew about the matter the better.' If Mary's prospects
had not been so complicated, it is to be feared that Philip
would have been less considerate of his Austrian relative —
but, as Throckmorton remarked, he was loath that his son
should marry a process.

This was August, 1564. Frustrated of her husband on the
Continent and of her title in England, Mary now professed
herself ready to marry Dudley if the succession went with
him. Whether she was sincere in her acceptance can no more
be determined than the sincerity of Elizabeth's offer. Her
closest advisers and the English ambassador, Randolph, were
convinced that she was in earnest; on the other hand, she
was still hoping to checkmate Elizabeth by a marriage with
Darnley. It was a battle of wits whose outcome was to decide which of the two Queens should die on the block.

Elizabeth answered agreeably to Mary's overtures, but
committed herself to nothing. She did not even insist that
Dudley was her sole candidate and made no promise regarding Mary's title if she married him, merely leaving it to be
inferred

inferred that her affection for him would cause her to do her best for his wife. A conference was arranged for November at Berwick, at which the representatives of both Queens would discuss the related questions of the marriage and the succession. De Silva wrote that Elizabeth had expressed herself ready to adopt Mary's cause at the conference if she agreed to marry any one of three Englishmen: Dudley, Darnley, or the Duke of Norfolk; if the Spaniard's information was correct, his report throws an interesting light on what follows.

Meantime Mary, in pursuance of her own secret design, instigated the Earl of Lennox to ask Elizabeth's permission to go to Scotland for the settlement of his estates. The English Council objected vigorously, but the Queen overruled them and sent Lennox on his way. As a further act of kindness to Darnley's family she released Lady Margaret from her confinement and made her welcome at Court. Shortly thereafter Darnley himself asked permission to go to Scotland on the same business as his father. The Privy Council took the request as pure effrontery: that Elizabeth would throw her two principal rivals into one another's arms was an idea too ridiculous to be entertained. Nevertheless the Queen, after some hesitation, directed that the young man should be given his passport. Cecil, Throckmorton, and their party thought she had gone out of her mind.

So did Randolph in Edinburgh. The news that Darnley was on his way North was the worst blow that sturdy servant received in the course of his long career. Believing that what his Queen most wanted was the Dudley marriage, he had worked night and day to bring it about. For months he had argued with Moray, with Maitland, with Mary herself, to that end; for months he had pleaded that Dudley should be sent to Edinburgh as the surest means of crowning his efforts with success. Randolph ran hither and thither and wrote letters by the ream. He described to the impressionable Robert Mary's physical charms in such detail as to bring blushes to his own bearded cheeks; he implored Elizabeth, Cecil,

Cecil, Sidney to set the laggard's feet upon the way North. The answers, when set side by side, told him exactly nothing. They read as if the Queen, the chief minister, and the suitor were reluctant to discuss the topic with one another or to give him any information that might be of the slightest use to him. One would have been justified in assuming that the heads of Government had quite forgotten the marriage of which they had made a policy.... There was something queer going on in London which nobody in Edinburgh and apparently no one in London could explain.

Darnley arrived and made an immediate good impression on Mary. Yet she said nothing of a betrothal, and Randolph plucked up heart as he saw that, despite her success in bringing Darnley into Scotland, she was obviously still torn in mind. It might be best after all to please Elizabeth and marry her lover with the promise of the succession — it could not be denied that Elizabeth was nine years older and not in nearly as good health as herself. But while she waited, she began to see in Darnley personal attractions as pronounced as the political advantages for which she had wanted him: 'he was the properest and best proportioned long man she had ever seen,' she exclaimed enthusiastically as she saw him riding on Leith sands. Randolph's hopes drooped and his letters flew faster.

And all the while Elizabeth kept Robert by her side, their fondness becoming if anything more conspicuous and their familiarities more unconcealed than ever. She had at last given him the earldom of Leicester, and scandalized the by-standers by tickling his neck during the ceremony. Shortly thereafter he coolly took her kerchief out of her hand and wiped the sweat from his face after a tennis match, to the fury of the Duke of Norfolk, who at once challenged him to a duel for his insolence. These reports coming to Mary's ears helped at last to convince her that Elizabeth had no intention of parting with her lover. Stung in her pride, mocked and jilted, Mary swore that she would bear it no longer. Randolph, warned by Moray, who was himself awed by her

temper

temper — '"The devil cumber you," saith he, "our Queen doth nothing but weep and write"' — attempted to mollify her, but she broke into tears, damned Elizabeth roundly, and went off to nurse Darnley, who was suffering from an attack of the measles. The next thing Randolph learned was that she had decided to marry him.

The English Protestants were aghast. The Council implored Elizabeth to stop the marriage by any means, even force if necessary, else there would be a Catholic rising. Elizabeth herself seemed to share their alarm: she forcibly forbade Mary to carry out the engagement, and appointed Throckmorton to carry her formal protest to Edinburgh. Yet she delayed his going on one excuse after another, as if paralyzed by doubt and urgency: it was no surprise that he arrived in Scotland too late to do any good. So far as the world could see, she had been completely outmanœuvred.

There were one or two wise observers, however — Castelnau de Mauvissière, a highly experienced French diplomat then in London, and de Silva, for instance — who penetrated to the astounding truth. Perhaps it took a Latin to comprehend one of the most ingenious and diabolic schemes ever hatched in the brain of a ruler; it is doubtful whether any man, Machiavelli himself, could ever have conceived it. In brief, Elizabeth had inveigled Mary, with devilish deliberation, into taking the very husband she had intended for her. She knew Darnley, had long known him, for the worthless scoundrel that he was. She could not, of course, have counted on Mary falling in love with him, but she had certainly had him in mind as the man most likely to tempt her: in chaffing with Melville the year before she had pointed to him and remarked with a smile that no doubt his mistress 'would like better of yonder long lad' than of Dudley, whom they were discussing. If her offer of Dudley was genuine, she could have sent him to Scotland; if her objection to Darnley was sincere, she could have prevented him from going. By first offering the one and then withholding him, she had goaded
Mary

Mary into taking the other. And if her later protests expressed her real mind Throckmorton would not have been kept hanging about London when he might have been working upon Mary and her ministers in Edinburgh.

Mary, of course, protested that she had accepted Darnley with Elizabeth's entire consent, which bears out de Silva's words on the abortive Berwick conference. But it was Elizabeth's intention that Mary should so believe, for it considerably added to the attractiveness of the bait. Had she insisted on Dudley exclusively, Mary would either have accepted him outright, which would have been awkward for Elizabeth, or refused him instead of being as it were refused by him. It was the essence of the whole scheme that the Queen of Scots should marry without any promise, explicit or implied, of the succession, and that is exactly what she did. It is clear that Mary herself recognized the weakness of her position, for before her marriage she wrote secretly to Philip offering to throw Darnley over if he would now give her Don Carlos: if she had really believed what she said, she would never have sacrificed the English bird in the hand for the Spanish bird in the bush.

'*L'Inglese italianato è il diabolo incarnato*' ran a sixteenth-century proverb. The English Queen had designed her snare with the cunning, patience, and cool ruthlessness of a Borgia, and laid it with an insight into motive and feeling of which no Borgia had ever proved himself capable. But it still remained to be seen who would be caught in it. If Elizabeth had gauged the situation wrongly, she had by her own act united her enemies for her own destruction; if rightly, she had neutralized their capacity for harm by setting them to destroy one another. It all depended on how sound was her knowledge of human nature and how reliable the axiom that character is destiny.

Chapter VI

The Unwelcome Guest

MARY and Darnley were married 'with all the solemnities of the Popish time' at the end of July, 1565. They did not, murmured gossip, wait for the priestly blessing on their union before consummating it, nor, lamented good Catholics, for the Papal dispensation which as cousins they required and which arrived two months later. But these technicalities in no way detracted from the significance of that ceremony, which no man alive was too humble or dull-witted to grasp. The order established by the Treaty of Edinburgh was at an end, and with it the tentative peace between the two Queens. The newly wedded couple had been offered and had accepted the Church's commission to restore her sway over the whole of Britain.

It was the dawn of Mary's short day of triumph. From Pius V and Philip II came messages of approval and congratulation, money and promises of more money for use in the great crusade for whose beginning such elaborate if dilatory preparations were being made. At Bayonne were foregathered the Queen of Spain, the Duke of Alba, the Queen-Mother of France, and various Roman dignitaries to found, so it was universally believed, an offensive league for the suppression of all heretic kingdoms. Mary had, so far as human foresight could contrive, assured herself of the English succession, but she might not, it now appeared, even have to wait for Elizabeth's death before assuming her throne. In Scotland she was all but supreme: various of the Lords had revolted against the Darnley marriage, but she had overcome them with ease, and now reigned with no friend or pensioner of England to gainsay her will. Moray and Lethington were removed from her councils and in their stead she installed the ex-choir singer,

singer, David Rizzio, who combined the functions of secretary and liaison officer with the Vatican.

As Mary's star rose, Elizabeth's sank. The Catholics of the North were openly in treaty with the Queen of Scots, offering their help if she would descend into England when her conversion of Scotland was complete. It was scarcely a secret that important members of Council and Court in London were endeavouring to come to terms with their future mistress. The Protestant ministers implored Elizabeth to do something — help the Scottish rebels with arms and money, deal with Mary as her mother had been dealt with, before all the good work of the reign was undone. They were justified in their fears, but she was right in her refusal. Conditions in 1565 were vastly different from those of 1560. The lawful Queen now ruled in Scotland, and to attack her would have violated a fundamental tenet of Elizabeth's creed. Moreover, the French war had left her poor, her friends no longer ruled at Edinburgh, the Scots might well have united in force to resist her interference. Nor dared she move until the result of the Bayonne Conference was known, lest she invite the united hostility of the strongest part of Europe.

Elizabeth merely waited: if one puts one's trust in the belief that character is destiny, one must give the character opportunity to assert itself.

She had not long to wait. The most extraordinary aspect of Mary Stuart's tragedy is its swiftness — a year of success, a year of error, and then the cataclysm. A few days after her wedding, Randolph wrote of her and Darnley, 'All honour that may be attributed unto any man by a wife, he hath it wholly and fully.' Two months later every dispatch from Edinburgh graphically described her loathing and contempt for him. She had already learnt all there was to know about him, his greed, his selfishness, his swinish debaucheries. He was a liar, a drunkard, a pervert; she and her visions of greatness were nothing to him so long as through her he could gratify his mean little lusts and ambitions. This was the lover
for

for whom her heart had yearned, the consort with whose aid she had expected to scale the heights. There were daily scenes of bickering and tears, over money, dignities, personal jealousies. The husband demanded the high office of Lieutenant-General of the kingdom for his father and the Crown Matrimonial for himself; the disillusioned wife gave the first to Bothwell and scornfully refused the second. Darnley sulked, stormed, and looked about for revenge.

His toadies whispered that it was Rizzio who was responsible for his disappointments. He was the man who had usurped the husband's rightful place in his wife's councils; nay more, he had availed himself of other and more intimate privileges. Darnley listened and believed. There were only two recognized means of dealing with human obstacles in Scotland, the dagger and the arquebus, with the result that for several generations every important Scottish death was a matter for the coroner. The offended Prince, not daring to avenge himself on his wife's favourite unassisted, laid his grievances before the Protestant Lords, who had drifted back into the country since their banishment in the early autumn. Moray, Lethington, Argyll, and their friends were only too glad to be rid of the foreigner who had supplanted them. A bond was drawn up between them and 'the mighty Prince Henry, King of Scotland, husband to our sovereign lady'; in return for assisting the royal party of the second part to do away with the Italian and obtain the coveted crown, the signatories of the first part were to have their confiscated lands restored and their power re-established as on Mary's homecoming. Apparently everyone knew of the prospective assassination except its victim and the Queen against whom it was aimed; several days before the actual event Randolph and the Earl of Bedford received a copy of the bond at Berwick and sent it on to London. On the night of March 9, Darnley, followed by Lord Ruthven and a band of ruffians, broke into Mary's closet, dragged the screaming Secretary from behind her skirts and hacked him to pieces in the corridor outside. The Queen

Queen herself the conspirators bore away to Stirling Castle for 'warding.'

Character proved itself swiftly, completely, melodramatically. Alone in the company of his wife Darnley's courage oozed out of him. Cringing under her anger he cut loose from his accomplices, attempting to whitewash himself by blackening them. For Mary it was an important achievement, since it disrupted the cabal against her. A few days later she contrived her escape with the aid of Huntley and Bothwell, and after a wild night-ride of twenty miles — the Queen, though in the seventh month of her pregnancy, bearing herself like a strong man — clattered into Dunbar safe from the pursuing captors. Her magnificent spirit had saved her throne and brought her unscathed through her terrible ordeal, but the vision of absolute sovereignty and a Catholic restoration had temporarily to be put aside: the general joy at Rizzio's death revealed once again the Scottish people's invincible hatred of all things Papist, while Darnley was clearly past praying for as the partner of so grandiose a dream. After a short negotiation Mary compromised with her enemies by forming a council in which Protestants like Moray and Lethington sat side by side with Catholics like Argyll and Huntley.

Detached and impartial, Elizabeth observed the tumults across the Border. Everybody turned to her, but none succeeded in stirring her to interference. Her Protestant ministers on bended knees pleaded with her to intervene on behalf of Rizzio's murderers for Christ's sake as well as her own; she sternly bade them keep out of their neighbours' business. Mary, half defiant, half pathetic, requested her to send back those of Darnley's confederates, such as Ruthven and Morton, who had fled into England. Ruthven was dying and Morton too potentially useful to be served up to the Scottish executioner, so Elizabeth declined, but instructed her officers to keep a close watch on the various fugitives and prevent their brewing further trouble during their residence in her dominions.

ions. Her admiration for her cousin's pluck was outspoken and sincere, and she promptly dispatched a messenger to convey it, together with her sympathy. When Darnley wrote begging her not to believe his enemies' inventions, swearing by all the gods that he had had no hand in the murder or his wife's kidnapping, she loudly exclaimed that he was a liar and told de Silva that in Mary's place 'she would have taken her husband's dagger and stabbed him with it' on the spot for the disrespect shown her; but remembering suddenly that de Silva was trying to bring the Archduke into England to please her, she hastily added that he must not think that she meant to treat her Austrian suitor in that fashion if he came. Certainly Mary had no cause to reproach the Queen of England for her conduct during those critical days.

On June 19, 1566, Mary bore the child so miraculously preserved through that week of fierce excitements and physical hardship. Whatever came of her own ambitions or her luckless marriage now, she had with Nature's aid made good the Stuart claim to both the thrones of Britain in the tiny person of her son. A million Englishmen who would have resisted her own pretensions to the death knew in their hearts that she had borne them their future King. Elizabeth knew it too, though policy kept her from acknowledging it until she lay on her deathbed. Scores of times she made it plain, often by the very acts or words designed at the time to prevent James's recognition, that she expected him one day to succeed her.

It was Sir James Melville, the emissary three years before for the Dudley marriage, who now rode into Greenwich on the evening of the twenty-third to inform the Queen of England of the happy event. The palace was gay with festivity and Elizabeth herself merrily dancing as the Scot entered its portals. Not being attired for the occasion, he sought out Cecil, whom he found working, as one might expect, in an ante-chamber, and delivered his message. The Secretary entered the ballroom, quietly threaded his way through the dancers

dancers till he reached Elizabeth's side, and whispered the news in her ear.

The Queen tottered to a seat and rested her cheek in her hand. The dancing ceased, the musicians laid down their instruments; everyone in the room felt the silent rustle of fateful tidings, and in that hush Elizabeth for once allowed her heart to betray her. 'The Queen of Scots,' she burst forth in tearless misery, 'is mother of a fair son, while I am but a barren stock.' It was Mary's last and one lasting triumph.

Although James's birth influenced moderate English opinion in his mother's favour, it had precisely the opposite effect on the militant Protestants. The Stuarts had effected an insurance against the risks of mortality and were by so much the more certain of their goal on Elizabeth's death. Then, unless the law stepped in to bar the Scottish line, would come the day of reckoning for the class that had risen to wealth and power during the previous generation. It was not the moment that Elizabeth would have chosen to meet Parliament, with the hateful question of the succession certain to arise in an acuter form than ever before. But she had no choice: the treasury was nearly empty as a result of the Huguenot war and the first of her Irish rebellions, so she sent out the summons and prepared for battle.

The personnel of the House of Commons was the same as that she had last confronted in January of 1563, and its mood even uglier and more uncompromising. For nearly eight years Elizabeth had deluded the country with hopes of her marriage and an heir, yet there was no indication that she was any nearer to fulfilling them than in the beginning. It was true that she was still flirting with the Archduke, but so she had been during the previous session nearly four years before. The suppressive measures against the Catholics lay harmless on the statute books since she refused to enforce them with anything like the rigour their language called for, and

and as a result (so argued the furious legislators) Papistry was again raising its head. It was an indignant as well as bigoted Commons that assembled on September 30, 1566, in the determination that its wishes must be respected in return for whatever money it might decide to grant.

The House showed its temper by proceeding to the immediate election of one Onslow, 'a furious heretic,' as Speaker and sending a petition to the Queen demanding that she either marry or nominate a successor without delay. Elizabeth returned the paper with the answer that her marriage was her own business, while it was theirs to get on with the financial bills. It was scarcely an answer to turn away wrath: the ministers tried to soften its effect, but were shouted down, a general exchange of blows followed and the assembly adjourned in a deadlock.

It met again on October 17, when Sir Edward Rogers, Comptroller of the Household, moved a subsidy with the plea 'that the Queen had emptied the Exchequer as well in the late wars as in the maintenance of her ships at sea, for the protection of her kingdom and subjects...' He was not allowed to finish. A country gentleman leapt to his feet with the objection 'that he saw no occasion, nor any pressing necessity which ought to move Her Majesty to ask for money of her subjects': she had fought the wars for her own purposes and it was more important to examine into how the last subsidy was spent than to vote a new one.

Mr. Basche, Purveyor of the Marine, was ready with an accounting both for previous expenditures and those for the new ships in building, but another country member interrupted him with the acrid observation 'that the said Basche had certainly his reasons to speak for the Queen in the present case, since a great deal of Her Majesty's monies for the providing of ships passed through his hands; the more he consumed the greater was his profit.... There were but too many purveyors in this kingdom, whose noses had grown so long that they stretched from London to the West.' Very little

little is known of Mr. Basche, but if he sold supplies to the
Government he was a suitable object of suspicion, and with
the House shouting its hearty approval the debate again
broke up in an uproar. When it was resumed next day still a
third country gentleman wanted to know why the Queen
needed any money at all: it had been his impression that the
subsidies voted four years before (which had raised at most
a few hundred thousand pounds) would suffice for the rest
of the reign. One begins to understand the reason for Elizabeth's celebrated parsimony.

The ministers entreated and argued, but to no avail. The
House, losing all interest in finance, broke into an outcry
that it was 'far more necessary for this kingdom to speak
concerning an heir or successor to their crown and of the
Queen's marriage than of a subsidy.' The ministers entreated them to have patience at least until the urgent needs
of the treasury had been provided for, but they were drowned
by cries of 'No! No! We are expressly charged not to
grant anything until the Queen resolvedly answers that which
we now ask; and we require you to inform Her Majesty of
our intention....' Various of the members swore with tears
in their eyes that their heads would pay for it if they returned
to their constituents without their answer.

It was beyond the power of the ministers to control that
assembly and they turned helplessly to the Queen. Elizabeth
refused to budge. 'The Commons,' she snapped, 'are very
rebellious... it was not for them to impede her affairs and it
did not become a subject to compel the Sovereign. What
they asked was nothing less than wishing her to dig the grave
before she was dead.' Her exasperation was not affected: her
marriage was an affair of high policy that did not concern a
popular assembly; she had promised them to marry when
she got down to it, and that should have been enough
for them, as it seemed to be enough for the foreign powers.
'I know not what these devils want,' she complained in her
vexation to de Silva, who was thoughtfully observing the
situation

situation for whatever light it might cast on the Archduke's chances.

The Lords, alarmed at the rupture between Crown and Commons, tried to arrange a compromise, but the Queen would not hear of it. 'My Lords,' she dismissed them angrily, 'do what you will; as for myself, I shall do nothing but according to my pleasure. All the resolutions which you may make can have no force without my consent and authority; besides, what you desire is an affair of much too great importance to be declared to a knot of hare-brains.'

After this rebuff the Upper House and the Council fell a prey to nerves and the Duke of Norfolk incautiously allowed himself to criticize the Queen for taking 'no other advice than her own.' Elizabeth threatened to have him arrested, so four of her best friends among the Lords, Pembroke, Leicester, Northampton, and the Lord Chamberlain, waited upon her to apologize for the Duke's tactlessness and prevent the already delicate situation from becoming more strained than it was. Within five minutes they wished themselves elsewhere. Elizabeth scathingly told Pembroke that he talked like a swaggering soldier and Northampton that he had better save his breath to explain how he happened to marry a second wife while his first was still living instead of using it to mince words with her. To Leicester she said reproachfully that she thought if all the world abandoned her he at least would not have done so. By way of answer Robin contritely offered to die at her feet, but she spurned the offer with the irritable comment that that had nothing to do with the matter. Shutting her ears to further expostulation she flounced out of the room threatening to arrest all four if they dared show their faces in her presence again.

The bishops tried next, but found their cloth no protection against the royal tongue. The Queen reminded them that they were merely her creatures — doctors, not bishops — who had 'dared to say in past times that the Queen my sister and

and I were bastards' and threw in their faces the universal complaints against their avarice and immorality.

The Commons and the Lords spiritual and temporal made one last attempt at conciliation: a mixed commission was sent to say humbly that if the Queen would only marry she might do so whenever, with whomever, and under whatever conditions she pleased. Naturally this petition fared no better than its predecessors; no one apparently guessed the root cause of Elizabeth's exasperation. She would not, she dared not, barter a promise which would jeopardize the peace of the kingdom for the sums she needed to carry on the kingdom's business; she felt that she had done her duty if she used her people's money wisely and thriftily. She told the commission that she was not surprised at the Lower House treating so grave a matter like a lot of inexperienced schoolboys, but she marvelled greatly that the Lords would not understand the danger of what they were asking. And in truth they were trying to blunt the very weapon, her eligibility for marriage, by which she was securing for them order and safety such as they had never known before. 'I might well excuse myself from marrying in the face of pressure from all of you, but having in view the good of the country, I am determined to marry. It will be, however, with someone who will not please you, which has been partly my reason for avoiding it hitherto, but I will refrain no longer.' This was, of course, for the benefit of de Silva and the Archduke. She concluded with the ominous warning: 'The man who is to be my husband is a foreigner and will not think himself safe in your hands if I, your lawful Queen, am to be so thwarted, and I will not put up with it.' In other words, if they compelled her to marry, they would have only themselves to blame if the husband she chose were one from whom they might expect little favour.

The peers and bishops saw the point and withdrew from the contest, but the Commons were made of sterner stuff. Not a penny until the marriage or the succession was definitely assured.

assured. One member threw down a paper in the House stating that if the Queen would not lift the ban on the discussion 'she would see something she would not like.' Another, a Mr. Dalton, launched a fiery oratorical attack on a recently published book upholding James and the Stuart succession: 'Prince of England, and Queen Elizabeth having as yet no child! Prince of England, and the Scottish Queen's child! Prince of Scotland and England, and Scotland before England! Whoever heard or read that before this time?... If our mouths shall be stopped... it will make the heart of a true Englishman break within his breast.' The author of the paper prudently remained anonymous, but the patriotic Mr. Dalton was sent to break his heart in the Fleet.

Then indeed there was a tempest such as the Stuarts were to know only too well when their turn came. Where were the sacred liberties stretching back to Magna Charta if a member of the House was to be arrested for speaking his mind? The Queen had overstepped her bounds and the enraged Commons were now as keen to defend their privilege as she her prerogative.

But Elizabeth knew better than to seek battle on grounds consecrated to her opponents by centuries of tradition. In answer to the House's protest she at once ordered Dalton's release, gracefully apologized for having detained him, and vowed that the last thing that would ever enter her mind was a trespass against Parliament's freedom of speech.

The Commons, overjoyed at their victory, applauded the Queen's magnanimity and folded her again to their hearts. The subsidy was voted without further debate or attempt to coerce the Queen into marriage. Before Parliament rose on January 2, 1567, she voluntarily reduced the appropriation by a third and dissolved the session with one of those speeches, both candid and matriarchal, which enables one to understand why the nation adored her to the point of idolatry. 'Do not think that I am unmindful of your surety by succession, wherein is all my care, considering I know myself
self

self to be mortal. No, I warrant you. Or that I went about
to break your liberties. No, it was never in my meaning, but
to stay you before you fell into the ditch.... Whether I live
to see the like assembly or no, or whoever it be, yet beware
how you prove your Prince's patience, as you have now done
mine.'

It was the decisive Parliamentary conflict of the reign,
and superbly conducted by Elizabeth. She had known when
to stand fast, when to give way; her adroit seizure of an
untenable position and subsequent retreat from it in order
to catch the enemy in flank was a master-stroke of strategy.
The future was to demolish the supremacy she then established of Crown over Parliament, partly because her
successors lacked her tact and skill, chiefly because another
age would require a different balance in government. But
her victory preserved England from the horrors of bloody
disunion for seventy-five years. Heaven knows what would
have happened in the troubled days so swiftly approaching
had the Queen allowed herself to be subjugated by a fractious
and divided popular assembly. A torn country inevitably
turns to an autocrat, and it was England's blessing that she
already had hers in her lawful sovereign.

The foreign ambassadors in London naturally reported
the proceedings with keenest interest. De Silva in particular
observed them with alert attention, while labouring with all
his wit to turn the antagonism between Elizabeth and the
Commons to his King's advantage. He followed her about
like a shadow, urbanely, sympathetically expatiating upon
her difficulties under this mad system of popular representation, urging her to wed his Archduke and make her peace
with Rome so as to be free of her subjects' interference.
Elizabeth listened with apparent agreement and sent still
another agent to see the Holy Roman Emperor. The ambassador promised that if she were reconciled to the Pope he
would use his good offices with His Holiness to obtain for her
a decree of legitimacy and the formal investiture of the kingdom.

dom. Elizabeth must have smiled inwardly: after thirty-
three years of life and eight on the throne she could have felt
no pressing need of Papal sanction for either. She professed
herself grateful for his kind offer, however, adding thoughtfully, 'I am well aware of the good-will of the Pope, and who
knows? It may happen that after all we two will marry.'
De Silva apparently received this remarkable suggestion
without turning a hair and passed it on to Philip in the ordinary routine of business.

Not the least intent spectator of the row at Westminster
was the Queen of Scots. She had it fixed in her mind that
only Elizabeth's failure to speak the necessary word prevented her from receiving full recognition as heir, suspected
that the opposition in Parliament had been, in part at least,
manufactured to serve as an excuse for delay, and considered
herself deeply aggrieved by the release of Dalton after his
expressions against herself. There was an acrimonious inter-
change of letters between the cousins, and a rupture would
in all likelihood have followed had not the shadows of Mary's
own doom been sweeping across Scotland with appalling
speed.

It had proved impossible, as was to be expected, to keep
harmony in the Council improvised after Rizzio's death.
There were too many political enmities, personal feuds,
conflicts of greed in that unnatural coalition. Mary's lean-
ings towards the Catholics set their opponents against her,
while the Protestants themselves were divided by their
individual hatreds. Bothwell and Moray frankly wished
each other dead, and Lethington was waiting in his own
patient way for revenge on the former, who had been awarded
his estates after the rising in the spring. On only one subject
were the Queen and the ministers in agreement, that it
would be better for all if Darnley, who had betrayed each in
turn, were out of the way.

To Mary in particular the sight of her husband had become

come unbearable; not only because she loathed him, nor because his existence was an insupportable handicap to her — both had been true since the second month of their marriage — but because she had fallen in love with Bothwell, that 'rash, glorious, and hazardous young man' against whom Throckmorton had long ago warned Elizabeth. He was a glorified Border bandit, without loyalty, principle, or judgment, who acknowledged no master and had never been true to a friend, a man who preyed on women for his pleasure as unscrupulously as on men for his profit, and despised both. Mary had once banished him for treason, whereupon Elizabeth had shut him in the Tower for a year by way of joint punishment and precaution. When he was released he departed for France with the contemptuous comment that 'both Queens together would not make one honest woman.' It was to this brigand, philanderer — and self-styled Protestant — that Mary Stuart had given her heart and trust, passionately and utterly. Six years of disappointment and unhappiness had spoiled every fine desire and dream; all she now yearned for was a man's strength to lend her support in the homeland to which she had been exiled.

Darnley's fate was sealed. In the circle into which he had married wish lived next door to deed, and every cabinet in Europe was merely waiting for such particulars as the time and manner of his impending demise. The doomed man himself wandered like an uneasy ghost on the fringes of his wife's Court, afraid to stay yet reluctant to leave the field wholly to his enemies. Taking no notice of him, the warring nobles, at Mary's request, shook hands all round, with the result that they sat down together at Craigmillar early in December to decide on ways and means of removing her impediment. A divorce was suggested, but Mary vetoed it for fear it might affect her son's legitimacy. Poison was also considered, but temporarily set aside, and Darnley reprieved for a little while longer, since it was thought desirable for form's sake that he should grace James's christening; also because

his

his presence might set at rest the doubts of the infant's
paternity which prevailed in various quarters and for which
his own words were not least responsible. The respite nearly
saved him: before the ceremony he asked Mary's permission
to go abroad, but she with smiles and promises of reconciliation prevailed on him to change his mind. A woman with a
love-affair she must conceal seldom finds it convenient to be
publicly deserted by her husband. At the christening the
father stood forlorn and unheeded by the church door, from
which he could see the first 'bishop in pontifical habits' to
gladden Papist eyes in Scotland for over seven years, and the
glittering gifts from all the Princes of Europe, including
Elizabeth's 'font of massive gold of sufficient proportions to
immerse the infant Prince and of exquisite workmanship
with many precious stones so that the whole effect combined
elegance with value'— the value was publicly declared, according to the custom of the time, at one thousand pounds.

When the ceremony was over, Darnley fled to safety
amongst his kinsmen at Glasgow. His wife pleaded with
him to return, but he could not even if he had wanted to, for
he fell ill of smallpox. She followed him to Glasgow and nursed
him as she had nursed him through his attack of measles two
years before. At his bedside she promised that all should be
well between them in the future, and sealed the promise with
a kiss. She was not altogether insincere — her pity for him
is one of the glowing threads in that lyric of love and death,
the letter she composed to Bothwell in the sick-room after
the patient had fallen into a feverish slumber. A few days
later she brought him with her to the capital and installed
him in an old house at Kirk o' Field outside the city, whence
he wrote his father on February 7 that his health was much
improved 'through the good treatment of such as hath this
good while concealed their good-will; I mean of my love the
Queen, which I assure you hath all this while, and yet doth,
use herself like a natural and loving wife.' It is not easy to
be sorry for Darnley, but there is something touching in his
                                                      trust

trust and the clumsy schoolboy's phrasing in these the last words he ever wrote.

Two days later, in the evening, Mary kissed him tenderly good-night in his bedroom and gave him a ring as pledge of her undying affection, before going out to attend the wedding festivities of one of her courtiers. When she left he began to undress, but suddenly hearing men's footsteps below he went to the window, and saw in the moonlight the gleam of armour.... Frantically he tried to escape by climbing down the vine outside the window, but his enemies seized him in the courtyard, strangled him with the lace sleeves of his shirt, killed the servant who had followed him, and laid both bodies on the grass. An instant later the gunpowder which Bothwell's men had laid beneath his room, intending to blow him up while he was asleep, exploded with a crash that shook the countryside around.

The voluminous annals of assassination can show few meaner sacrifices to political or private passion than Darnley, but it would be hard to discover another whose death more deeply shocked his fellow men. The murder was so expected yet so sudden, so dramatic yet so commonplace. It had the quality of great tragedy in that it raised the particular to the general, troubling the obscure places of the ordinary human heart, awakening in every hearer a sense of awed kinship with the proud Queen who had obeyed the primal impulse to destroy what stood between her and her desire. No listener has ever been indifferent to that story: whether his feelings were of pity, terror, dismay, cynicism, or approval, he has clung to them without measure or temperance. And it is perhaps not too much to say that they love Mary more and are nearer to an understanding of her spirit who believe in her guilt than those who so gallantly argue her incredible innocence.

As the reverberations of the explosion hurtled across Europe, Mary stood almost alone in the company of Bothwell and his band of murderers. No one at the beginning doubted her

her guilt; her defence was laboriously constructed later. Across Scotland rang such a cry of horror and hatred that it was dangerous for her to show herself in public. The English Catholics resigned themselves in despair to an immediate declaration in favour of Katharine Grey. The rulers of Spain and France listened to her ambassadors' incoherent apologies with polite scepticism and shrugged their shoulders over a crime that was like to be aggravated into a serious error. Even the Pope hardened his heart against a lost daughter. The only sovereign to withhold unkind judgment was the Queen of England.

Mary sent Robert Melville to acquaint the English Queen with her own version of the affair. Elizabeth responded with a message of condolence for his mistress in her bereavement, breathing no word of the suspicions with which the world was ringing. Mary's guilt was no affair of hers unless or until it affected the peace of England. In her own hand she wrote to the Queen of Scots one of those straightforward letters so characteristic of her when she was in earnest; no one can question its sense, and not many would deny its nobility:

> MADAME, — My ears have been so astounded and my heart so frightened to hear of the horrible and abominable murder of your late husband and my dead cousin, that I have scarcely spirit to write: yet I cannot conceal that I grieve more for you than for him. I should not do the office of a faithful cousin and friend, if I did not urge you to preserve your honour, rather than look through your fingers at revenge on those who have done you *tel plaisir*, as most people say. I counsel you so to take this matter to heart, that you may show the world what a noble Princess and loyal woman you are. I write thus vehemently, not that I doubt, but for affection....

Had Mary taken that advice she might even yet have saved herself. There were two powerful factors on her side: she was mother of the future King, and the Queen of England would have prevented her pensioners of the Congregation from raising a rebellion against her. But the unhappy woman

was

was no longer responsible for what she did. She allowed Bothwell to stand a trial that was a travesty of justice and attempted to appease the outraged populace by sacrificing a few of his lesser confederates. The dead man's father, come to claim vengeance for his son's death, was silenced by Bothwell's pikemen; he besought Elizabeth to intercede for him, and the English Queen wrote asking her cousin 'to grant this request, which if it be denied, will turn suspicion largely on you. For the love of God, Madame, use such sincerity and prudence in this matter, which touches you so nearly, that all the world may feel justified in believing you innocent of so enormous a crime....'

The appeal was ignored. A few days after Bothwell's 'cleansing,' Mary, whom the massive walls of Stirling had been unable to hold, meekly allowed herself to be carried off and kept in captivity by her lover, while suborned priests of her faith and ministers of his arranged for his divorce and their marriage. The Scots could stomach no more. Seizing gun, scythe, and staff they marched on the capital to put an end to that reign of blood and indecency. At Carberry Hill they met the royal forces in a battle of few blows but many words; half the nobility of Scotland wanted to fight the quarrel out with Bothwell in single combat, but that hero, at his wife's insistence, fled the field, leaving her to be carried off by the victors to Edinburgh. There the mob lit a bonfire under the walls of Holyrood and shouted hoarsely for her to be delivered to its flames, while she shrieked defiance back at them. The Lords hastily removed her to the island castle of Lochleven for safety.

Again no one stirred a finger to save her except the Queen whose advice she had consistently flouted. Elizabeth was not only sorry for her cousin and indignant at the affront put upon a fellow sovereign, but alarmed lest the troubles of Scotland should serve as an invitation to French interference. She ordered Throckmorton to Edinburgh, with considerably greater expedition than she had sent him to protest
against

against the Darnley marriage, to demand of the Lords that they at once enter into a composition with their Queen for her release and the future government of the country. He was also instructed to see Mary and offer her support and sympathy if she would consent to have her son brought up under English tutelage — a piece of hard bargaining, perhaps, with a woman in distress, but in the circumstances a reasonable precaution; the French were trying hard to get possession of the infant Prince, and the English people would have frowned upon any attempt to help the Queen of Scots unless they obtained some security with regard to the heir.

But the Scots received Throckmorton coldly, recalling the barren welcome Elizabeth had extended them during their exile the year before, and flatly refused to allow him or any other foreigner to go to Lochleven. They made it plain that they dared not risk letting Mary get free, for her first act would be to summon foreign assistance and her second to behead everyone who had offended her. Throckmorton, impressed by their fears and the gravity of Mary's situation, warned Elizabeth not to persist, else the prisoner would be done to death by her captors for their own safety. Three days later, on July 21, the Lords laid before Mary a demand for her abdication, which she signed after a stormy scene. James was then proclaimed King with Moray as Regent. Elizabeth refused to recognize the new Government, but there was nothing else she could do to show her displeasure short of going to war — the first consequence of which would have been Mary's abrupt disappearance into an anonymous grave.

For ten months the deposed Queen filled the Courts of Europe with her laments and her prayers for help, exactly as she was to do during the subsequent nineteen years of her captivity in England. Few of the fellow sovereigns she addressed even troubled to answer — whether or no she was guilty of Darnley's murder the Bothwell marriage had ended

for

for the present her usefulness to European diplomacy. Only Elizabeth kept up a friendly correspondence with her, a kindness which was to bring the Queen of England more evil than all the ill she ever did. After unwearying effort Mary escaped from Lochleven on May 2, 1568, and was carried off by Lord Herries to the neighbourhood of Glasgow. The Hamiltons, who three months earlier had advised her quiet assassination, rallied round her in hopes of making themselves masters of the country; eleven days later they were defeated by the Regent Moray's forces at Langside near Glasgow, and Mary fled blindly once more, never pausing until she had put ninety miles between her and her pursuers. At the English border she hesitated momentarily: her friends pleaded with her not to put herself in Elizabeth's power, but no other sovereign had held out to her the slightest prospect of welcome. On May 15 she wrote to Elizabeth: 'I am now forced out of my kingdom, and driven to such straits that, next to God, I have no hope but in your goodness. I beseech you therefore, my dearest sister, that I may be conducted to your presence, that I may acquaint you with all my affairs,' and enclosed with the letter the diamond Elizabeth had sent her long before. Next day she crossed the Solway in a fishing-boat and landed on the coast of Cumberland.

It was not quite seven years since she had set out, with hopes as brilliant as her retinue, to claim her royal inheritance, then the one fear in her heart had been that she might be forced by the elements to take refuge on the coast of England. Now, driven forth by her people, a suppliant for the very clothes she needed to keep her warm, she had of her own accord come to that dreaded shore as the one place where she might receive shelter from a bleak and hostile world.

If Elizabeth had been actuated by mere personal animosity towards her cousin she must now have been satisfied; without lifting a hand to encompass it she had her rival a helpless beggar at her door. Yet Mary's arrival was the last thing she would

would have asked for: it placed her in the cruellest dilemma of her life and kept her there for nearly twenty years.

For what was to be done with this uninvited guest? To bundle her unceremoniously back into Scotland was equivalent to handing her over to the waiting bonfires. To assist her to regain her throne by force would have been a quixotic adventure for which Elizabeth's subjects would have refused, quite properly, either to pay or to die. There was no justification for keeping her a prisoner, yet to let her go free in England would be to set up a beacon towards which all the dissatisfied would surge. And to grant the request, which she soon made, to be allowed to go to France, would sooner or later give the French an excuse to recover their old dominion in the North. There was not a single solution that did not conflict either with morality or England's good.

There were those of Elizabeth's ministers who urged cutting the knot by putting the Queen of Scots on trial for the murder of her husband and executing her, or even getting rid of her more expeditiously with a silent dagger thrust. John Knox, that godly and gloomy latter-day prophet, the greatest man in all Scotland, called sternly for her death with a wealth of invective and Biblical precedent. But Elizabeth would listen to none of them: there was no warrant for trying a sovereign for any crime, least of all one committed abroad; and Elizabethan England, alone amongst her contemporaries, had outgrown political murder.

The Queen sent her cousin, Sir Francis Knollys, to Carlisle, where Mary had been lent a house, to inform the fugitive that she could not be received at Court until the circumstances of her flight and the suspicions regarding the murder had been looked into. It was not a comforting message, but there was no other that could have been given at the moment — to have permitted Mary the triumphal entry into London that she had requested would have set the country by the ears. Knollys, like most men, was at first sight charmed by the Queen of Scots. 'We found her,' he wrote,

'to

'to have an eloquent tongue and a discreet head, and it seemeth by her doings she hath stout courage and a liberal heart thereunto.' But he quickly changed his opinion. When Mary heard that her welcome was to be put off, she flew into such a rage that he retreated wishing fervently that 'the Regent had her again,' and wrote advising Elizabeth to deal 'plainly and sharply with her.'

If ever there was a time for patience Mary should now have resigned herself to the practice of it; but this was the particular virtue she most conspicuously lacked. She turned upon Elizabeth like a tigress, demanding to be set free immediately. 'Dismiss, Madame, from your mind the idea that I came hither to save my life; neither the world nor all the Scots could have cast me out: but to recover my honour and to obtain support to enable me to chastise my false accusers, not to answer them as their equal but to accuse them before you.... I have chosen you from all other Princes as my nearest kinswoman and perfect friend, as if I supposed it an honour to be called the Queen's restorer....' The effrontery of it is beyond belief: a few weeks before when, spent and weary, she had stumbled across Elizabeth's threshold, she had written, 'I am now forced out of my kingdom and driven to such straits that, next to God, I have no hope but in your goodness'; now she haughtily informed her protector that she should consider herself blessed in having been chosen from all others to provide men and money for a war on Scotland! The exile peremptorily demanded the right, if the Queen of England failed to appreciate the honour, to send Lord Fleming into France to arrange for her reception there.

Elizabeth remained unmoved. She was not wise, she replied to Mary's torrent of arrogance, but not so wholly bereft of her senses as to allow Fleming, the master of the one fortress in Scotland, Dumbarton, available for a French army to procure an invasion by the Guises. If Mary would submit to her jurisdiction — which was not unreasonable, seeing that she had put herself under her protection — she would
. befriend

befriend her as she deserved; meanwhile she would be entertained as befitted her rank, provided she refrained from making trouble.

That was the one thing the Queen of Scots was incapable of doing. She wrote to the Duke of Alba in Brussels, to her cousin the Duke of Guise, to the Pope, to everyone who might conceivably derive advantage from helping her, promising that she would be Queen of England in three months if an armed force were sent to her assistance. She tried to seduce Knollys from his loyalty by taking an English chaplain and displaying a sudden affection for the Anglican faith, but Knollys refused to be cozened. She fared better with her Catholic neighbours, who flocked round to pay her court as if she were already in fact their Queen. When the English agents discovered a plot between these Northern gentry and the Hamiltons to abduct Mary and start a revolt on the Border, Elizabeth at once ordered the prisoner to be removed farther south to Bolton in Yorks. Mary declined to go: surrounded by her friends she could not be moved except by force and dared Elizabeth to put this indignity upon her. Elizabeth dared: Mary saw that she meant what she said and capitulated with 'tragical demonstrations.'

The Queen of Scots made herself a permanent prisoner by her conduct in England as surely as she was forced to take refuge there by her conduct in Scotland. Despite all pressure to deal 'plainly and sharply' with her, Elizabeth had thus far shown remarkable forbearance towards her guest's tantrums. The English Queen's letters were like those of an elder sister, packed with good sense and womanly understanding, and it is evident that they were not meant to be the whole of her effort. The ministers who saw her daily were convinced that she meant to go to the point of rashness in helping her cousin, and communicated their fears so strongly to Moray that the Regent considered inviting her back before he was compelled to receive her by force. Had Mary only had the sense to keep quiet while the discussions for her release were going

going on, something better than captivity might have been devised for her after time had cooled her subjects' anger, but she forestalled every helpful move of Elizabeth's by her reckless intrigues against the peace of England and her only too obvious intention to get even with everybody the moment she was free. Meantime her enemies ceaselessly dinned into Elizabeth's ears that no promise the captive might make could be relied upon. They brought up her repudiation of the Treaty of Edinburgh and of her recent abdication; they dwelt upon the ease with which she could obtain Papal absolution for a broken pledge, until Elizabeth was finally persuaded that she must do something to restrain her rival's capacity for mischief.

The way that was chosen was typical of the sixteenth century, crooked, subterranean, yet ingeniously constructed to comply with the law. Since there was no legal method of bringing Mary to trial for the murder, it was decided to hold a political conference at which the English Government would seek such information as was necessary to determine its future policy. The Lords of the Congregation were to be summoned to answer charges of unlawful conspiracy against their Queen, hence the Queen of Scots would be the plaintiff and her rebels the defendants, as she had desired in her first letter to Elizabeth. To make sure that the Scots would appear, Moray was told privately that if he proved Mary guilty of Darnley's murder it would be a sufficient answer and she would be kept in captivity. Since the contents of the Casket Letters had already been disclosed to Elizabeth in secret, there was no doubt that he would prove his case. Mary was induced to participate by an intimation that the hearing would be perfunctory, a mere formality before she was restored under certain specific guarantees for future peace. At first she refused outright, indignant at the very idea of a sovereign answering charges brought by her subjects. Knowing that her accusers would rely on the Casket Letters, she denounced them in advance as impudent for-
geries

geries and demanded to see them, but was told that they
could only be shown to her representatives at the conference.
It was as fatal to be damned by default as by evidence, so
she sent the Bishop of Ross and Lord Herries to act for her,
though still declining to submit herself to any judgment
whatever.

Early in October, Moray, Lethington, and the Earl of
Morton joined Mary's two defenders and the English commissioners, Norfolk, Sussex, and Sadler, at York. It was a
strange assembly: a jumble of judges, jurors, prosecutors,
defendants, accomplices, witnesses, counsel and holders of
watching briefs, with every man filling two or more of these
places simultaneously. They were there ostensibly to seek
light, but each was trying earnestly to create some form of
self-protective darkness. The Scots, supported by very
limited faith in Elizabeth's promise, were determined to
damn Mary universally and forever lest the English Queen
use any flaw in their proof as an excuse to foist her on them
again; yet they dared not allow too close a scrutiny into the
circumstances of the murder. Moray himself had been
abroad at the time — it is curious how often he was elsewhere when trouble was approaching — but Lethington had
been able to promise for him, with sardonic assurance, that
'he would look through his fingers' at the crime. Lethington,
if Mary's champions are right, had written the letters himself; and even if they are wrong he had been the leading
spirit at Craigmillar. Morton, the Black Douglas, a desper-
ado of many talents, knew so much about the homicide of
which he was accusing his Queen that he was to expiate his
knowledge on the scaffold thirteen years later. The Englishmen were fully aware that they had been appointed not to
discover truth for truth's sake, but to obscure it for the
State's. Of Mary's pair Ross had confessed his private belief that his mistress was guilty of her husband's death, and
Herries's whole fortune was involved in her acquittal.

The silver casket was produced and the letters — those
tear-splashed

tear-splashed pages in which a Queen traced the imperishable confession of her love and misery and guilt — laid before the fascinated gaze of the English commissioners. All three declared without hesitation that there was a *prima facie* case which the Queen of Scots must answer before they could advise their sovereign of her innocence. But a new complication arose in the form of a plan to free Mary by marrying her to the Duke of Norfolk, the chief English delegate, and Elizabeth promptly adjourned the conference to Westminster, where it would be under her own eye.

When it reassembled on November 25, the English delegation was increased by the addition of Cecil, Bacon, Leicester, Clinton, and Arundel; the last named, like his son-in-law Norfolk, was one of Mary's partisans. Morton testified to the finding of the casket, the letters were submitted to detailed examination over the strenuous protests of Ross and Herries, the depositions of the witnesses read, and the English commissioners retired to make their report to the Queen.

On December 14, Elizabeth presided over the final session at Hampton Court, when the foreign ambassadors and several of Mary's friends amongst the Northern earls were invited to be present. The company was informed of the result of the previous inquiries, saw the letters, and, with thanks to the Queen for having 'imparted the state of such great cause in so plain a manner,' admitted that 'they had seen such foul matters as they thought truly in their consciences' made only one conclusion possible. There was no verdict, as there had been no trial. Neither the letters nor the findings were published. The sole result was what had been intended from the beginning: Mary and her accusers had both been put off with a verdict that was no verdict; Mary could be kept under restraint with the danger of exposure still held over her head and the threat of her restoration held over the Lords' if they at any time displeased Elizabeth.

If the series of conferences be regarded as a judicial trial, the

the whole business was of course iniquitous. But Elizabeth never pretended that her commissioners were a court nor would Mary ever have submitted to its jurisdiction if she had. The inquiry was simply a device for finding a moral warrant to detain a dangerous political personage. It would not have been necessary had the Queen of Scots not shown herself an enemy to public order, in her own realm and in England; it would have failed had the evidence not richly proved her guilt. The documents may have been tampered with, and probably were, since Moray and his colleagues, afraid for their necks and not too trustful of Elizabeth, would have stopped at nothing to shield themselves at Mary's expense: they burned the compromising Craigmillar bond without compunction. Nevertheless the letters were viewed by a great many astute eyes, not all of them belonging to Mary's adversaries, and found authentic. Many plausible arguments, based chiefly on external inference, have been adduced against them, but it is impossible to believe that any forger, even a far greater literary genius than was yet writing in the two kingdoms, possessed either the pen or the insight into a woman's heart needed to compose those superb specimens of epistolary literature. In any event the Queen of Scots' guilt by no means rests on the Casket Letters alone.

The scheme for Mary's detention was not concocted by Elizabeth, though she must bear the responsibility for it. She neither favoured it at the beginning nor was she satisfied with it at the end, not fancying herself in the rôle of jailer to a sister-queen. Scarcely had she dismissed the conference than she was again looking round for a way to be rid of her burden. She offered, 'for avoiding of extremities,' to give the prisoner her freedom if she would voluntarily retire from the active exercise of power (though retaining the title of Queen) on the plea of weariness and of consideration for her son's future; if he were brought up under English tutelage, Elizabeth would undertake both to treat him as her
heir

heir and protect him in his Scottish rights. Mary must also
— one of the conditions on which Elizabeth was inflexible
throughout — divorce Bothwell and agree to his punishment.

For a few days, on the eve of Christmas, 1568, Mary
thought of complying. But her friends whispered that Elizabeth's proposal was a mere mask for her fears: if the Queen
of Scots would but wait a little while longer events would
make her instead of Elizabeth the dictator of terms. The
peace of Europe had that summer been shattered into fragments, with civil war in France, revolt in the Netherlands,
and unrest everywhere. Who could tell what the world
would be like when the pieces were reassembled? The dis-
dainful rulers of the mainland were beginning to take notice
of the captive as a potential menace to her heretic captor.
The clash of arms and the cries of the massacred on the
Continent were sounding in the ears of the English Catholics
like the strains of martial music, and they exhorted the
Queen of Scots to stand firm, vowing that if she would but
persuade her friends abroad to send help they would carry
her in triumph to Westminster.

Mary heard and weighed. On one side lay safety and
oblivion, on the other danger, but the vision of retrieving all
she had lost, gaining all she had dreamed of. If she refused,
Elizabeth might have her killed. Worse yet — for the young
woman had small fear of death — she might publish the
casket's contents. On the other hand, that might not matter
so seriously now. Men were thinking of graver questions
and her friends had already, and forever, confused the issue
of her guilt or innocence. As early as July, de Silva, who as
Spanish ambassador was drawn to her support regardless
of his private convictions, had written to Philip: 'The accusations of complicity in the murder of her husband are being
forgotten and her marriage with Bothwell is now being
attributed to compulsion and fear. This view is being spread
and friends easily persuade themselves of the truth of what
they wish to believe, specially in this island.' Six months
later,

later, with the Catholics in arms, the new story had vastly extended its currency. Those damning letters would do little harm to a Queen of Great Britain and Ireland....

Had Mary loved Scotland as Elizabeth loved England, she might have accepted the offer. But her heart was elsewhere — with her kinsfolk in France and the Spanish soldiers in Flanders, both fighting for her religion and indirectly for herself; with Bothwell, now a fugitive in Denmark, whom she had once sworn to follow through the world in her petticoat. She declined Elizabeth's terms without thanks, saying she had been born and would die Queen of Scotland.

It was a declaration of war for which she was to pay the supreme indemnity. Yet the first campaign was soon to carry her beyond the boundaries of her claim to be Queen of Scotland to within sight of the English throne itself.

Chapter VII

The Rebellion

THE tidings that brought fresh heart to Mary Stuart in her prison and prompted her scornful rejection of Elizabeth's overtures were the preliminary rumblings of the greatest struggle the West had known since the fall of the Roman Empire. For nearly a thousand years the Catholic Church had united Europe in a social order that had been able to survive the most savage quarrels between its various parts. She had been able to dictate how people should live, think, and worship. She had imposed her will on kings and emperors, and conferred, in return for their submission, the benefits of their subjects' obedience and their only respectable titles to the treasures of the East and the New World. But in the first half of the sixteenth century had risen in Germany the first serious challenge to that millennial order; all efforts to settle peaceably the differences between adherents and antagonists had broken down, and it was now to be determined whether force would succeed where persuasion had failed. In that struggle there could be no neutrality, for no living person could remain unaffected by the result. Either society would be more or less restored to its ancient mould or all human life would be radically altered, all wealth drastically redistributed. Eighty years were to pass before the contending hosts agreed to call quits.

In the spring of 1568, William of Orange was summoned before the Council of Blood, Egmont and Horn were executed at Brussels, and the Netherlands broken out into the long-awaited rebellion against Spain. Simultaneously the Huguenots and the Guises flew at each other's throats in the second French war of religion, the former, under Coligny and Condé, establishing themselves as an independent power in the
west

west with La Rochelle as their naval base and capital.
Their fleet joined hands with the Dutch privateers, and the
seamen of Devon and Cornwall hurried off to combine duty
with profit by expropriating the Papists' vessels on the high
seas.

The supreme test of Elizabeth's policy and of her character was at hand. For ten years she had kept England
secure from invasion by playing Spain and France against
each other, and from civil war by discouraging with impartial
frowns the exuberances of party strife. If she had at times
tempted Spain and France to anger, the one by the breach
with Rome and the trespasses of her sailors, the other by her
course in Scotland and her encouragement of the Huguenots,
she had never tempted them so far as to make either lose
hope of winning her away from the other. If she had not
altogether reconciled her own irreconcilables, she had at
least prevented the Catholic and Protestant fanatics from
adapting the country to the uses of guerrilla warfare. By
a system of delicate balance and compromise, by transferring
to the Crown the authority formerly exercised by the various
religious and geographical factions, she had given England
a cohesion it had never before possessed. It was now to be
seen whether that system commanded greater devotion from
the people than did the older political and spiritual creeds
it had displaced.

The transformation had naturally not been achieved without offence and hurt to many. It is as impossible to alter a
society without taking from some and giving to others as to
divert the course of a river without drying up the original
bed. England was as yet less than a hundred years distant
from the Wars of the Roses, from the mediæval constitution
under which the barons were the masters and the king their
creature. The highly organized, all-powerful central government as a synonym for the State was yet new in the sixteenth
century. It had barely reached its majority in Spain under
Charles V; it had yet to be imposed on France by the strongest

est of her kings, after she had fought eight civil wars in thirty
years. The work had been begun but by no means completed
in England under Henry VIII. The farther one travelled
from London, the less were the great local magnates disposed
to accept the new forms introduced into English life by the
Tudors. Especially in the North the old ruling families
opposed with proud bitterness the efforts of the monarchy
to substitute for their ancient privileges a novel conception
of ruler and subject. For centuries Nevilles, Percys, and
Dacres had made and executed the law between the Trent
and the Scottish marches. Apart from a nominal allegiance
— the supply of a stipulated number of troops in a national
emergency, the grudging payment of special subsidies decreed
for special purposes by Parliament — these local potentates
recognized no particular obedience to the Crown. The
men and women living on their broad lands were their subjects, to whom they dispensed justice, from whom they
collected taxes, for whose very salvation they assumed personal responsibility. At times they went even further in
their claims to a quasi-sovereignty, for when it suited their
purpose they made treaties with foreign powers and declared
war on their enemies within or without the country independently of the Government by the bank of the Thames.

Fair as the Queen had been in the division of offices,
shrewd in her preservation of autonomy in local affairs,
tolerant in the spirit and method of her ecclesiastical reformation, nevertheless it was soon obvious that the new Tudor
meant to outdo her predecessors in stretching the royal
prerogative to the remotest corners and oldest institutions of
the land. Not only did the Government in London claim the
complete direction and control of foreign policy; it brushed
by earl and squire and went direct to the subject in mustering
troops for the army and navy, in assessing taxes, in deciding
causes and haling offenders to the seats of justice. More, it
had now set itself up as supreme arbiter of religion, and since
1563 claimed the right to exact from every man an oath
in

in acknowledgment of its supremacy. And the ministers through whom the Queen devised and enforced her rule were as obnoxious as the system they represented — upstarts from the dissenting middle classes like Cecil, Bacon, Leicester, and various of her maternal relatives, whom any aristocrat from the days of chivalry was bound to find objectionable. It was true that the Queen had included in her Council such men as Howard, Arundel, and Derby; but even they had been made to conform and in any event were of lesser importance than their colleagues.

The war between the past and future is the fiercest of all conflicts of the human spirit, a struggle forever renewed and forever hopeless. For the future must win, else it would not be the future. In order to make the England that was to be, Elizabeth had to circumvent Mary Stuart as she did, had to come into ultimate collision with the power which sat jealously on the coveted riches of the New World and was able at its pleasure to exclude English goods from the Continental markets. Nationalist policy could not but evolve into imperialist — the island was too small to afford sufficient scope to its inhabitants once they were united amongst themselves. Yet to the Northern Catholics Mary Stuart was the symbol and Spain the secular rock of their faith, far more dear than Elizabeth to those thousands of men and women who beheld with sadness or a sense of injury their old manorial interests, affections, and feuds overridden by the arrogant monarchy which required a world for the employment of its energies.

Elizabeth was caught between the Devil and the deep sea. The followers of Orange and Coligny were the partners spiritual and commercial of her own Protestant and mercantile classes; if she allowed Dutch and Huguenot to go under, she would estrange these powerful subjects. But if she openly gave help to Rome's enemies, she would drive into revolt those of her people who knelt daily in prayer for a Catholic victory. The collections in the Anglican churches and the volunteers

volunteers who flocked to help the rebels have received much advertisement, but little has ever been written of those other thousands of Englishmen who gave their money and laid down their lives to sustain the Catholic empire.

In the hope of stilling the disaffection at home, Elizabeth announced loudly that England was and intended to remain neutral. In a sense she meant it, as her record of the next twenty years was to prove many times over; in another it was a lie from the beginning — the lie by which she was to conserve England's strength for the mortal combat to come. For there was no earthly chance of England remaining completely aloof. In the very first months of the European struggle, both hemispheres resounded with two separate and inevitable clashes between her interests and Spain's.

In the spring of 1568, the Duke of Alba, Governor of the Netherlands, issued a proclamation forbidding heretics to trade with the Low Countries. By a stroke of the pen England lost her most flourishing commerce, and her merchants of course complained bitterly to their Government that religion was being used as a pretext to ruin them. Elizabeth instructed her ambassador in Madrid, Dr. Mann, to protest to Philip against the violation of her subjects' rights. Mann's language was unnecessarily heated, while Philip was too interested in recovering his rebels' obedience and saving their souls to interfere with Alba's discipline. The result was a scene in which the ambassador was told that if he wished to remain in Spain 'he must live like a good Christian.' Mann wrote to Elizabeth to complain of Philip, Philip to complain of Mann and demand his recall. The Queen stood by her ambassador, but his position at the Spanish Court became impossible and in July he returned home. At about the same time Philip recalled de Silva, and the two countries looked to be on the verge of a serious diplomatic rupture. Almost simultaneously the English privateers, ostensibly in the employ of Condé, were let loose in the Channel and virtually blockaded it against reinforcements from Spain to Alba.

Philip,

Philip, with the Turks as well as the Dutch to fight, had no desire to take on England at the same time. He sent Don Guerau de Spes as successor to de Silva, with instructions to pacify Elizabeth and arrange an amicable settlement of differences. But before the new ambassador landed, a fresh incident occurred that seemed certain to lead to an immediate declaration of war.

A year earlier John Hawkins had sailed on a slaving expedition to the West Indies; it was his third offence of the kind and one of the chief complaints which Don Guerau had come to adjust, for foreigners were strictly forbidden to carry on commerce with the Spanish overseas possessions. But the grievance was distinctly reciprocal: Hawkins was long overdue, a great deal of English capital was invested in his voyage, and sinister rumours were coming in of some dreadful calamity that had befallen him at the hands of Spain. The investors, Hawkins's relatives, nearly the whole of the Protestant leaders, begged Elizabeth to take revenge by a spectacular raid on Spanish shipping. Elizabeth sympathized — she was the largest investor — but she hesitated. She wanted her money back, but even more she wanted to keep the peace. At that critical instant an irresistible temptation was thrown in her way. Her agents discovered that Philip had borrowed a hundred and fifty thousand pounds from his Genoese bankers for the payment of Alba's troops, and that it was now on its way to Brussels by sea. Still she hesitated: then word arrived that the ships carrying gold had sought refuge in her harbours from the pirates in the Channel. She seized on the word refuge — and on the ships. The pirates were sent away with a scolding; the vessels remained. When she learned of the disastrous end of Hawkins's expedition in Mexico through Spanish treachery, it became a moral certainty that the treasure would never find its way back to Spain.

The task of inducing Elizabeth to return it was the first that confronted Don Guerau on his arrival in November. No

No man could have been less suitable. He was inexperienced, obstinate, narrow-minded, and so puffed up with his own importance that he was incapable of recognizing that his adversaries might have their share of brains. Why Philip ever chose him is a mystery; he never trusted him, and Alba, under whose orders he was placed, openly despised him. He charged at Elizabeth like a bull and naturally sprawled headlong. The Queen opened her eyes wide at the insinuation that what she had done was no better than theft. In injured tones she explained that the money had virtually been forced on her... she was only keeping it safe while she looked into the question of its legal ownership... there was absolutely nothing in the story that she intended to hold it permanently. The bewildered Don Guerau got up, brushed himself, and ambled away to await her decision.

She did look into the question of the ownership, as she had promised, and found that the money only became Philip's property after its debarkation at Antwerp: until then it belonged to the lenders. Thereupon she informed the ambassador that, being hard pressed herself, she had decided to borrow it and thus absolve Philip from the need of repaying it. Even this arrangement, she added, was only temporary; it might be that one day she would let Philip have it back, and in that hope the King of Spain sent other and shrewder agents to argue with her for a period of many years. But meantime he could raise no more on his credit, and Alba, deprived of the means of paying his troops, was driven to those desperate expedients which widened the whole area of the rebellion and ultimately drove the Spanish soldiers to mutiny.

It was a dangerous game Elizabeth was playing as well as a dishonest one. She coolly reckoned up Philip's resources and deliberately gambled on the theory that he would suffer almost any provocation rather than make war on her for the present; if her calculations were correct, she might derive all the benefits of a belligerent and a neutral at the same time.
Philip

Philip himself acknowledged how uncannily she had read Spain's plight, for in answer to Alba's request for instructions he wrote that 'it was undesirable to embark upon a war with the Queen, as however great the damage we may do her, she will not by this means restore what she has taken. We think that she should be treated with a certain show of gentleness, united with an attempt to rouse her fears and suspicions that, if she does not make the restitution, we may declare war.'

Spain attempted another form of retaliation, however, by confiscating all English goods in the Netherlands. But this weapon cut both ways: Elizabeth promptly ordered the seizure of all Spanish property in England, and since this, with Flemish goods and ships included, considerably exceeded the value of her own subjects' losses, Alba was forced to report that she had had the best of it.

Some years earlier the great soldier had written to de Quadra, who was as usual urging a Spanish invasion, that Elizabeth's success in expelling the French had proved that no single foreign power had much chance of forcing a landing unaided on the coast of England, since such an enterprise would require the co-operation of the Catholic forces within the country. It now became the keystone of Spanish policy to obtain that internal assistance. The time was favourable for the attempt: the discontent in the North, already aggravated by the coming of Mary Stuart and the aggressions against Spain, had grown intense under the widespread hardship in those parts resulting from the stoppage of the wool trade. The Spanish ambassador, to whose talents intrigue was more congenial than the plainer courses of diplomacy, undertook to unite the various disaffected elements by reviving the project of a marriage between the head of the greatest house, the last surviving duke, in the country and the prisoner who was the symbol of all Catholic hopes.

The suggestion had originally been put forward by Mary's friends as a plausible solution for all the difficulties underlying

ing the York Conference. Norfolk had at first been doubtful: both Mary's previous husbands had died extremely young, and after a sight of the Casket Letters the Duke was disturbed by the thought that she was not without responsibility for her second widowhood. Then Elizabeth's interference had caused the matter to be dropped until the Hampton Court Conference in December.

By the time of its revival Norfolk's scruples had become less poignant. He had got over his shock and probably reflected that having, at the age of thirty-four, already survived three wives, the chances were he might outlive still another. From his previous marriages he had derived such considerable estates that he was now the richest as well as the first of Elizabeth's subjects. It would be a dazzling climax to his matrimonial career if he were now to wed a queen with the partnership in a throne to look forward to — perhaps two thrones.

Don Guerau and the Bishop of Ross took the affair in hand. Through their agents Mary and Norfolk wrote each other letters of tenderest affection; through other agents they carried on separate intrigues unknown to each other. Mary addressed Norfolk as 'mine own lord' to whom she would be 'faithful unto death,' simultaneously writing to Philip that the marriage was not to her taste, that she would prefer to accept a husband related to His Majesty, and would wed the Duke only with Philip's consent. The Duke, though courting her ardently and swearing that her freedom and subsequent greatness were the sole aims of his life, privately tried to guard himself against possible trouble by securing as sponsors for the marriage the two people Mary hated most on earth, her brother and, presently, Elizabeth.

Moray said neither yes nor no. He thought that it might be to his advantage to have his dangerous sister under the supervision of a responsible Englishman, and Norfolk was both a member of the Privy Council and at least as much of
a Protestant

a Protestant as the law required. On the other hand, the match might be used as a means of organizing a powerful party to force her back on Scotland. The Regent did not discourage the project, but passed it on to Cecil; his uncertainty gave him another year of life, for a plot to assassinate him on his return to Edinburgh was called off in consideration of his unexpected open-mindedness.

Elizabeth herself was not yet told. How much she knew is uncertain, though it is obvious from her subsequent words that she knew something. But it was not her way to precipitate a row unnecessarily: she sat back and waited until she should be approached.

The plans of the Duke and his party did not yet contemplate armed rebellion. There was no question of turning Elizabeth off her throne. It was merely intended to remove Cecil from office, obtain Mary's recognition as heir, reverse the foreign policy of England, and work for a Catholic restoration in the near future. Only by a broad policy of reform rather than a narrow one of revolution could the Duke hope to win over the moderate mass of the people. But, as frequently happens in such a programme, the tail began to wag the dog. The extremists of the North were not likely to be long content with the methods of compromise upon which the Duke's colleagues in the Council, who had no wish to jeopardize their profitable offices at Court, insisted. Indeed, so timidly did the Duke's party plot their rebellion that they tried to win over Cecil himself, the very man against whom it was chiefly aimed, to support the marriage with Mary Stuart. This was rather more than the belligerent Catholic earls would swallow, and their enthusiasm for that marriage, never very great, rapidly gave way to a scheme of their own for marrying the Queen of Scots to some candidate of Spain's.

The original objects of the Duke's party were thus quite legal at the beginning, since they contemplated no armed attack on the throne, but the steps taken to carry them out

look

look remarkably like treason to the less complex political
vision of later centuries. The conspirators, through the
Spanish ambassador, approached Alba and invited his
co-operation. If Spain would stand firm in the exclusion
of English goods from the Netherlands, if Alba would seize
the English fleet which the City of London merchants
were sending to Hamburg (a venture intended to replace
the lost Antwerp trade), the resulting business depression
would discredit Cecil and make it possible to remove him
abruptly from office. A similar suggestion was made to
the King of France. It did not matter, apparently, to the
reactionary party how much they injured their country if
the blame could be made to fall on the hated Secretary.

Alba complied to the extent of issuing the desired proclamation against English commerce. France, already em-
broiled with England over the activities of her seamen,
had just handed in an ultimatum (which it was hoped
Elizabeth would not take too seriously and which she
obligingly ignored), and could in consequence do nothing
more. The one step that remained was to remove Cecil by
force and confront the Queen with a demand that the
direction of policy be placed in his enemies' hands.

There was every possibility that the *coup* would succeed.
The great majority of the Council were involved in it to
some extent. Even Leicester, through hatred of Cecil, was
in the plot, and hoped that Norfolk would succeed in marrying the Queen of Scots so as to encourage his own Queen to
marry another worthy subject. The Secretary was by now
almost his own sole faction; even his old friends and kindred
were frightened to stand by him. His days as Prime Minister,
wrote Don Guerau exultantly to Alba, were almost ended.

But Cecil had one friend worth the whole lot of politicians
and plotters together. Elizabeth had been badgered by
his enemies to get rid of him until she was frantic and ill;
it had been more than hinted that if she resisted his removal
she herself might be put under constraint. But to bully
Elizabeth

Elizabeth was the surest means of putting her on her mettle. At times she doubted the wisdom of the policy she had undertaken, and once she wished publicly that the Devil would fly away with the men who had advised her to take the Spaniards' money. As she saw the gloom in the City, heard of the unrest in the North, allowed herself to think of the possibility of bloodshed, she cried miserably that she wanted no war —'*Point de guerre, point de guerre,*' she exclaimed shrilly before the French ambassador. Yet no more would she apologize to Spain and restore the stolen money, as Norfolk's party wanted her to, or throw overboard a useful servant. And above all she would not be dictated to by her Council. She was still Queen of England and believed she knew what was best for her people.

The capture of Cecil was planned for Easter, and the conspirators came to the council-board with the full intention of departing with the Secretary their prisoner. It was what had been done to Henry VIII's minister Cromwell a generation before. But Elizabeth was made of loyaller stuff than her father. Awed by her presence and that pervasive sense of the almost religious bond between her and the people, the conspirators withdrew in fear, leaving Cecil unmolested. Twice more they came resolved to kidnap the Secretary and assert their ascendancy over her, twice more they postponed the kidnapping in dread of provoking her displeasure. Then they gave the attempt up and retired to discuss, with courage derived from each other's presence and Elizabeth's absence, even stronger measures, Mary's forcible liberation and an attack on the throne itself.

From the beginning the various groups hostile to Elizabeth and Cecil — the majority faction in the Council, the Northern Earls, Mary Stuart's agents — had been dealing with the Spanish ambassador, unknown, as they thought, to the Queen and frequently unknown to one another. Don Guerau encouraged them all and Alba to support them all,
with

with the result that he was put under arrest in January, 1569, by the Queen's orders. But an arrest might be technical or actual, and in Don Guerau's case it was merely a means of keeping him in bounds and his doings under surveillance. He was free to carry on his intrigues as long as nothing serious happened, and it was to him, therefore, that Norfolk turned when he found that he lacked the courage to lay violent hands on Cecil. The Duke promised to marry Mary and render obedience to Spain if Alba would send him help. Don Guerau wrote as asked; but Alba, far wiser, declined to be drawn into an invasion of England at the invitation of a confederacy which had so far shown nothing but indecision and incompetence. When Norfolk had carried off the Queen of Scots, overcome Cecil, and collected a sufficient force to guarantee a successful Spanish landing, he would come — not otherwise. Meantime he sent, with unconcealed contempt, a draft to cover the Englishmen's immediate needs.

The conspirators still hesitated and the initiative passed to Elizabeth and Cecil. The Secretary took a hand in a lawsuit between Norfolk and Leonard Dacre, one of the most influential of the Northern magnates, over the property left by Dacre's nephew, who was also the nephew of Norfolk's late wife, and obtained an award in favour of the Duke. The decision enriched Norfolk while it embittered Dacre against him, and the rift between the Southern Catholics, who clung to the constitution, and the Northern, who disdained Norfolk's pusillanimity, grew wider.

At the same time London's merchant fleet set out on its momentous voyage to Hamburg. It carried a substantial proportion of the wealth of London, all the goods that had been stored during the past year of excitement on land and danger at sea. But it carried more than wealth: with it went the hopes of English farmers, wool merchants, artisans and traders, for if it failed to get through, English commerce was utterly ruined. It carried also the contrary wishes of
the

the Queen's adversaries: they had first counted on fear to restrain its sailing, then hoped that Spanish or French privateers might prevent its arrival, for others could play Elizabeth's game, as Norfolk had pointed out to Don Guerau. If the voyage were successful, a new port would have been found to replace Antwerp, and England could afford to ignore Spain's boycott; if it failed, there was no alternative but an apology for past misdeeds, restitution, and a humiliating composition with Philip. Elizabeth took no risks. She sent a squadron under Admiral Winter to convoy the merchantmen across the North Sea, and instructed Sir Henry Killigrew at Hamburg to prepare for their reception and the sale of their cargoes. The voyage was a triumphant success. No marauder dared lift a finger against the ships as they made eastward under the protection of Winter's guns, and when they arrived at their destination they found the Hanseatics, thanks to Killigrew's preparations, swarming to meet them. It was the most lucrative trading venture in the history of England, and its success was worth many battalions to the Queen when the hour of rebellion struck.

It could not be long delayed. In the North the small Catholics, impatient at their leaders' delays, turned out the Government's officials and sent the Anglican priests flying for their lives. In the South the Protestants were equally getting out of control and their private vendettas against the recusants became an acute embarrassment to the Crown. In London a prominent Spanish merchant's home was raided and the images in his chapel publicly burned to the accompaniment of jeers from the crowd at 'the idols of the Spaniards.' The Catholics saw that if action were delayed much longer, the Queen and her First Minister would be impregnable; yet their leaders could not decide on what was to be done. Norfolk, Arundel, and their confederates still dallied with the idea of a peaceful revolution through the agency of existing government; Westmoreland

Westmoreland, Northumberland, and theirs pinned their faith more and more to a rising which should attract the legions of Alba to their aid.

The Spanish ambassador, who feared that the whole enterprise would fall to earth if the two wings of it failed to flap in unison, prevailed on the earls to agree to Norfolk's marriage with Mary, and secured from the Duke a promise to restore the Catholic religion in England immediately, as the North wished, if Philip approved of the wedding. The ambassador, somewhat subdued after various snubs from his superiors for his excessive zeal, also agreed with Norfolk that an effort should be first made, unknown to the earls, to secure Elizabeth's consent to the match before actual insurrection was resorted to. With difficulty he induced the Northerners to keep their swords in their scabbards while that possibility was being explored.

Norfolk, concealing from all but his intimate friends the obligation he had entered into with Don Guerau, met the whole Privy Council and presented his case for his marriage with the Scottish Queen. The response was favourable: few of the ministers would have endorsed Norfolk's promises to Spain and to Mary, but the majority of them were quite willing to see the dangerous and vindictive exile delivered over to the first peer of the realm for safekeeping so long as he was loyal, and few yet doubted Norfolk's loyalty — opposition to Cecil did not make a man a traitor. Some of the oldest of Elizabeth's advisers, such as Pembroke and Bedford, favoured those of the Duke's plans that had been imparted to them. Even the Secretary agreed to lend his support to the marriage: not that it appealed to him — his estates and his head too, if she wished it, would have been the Duke's wedding present to his bride, but Cecil knew Elizabeth better than did his fellows, and while they supposed that she must give way to the wishes of the Council, he was not so sure. It was better, however, to be on the safe side. As chief of the secret intelligence he also happened

to

to know of Norfolk's Spanish dealings, which could be conveyed to the Queen as convenience and his own safety dictated.

The Council had agreed; it remained then only to present their united resolution to the Queen. But here a hush fell on the assembly. It was one thing to draft a demand, but quite another to bell the cat and tell Elizabeth that her ministers had decided on a plan and expected her meekly to ratify it.

Leicester suggested a committee. The suggestion was hailed with relief — until it came to a question of who should serve on the committee, when there appeared to be no volunteers. The favourite then offered to go himself if Cecil would go with him, but the Secretary had discreetly retired, as was his way, before the vote was taken, and though sought everywhere could not be found. The meeting broke up without coming to a decision. Norfolk went to the palace in the hope of making an opening for himself, but in Elizabeth's presence his courage failed him; he fell ill, and went to bed without his dinner. Elizabeth then left London for Richmond with Leicester, of course, in her train.

The Duke followed after and came upon Robert placidly fishing in the Thames. He inquired what Her Majesty's mood was. Leicester could not say: all he knew was that the Queen would be furious if Norfolk attempted to marry without speaking to her about it first. The Duke went on to Richmond and there Cecil advised him to make a clean breast of everything: it was the only way of removing any suspicions from Elizabeth's mind. The Duke tried to take his advice, but at sight of Elizabeth he felt his illness coming on him again. He gulped and wanted to retire, but Elizabeth helped him out by 'merrily inquiring what news was abroad.'

'None,' mumbled the head of the great house of Howard.

'None!' echoed the Queen archly. 'You come from London and can tell no news of a marriage?'

The

The Duke took courage and was about to fall on his knees and ask for what he wanted, but was interrupted by a lad with a bouquet of flowers for Her Majesty, and went away. It was the nearest he came to speaking out, though Leicester encouraged him, and the Queen gave him a nip on the ear and a friendly warning to 'take heed to his pillow.' But the poor man was beyond words; his mistress's inscrutable blue eyes and smiling lips gave him no clue as to how far she had read into his secret mind. He left Richmond and returned to London. Once out of Elizabeth's sight his courage came back: he would trust to action instead of words, kidnap Mary, call in the help of his pugnacious friends in the North and assume the leadership in the realm to which his birth and talents entitled him.

Elizabeth was content to play out the little comedy as long as she was neither threatened nor coerced. But she had no intention of allowing the marriage, for she knew — perhaps by her own instinct, perhaps through Cecil's spies — what it would signify for her. If she consented, she told Leicester, she would be in the Tower before four months were over. When the Council ventured to convey its approval of the project, she ordered them not to mention the subject again or she would behead the lot of them. Norfolk's abrupt departure at once aroused her suspicions and she peremptorily ordered him back to Court.

He hesitated, consulted with his friends, returned the sorry answer that he was ill and had not seriously considered marrying the Queen of Scots in any case. Then he fled to Kenninghall, his Norfolk estate, intending to rouse his tenants, secure possession of Mary, bring the earls into the field, and get in touch with Alba and his friends in France before Elizabeth realized what he was up to.

But her acts as well as her mind bounded leagues ahead of his. Before he could move to deliver the Queen of Scots, Elizabeth had sent her cousin the Earl of Huntingdon, one of Mary's rivals for the succession, to bring her from Wingfield,

field, where the amiable Earl of Shrewsbury was keeping her as guest rather than captive, to the safety of her former prison of Tutbury. While Norfolk was writing to excuse himself for not obeying his Queen's invitation to return to Court, Mary, protesting and threatening, was already riding into Tutbury under strong escort. The Duke's appeals to Alba and to France were intercepted with similar energy: the ports were shut by Elizabeth's orders, the couriers arrested on arrival and their dispatches seized. And an imperious order arrived at Kenninghall for the Duke to report at Court immediately or take the consequences.

Norfolk still hesitated. His followers urged him on, his fears held him back. The armies in the North were waiting for him to come and lead them; he could be reasonably sure that at the first sign of victory Spain would give him the help necessary to turn the balance against the forces of the Crown. In material strength he was probably at the moment more than a match for Elizabeth. But her moral strength told, the weight of personality behind that royal command to report immediately, the indomitable spirit that had anticipated him with such bewildering speed at Wingfield and at the ports. The Duke sent off messengers to ask the men of the North to wait a little longer, and rode off to join Elizabeth in the complete belief that his position was too strong, his crimes too well hidden, for her to dare to touch him.

It was never safe to speculate on how much Elizabeth knew or what she would dare. She broke off her progress through Hampshire and returned to Windsor. On the Duke's arrival she sent four of the Councillors, including the adaptable Cecil, to examine him. The results were unsatisfactory — the examiners were naturally anxious not to learn too much — but Elizabeth knew as much as she needed to determine her present course. The Duke had undoubtedly plotted with her enemies to steal Mary and interfere in questions of high policy, whether he was actually

a traitor

a traitor or no. To the surprise of her own intimates, to Norfolk's amazed consternation, she ordered Sir Francis Knollys to take charge of her first subject and bring him by river to the Tower of London.

It was a brave thing to do, for the Duke's imprisonment might lead to the very outbreak which it was designed to prevent. The noisy demonstrations of the Duke's partisans on the banks of the Thames as he was rowed through London showed how great was the risk she ran. But the very daring of her conduct dispelled the danger: the Duke was safely locked up, his closest lieutenants, Arundel, Pembroke, and Lumley, put under arrest in private houses. Their followers, surprised and dismayed at this display of fearless energy, melted away. The Southern half of the great conspiracy had fizzled out without striking a blow.

But there was still the Northern half to deal with, and in a military sense it was the more formidable. Norfolk's party had been handicapped as rebels because to the end they had hoped to attain their objects by a limited *coup d'état* under a constitutional cloak. The Northerners were less disposed to stand on such quibbles. The mere substitution of one ministry for another was well enough for men who were willing to call themselves Protestants and were animated to a large extent by greed for an increased share in the plums of office, but the honest, fiery peasants who followed the Earls of Westmoreland and Northumberland expected considerably more. They had been willing to go with Norfolk for a time because union gave strength, though if he succeeded they would have revolted again almost immediately, as Elizabeth foresaw when she predicted that Norfolk's success would mean her own end in four months. Those men of the borders wanted nothing less than their old England back again, with its feudal liberties, its priests and the precious traditions inherited from their forefathers.

It was their own leaders who betrayed them. Alarmed at the

the collapse of the Southern half of the rebellion, the earls tried to stave off the rising until a better season. Norfolk's last message before leaving Kenninghall for Court had been a plea for such delay. Don Guerau, who had pumped them full of optimism when the general rebellion seemed certain, added his voice to the Duke's, knowing that he would have to answer to his superiors if the whole enterprise, to which he had deeply committed his country without proper authority, now miscarried. Westmoreland and Northumberland told the Earl of Sussex, President of the Council of the North, at York on the very day of Norfolk's conveyance to the Tower that they would try to keep their followers quiet. The last thing these nobles wanted was a rebellion on the grounds of religion alone, and they tried to soothe the humble folk who trusted them with the glib but feeble excuse that since Elizabeth had not yet been excommunicated it would be better to postpone the rising to another day.

But it was too late. The peasants and small tradesmen were already in the field, clad in their mediæval Crusaders' uniform of blue with the red cross on the breast and bearing their Crusaders' flags on which were depicted the Saviour's wounds. The compromises and quibbles of the politicians had no meaning for them, and their simple, single-minded fury swept their leaders along as all but the greatest leaders have always been swept on the tides of popular feeling.

Word flew to London that the rebels were on the march with the capital as their goal. A panic fell on the land. Loyalists in the North, leaving their homes behind, ran ahead of the gathering storm to find what safety they could in the South. The Spanish and French ambassadors, at first dubious of the prospects of the revolt, wrote to their respective capitals that the country was ablaze and had passed out of control. In the daily reports that came in of additions to the ranks of the rebels appeared in growing number

number the most illustrious names in England. The kingdom seemed ready to plunge into the worst deluge of blood since the Wars of the Roses.

The Queen alone kept her head. She summoned Westmoreland and Northumberland to Court on pain of being outlawed. Like Norfolk they hesitated; unlike him, perhaps frightened by his example, certainly fearful of what their examination would divulge, they refused to come. She sent an order to Sussex to arrest them. That brave and capable pro-consul also hesitated and advised the Queen to compromise, since the rebels were too strong to be overcome by force. Elizabeth ignored him and ordered out her army under Warwick and her cousin, the Earl of Hunsdon. She might temporize in many things, but never with rebellion.

The Northerners continued their march. On November 14 they were in Durham, where they burned every Bible and Prayer Book of the Reformed faith and reverently celebrated the Mass in all its ancient pomp. They proceeded to Ripon, their numbers increasing as volunteers flowed in from all sides like rivulets into a stream after a freshet. The main body pressed on to the capture of York, a detachment was sent to free their chosen Queen from Tutbury, while yet another took Hartlepool as a port of debarkation for Alba's troops.

But again Elizabeth had been too quick for them. Before the raiders arrived at Mary's prison, she was in a new one, Coventry, far to the south. The rebels halted in dismay, for the Queen of Scots was the pledge of their Church's approval and of the more material aid expected from their friends abroad. Further shocks came swiftly: the refusal of Norfolk's tenants in East Anglia to join them; the defection of Leonard Dacre, whom Elizabeth had won over by reversing Cecil's chicanery in the award of the disputed estates to Norfolk; the massing of Moray's troops on the border to keep the Marian Scots from joining in the struggle; and on top of all the swift advance of the Crown's forces

to

to the relief of York, followed by the tidings that the Queen
was gathering the greatest army ever assembled in England.
Disheartened by the vigour of the Government and the
failure of the promised reinforcements, the army of yeomen
and peasants began to retreat.

The retreat became a rout. Caught between the immovable body of Moray's Scots and the irresistible force of
Warwick's regulars, the unhappy soldiers of a lost cause
became a dispirited and bewildered rabble, with no thought
but to rid themselves of their arms and find again the peace
of their homes. By Christmas they had dispersed and their
leaders had escaped into Scotland, whence Northumberland was extradited, by a classic act of treachery, to die
on the gallows, and Westmoreland fled to permanent exile
in Flanders.

The conflagration was not yet entirely extinguished.
Leonard Dacre had, until Elizabeth awarded him the
disputed family estates in November, been considered one
of the mainsprings of revolt in the North. His glibness at
Court and his subsequent good conduct during the rebellion
had convinced the Queen that he was loyal, but the examination of the captives taken by Sussex raised fresh doubts.
To satisfy herself Elizabeth ordered him to London in
January. Dacre, at once apprehensive and arrogant, delud-
ing himself that Elizabeth would not attempt to enforce
her command and arrest him in the midst of his own people,
refused to obey and shut himself in his stronghold of Naworth at the end of January, 1570. The Queen sent Hunsdon to get him. It was not a simple enterprise; Hunsdon
had only fifteen hundred men, Dacre two or three times
that number. Most of the royal forces had been withdrawn
after the subjugation of the main rebellion, while Moray's
assassination on the twenty-second of that month had left
the Scottish Catholics free to pour over the Border. But
the royal troops were trained men from Berwick, their
opponents largely 'rank-riders' of the marches, more
accustomed

accustomed to cattle-stealing than organized fighting. Dacre unwisely left the shelter of Naworth to fall upon his pursuers and after one fierce charge ran away, leaving his men to escape as best they could from Hunsdon's disciplined soldiery. It was a short battle but an important one, and Hunsdon said afterwards that had it been lost England would have been lost with it, for the scattered fragments of the rebellion would at once have assembled under Dacre's victorious banner. Possibly he exaggerated, but it was certain that as long as any part of the cancer remained in the national body it would reappear until the whole of it was cut away.

Unfortunately, the Queen who could be a commander of men in time of danger could also be an hysterical woman when the danger was past. She ordered the most brutal punishments to be inflicted on the wretches in the North, whose only offence had been fidelity to the faith in which they had been born and the leaders they had been taught to obey. Hundreds of the poor were hanged, scores of the wealthier were condemned only to be spared later by the sacrifice of their property. In contrast with contemporary proceedings on the Continent, her revenge was merciful; in comparison with the principles by which she had previously governed, it was savage. But Elizabeth had been frightened and, what was worse, disillusioned. Her feelings were like the reaction of a parent to a mischievous child who had run away and been recovered — relief mingled with resentment. She had felt so secure in the love of her people that she had never really believed they would rise against her. When the stress was over, her nerves gave way, and the consequence was the first and largest splotch of blood on the long panorama of her reign. There were to be further executions when the Jesuits stole in to plot her overthrow and death, but they were never again on a wholesale scale.

The great rebellion was over, and its failure declared that England

England would not retrace her steps into the past. No matter how gracious the ages on which Englishmen had finally turned their backs, no matter what ugliness the future might hold, the suppression of Norfolk and Dacre, of Percy and Neville, determined that the island kingdom was to go on its separate way, worshipping according to the strange but characteristic compromise of the Elizabethan establishment, conducting its affairs independently of the Continent, taking its leaders from amongst the descendants of the new Tudor squirearchy, exalting commerce until it overshadowed the cult of the soil, entering into competition with its neighbours until its energies had delivered a fourth of the earth to its government.

To that result the last of the Tudors had made the decisive contribution. When her ministers lost faith and courage, it was her indomitable resolution that there should be but one England and she its Queen that swept them on. In imminent danger of captivity or assassination she refused to hear of surrender or compromise. She knew how far to command men and they obeyed, how far to trust them so as to win their trust. The spectacle of Cecil and Leicester on their knees begging pardon for their part in the Mary-Norfolk marriage scheme is symbolic of the complete domination of her will over her ministers'; the military commands given to Bedford and Pembroke during the revolt in the North after Norfolk's conspiracy had failed illustrate her power to regain shaken loyalty by daring to rely on its fundamental strength. Had her intellect, her intuition or her courage once faltered, England would have known the succession of civil wars and invasions, the killings and the burnings that were to be the portion of her neighbours for most of the eighty years to come.

Her most formidable trials were only at their beginning: not until she sat tiredly waiting for death would she cease to be a mark for the assassin's knife nor be delivered from fear of the invading hosts of her enemies. But never while she

she lived would there be another such rising as that of 1569. Its failure had shown her people's approval of her labours for religious union and left her supreme over all leaders of party, including her own ministers. She could confront the future and its dangers with the proud assurance that at last she was Queen of all England.

Chapter VIII

The Reluctant Suitor

AT A distance of nearly four centuries it is plain that the rebellion's failure meant the ultimate triumph of the Elizabethan idea, but to the man of 1570 that lesson was anything but self-evident. He looked round him and saw that the embers of civil war were still smouldering, ready to burst into instant flame whenever the occasion or a bold leader should blow on them. The Scottish marauders, released by Moray's death, were again killing, stealing, and burning far south of the Border. Embargoes, blockades, and the promiscuous activities of the privateers were causing such losses to commerce that no ameliorative enterprises, such as the opening of the Hamburg trade, were adequate to make them good; piracy, which benefited the few, was hurting industry in general by flooding the country with cheap stolen wares. The popular nerves, already shaken by the political earthquake that seemed about to topple over the order and prosperity of the past ten years, were further frayed by secret agitators until the Queen was compelled to issue a sharp proclamation to 'the more simple of my dear subjects' warning them not to be 'misled by the false and mischievous inventions of foreigners,' and promising exemplary punishment both to those who distributed the seditious literature and those who, having read it, failed to denounce them. Even the highest circles of State and Court were whirling round in panic. A member of the Spanish embassy reports Cecil as saying, after returning home from an interview with the Queen, 'O wife, if God do not help us we shall be lost and undone. Get together all the jewels and money you can, so that you may follow me when the time comes, for surely trouble is in

store

store for us.' The specific words are probably a libel on the Secretary — who was shortly to be created Lord Burghley — but that they express his despondent forebodings is amply attested by his own letters and memoranda of the period. Not a few of his colleagues were already converting their property into cash and exporting it to Germany in preparation for flight, as so many had done in Mary Tudor's time. To aggravate the general unrest London was visited that summer by the deadliest plague it had known for years.

The fear of invasion by Alba and Guise was still acute. In the light of later knowledge the terror is seen to have been somewhat exaggerated, but it was by no means without substance. In December of 1569, while the North was still in arms, Philip at last instructed Alba 'to encourage with money and secret favour the Catholics of the North and to help those in Ireland to take up arms against the heretics and to deliver the Crown to the Queen of Scotland...' In the same month that Dacre hurled the last forces of the rebellion against Hunsdon at Naworth, Pius V launched his bull of excommunication, cutting off 'that servant of all iniquity, Elizabeth, pretended Queen of England... from the unity of the body of Christ.'

It was Elizabeth's good fortune that the Pope and the Catholic King did not move more quickly, for Alba's money and the Bull would have immeasurably strengthened the hesitating earls; but it was due to her own energy and courage that her enemies were no longer in a position to profit by either Spanish help or Papal decree. The appearance of the Bull was in fact so untimely that Philip was furious with his august ally for having published it at all. To enforce it was virtually out of the question, and any attempt to do so would only speed the Anglo-French treaty which Elizabeth, in reversal of her whole previous policy, was now negotiating. Not a word of protest was heard from Madrid or Brussels when John Felton was executed for his temerity in nailing the Bull to the door of Saint Paul's.

Yet

Yet, however King and Pope might disagree on the method of dealing with Elizabeth, they were at one in the conviction that she must be brought to heel quickly and by any possible means. Rebellion had failed, invasion was as yet impracticable; there remained a third way, narrower but no less efficient, assassination. The opportunity for this simple answer to their difficulties was soon offered to them and eagerly grasped by the ruler of the world's greatest empire and the spiritual head of Christendom.

In August the Duke of Norfolk succeeded in melting Elizabeth with his tears and promises of reform; it was her invariable practice, often a misguided one, to conciliate traitors by forgiving their treason, and she ordered his release after he had given a solemn oath that he would have no more to do with the Queen of Scots. Cecil, in the hope of distracting his mind from that temptation and of inducing him to turn over a new leaf, offered him his own sister-in-law, the rich widow Lady Hoby, as a fourth wife.

But Norfolk, weak, ambitious, and, despite his wealth, in debt, could not keep away from bad company. There was at that time in the City a Florentine banker named Rudolfo Ridolfi, who made a lucrative business of lending money to the sons of great houses and an avocation of dabbling in Popish plots. He had come under suspicion during the tumults of the previous year and been handed over by the argus-eyed Cecil to the most promising of the younger generation of politicians, Francis Walsingham, for examination. The Italian blandly insisted that his only connection with the rebel leaders was the fact that most of them owed him money and produced their notes of hand to prove it. Walsingham looked at the notes, kept Ridolfi in custody for a few days, and finally released him as an honest man fit even to be employed in the Queen's service. Elizabeth herself, after reading the transcript of the examination, thoughtfully remarked that if the Florentine had been more closely questioned more might have been learnt, but

but the sovereign cannot do everything, and various of the courtiers, including Leicester and even Cecil, had been trembling in their shoes for fear of what he might say.

During the first half of 1570, Ridolfi was in constant touch with Mary Stuart's agents, particularly the Bishop of Ross, serving as their intermediary with Alba and Rome. No sooner was Norfolk free than the Florentine sought him out and apprised him in vague terms of a great conspiracy that had been set afoot in his interest. The vagueness was inevitable, since the plot existed as yet only in Ridolfi's sleek head. The parties to it, besides the Duke and Mary Stuart, were to be the Holy See, the King of Spain, and the Guises, but none of them knew as yet that they had been chosen or for what purposes.

The original plan was contained in the letter from Norfolk that Ridolfi carried to Brussels in March, 1571. The Duke promised to raise an army of at least twenty thousand foot and three thousand horse and seize the person of the Queen if Alba would 'lend us his aid as well in money as in men, arms, and munitions'; Norfolk would then marry Mary Stuart and re-establish 'the ancient laws and the true Christian and Catholic religion.' Treason could not go much further than an attack on the sovereign and an invitation to foreign arms: Norfolk knew it and protested long and hard against signing his name to the document, but his will was weak, he owed Ridolfi money, and the Florentine patiently explained that he dared not approach the austere Governor of the Netherlands without full and sufficient credentials. Together with Norfolk's letter Ridolfi departed with a similar paper from the Queen of Scots and Don Guerau's blessing on the enterprise.

His reception from Alba was chilly to the point of rudeness. Suspicious of anyone recommended by Don Guerau, he contemptuously described the Florentine to Philip as 'a babbler' and sternly admonished him to keep his mouth shut while in Brussels. When Alba had completed his emendations

of

of the conspiracy, its originators would no longer have recognized it. He advised Philip that all those grandiose schemes for marriages and invasions be ignored, since if Elizabeth heard of them she would, quite rightly, execute both Mary and Norfolk at once and 'instantly marry the Duke of Anjou [this was in reference to Elizabeth's current courtship, then reaching its climax] and Your Majesty may consider how you will then stand with England, France, and Germany your enemies.' In his opinion the King's wisest course, for discretion"s sake and to save himself trouble and expense, was to hire some experienced assassin to get rid of Elizabeth. This was the gist of the message that the chastened Ridolfi carried with him on his further travels.

His next stop was Rome, where he secured the Pope's approval, the promise of some money, and a letter to Philip urging the King in God's name to proceed as rapidly as possible with the enterprise, whether of invasion or murder. Pius also annulled Mary's marriage to Bothwell so as to free her for Norfolk. The Holy Father might have been somewhat surprised to learn that his errant daughter, who in her petition for the annulment represented herself as the victim of a forcible abduction, was carrying on an affectionate correspondence with her abductor.

Ridolfi then went on to Spain, arriving there in July. Philip was more courteous than Alba, but equally cautious. He was as frightened as the Duke that Elizabeth might marry Anjou and anxious to do nothing that would encourage her. The Spanish Council met frequently during the summer to consider the various alternatives and in the end arrived at a compromise between the original design and Alba's substitute. Elizabeth should first be assassinated, then in the resultant confusion Norfolk's followers should rise, seize the Government and rescue Mary. When that was accomplished the Spaniards would land simultaneously in England and Scotland to consolidate the victory. Meantime Philip promised financial assistance to the extent of
fifty

fifty thousand pounds, while Chiapin Vitelli, Marquis of
Cetona, a famous Italian soldier in Spanish employ, who
had the previous autumn surveyed England while attempting to recover the stolen treasure from Elizabeth, volunteered
to undertake the murder. A complete programme was
drawn up: Vitelli explained that Elizabeth was notoriously
easy of access, recklessly admitting even strangers to her
presence; he would accompany her on her progress during
the early autumn and there the first and essential part of
the business could be dispatched. Ridolfi then returned
to Brussels, whence he wrote in elation to his principals in
London of his success.

That letter never arrived, for the prudent Alba unceremoniously stopped it. But the precaution was too late:
the Florentine had already written too many letters. Before
leaving Brussels for Rome, he had sent the Bishop of Ross
an account of his first conversation with Alba, together with
enclosures for Norfolk and Norfolk's follower Lumley.
Burghley, who, like his Queen, had remained suspicious
of Ridolfi despite Walsingham's exoneration, had the letter
opened before sending it on to its destination. At Brussels,
Madrid, and even the Vatican, the Florentine was under
the constant surveillance of English spies, and when he
sent a further report to London, Charles Baily, the courier,
and his packet were seized at Dover by Lord Cobham,
Warden of the Cinque Ports. The Spanish ambassador, who
was on the alert for Baily's coming, contrived with the help
of Cobham's brother to obtain possession of Baily's more
incriminating documents by a sleight-of-hand trick before
they could reach Burghley. Nothing was left in the packet
that could involve Norfolk, but there was quite enough to
show that Mary Stuart was again dealing with Spain. The
Bishop of Ross's ambassadorial privileges were revoked and
he was thrown into the Tower, while Baily went to the
Marshalsea.

All that summer, while Ridolfi toured Europe, Burghley in
London

London laboured to get to the bottom of the conspiracy, but at first failed for lack of a key to the conspirators' code. Ross was threatened with the rack and only saved by the intervention of Elizabeth, who loathed the use of that infernal instrument. In his terror, however, the Bishop denounced his Queen as the murderess of her husband, drawing from one of the examiners the exclamation, 'Lord, what people are these! What a Queen, and what an ambassador!' To loosen Baily's tongue the relentless Burghley introduced a stool pigeon into the Marshalsea. The ruse was successful up to a point, but the wretched courier could no more than Ross supply the information for which the Government was looking, the key to the cipher and conclusive evidence of Norfolk's treason.

Another and more illustrious stool pigeon meantime worked on the Spanish ambassador. Sir John Hawkins bore Philip a bitter grudge because a number of his crew were still in Spanish prisons as a result of the affair at San Juan d'Ulua in Mexico three years before. With Burghley's knowledge the great seaman offered to go to Spain and lead a Spanish fleet against his own country if his men were freed. Don Guerau believed him, they became great friends, and Philip released the prisoners with compensation. Yet deeply as Hawkins wormed his way into Spanish confidence, he could learn no more than that an invasion of England was projected. By this time even Don Guerau could not have explained the precise nature of the conspiracy he had framed with Ridolfi.

Another lucky capture brought the story to its close. Another messenger, carrying part of the promised money to assist in the uprising in Scotland, was captured, and on him was found the key to the cipher which had so baffled the examiners of Ross's original packet. Burghley and his iron-faced spies moved swiftly and darkly from cell to cell, compared confessions and deciphered letters. Revelation followed revelation until at length, in November, the way
was

was shown to the Duke of Norfolk's own correspondence with Ridolfi, which lay hidden under the tiles of Norfolk House in the Strand. In the twinkling of an eye the Duke was again in the Tower and Mary isolated under a reinforced guard.

The exposure of the conspiracy sent the country into ecstasies of excitement. The people flocked to their churches to give grateful thanks that their Queen's life had been spared, and in packed meetings shouted for the immediate death of those who had aimed at it. For days the streets of London seethed with roaring mobs and the printers did a brisk trade in pamphlets blackguarding Spain and 'the Pope who was more full of bulls than money.' Despite the suffering caused by the economic war the populace clamoured for a stringent boycott on all Spanish goods. The Queen of Scots was the special object of execration and in the eyes of the world she was already as good as dead.

Elizabeth herself, in her first outburst of anger against the woman who had callously plotted against her life and the peace of the kingdom, was capable of almost anything. When de la Mothe Fénelon, the French ambassador, tried half-heartedly to justify Mary's conduct on the plea of her ill-treatment, the Queen 'burst into a most furious rage and dwelt very strongly on the evils which...were brought upon this country by the Queen of Scotland.... She screamed this out with so much vehemence that everybody in the palace could hear her.' Yet, despite her rage, Elizabeth turned sick at the thought of exposing a fellow queen to the cruel machinery of a state trial and execution. Once again she stood solidly and alone between Mary and the revenge-thirsty public. Committees of aldermen and a delegation from Parliament waited upon her to demand that the law be allowed to take its course with the royal felon as with any other: Elizabeth, in one of those phrases of hers that move the heart as much by their felicity as by their sentiment, disarmed her petitioners with the simple explanation that 'she could

could not put to death the bird that had flown to her for succour from the hawk.'

She tried to save even Norfolk. He was sentenced to death in January by a court of his peers, many of them his accusers or accomplices, as was the way of sixteenth-century justice, and the warrant signed by the Queen, after much heartburning, on February 11. Three times she postponed the execution in the hope that the popular emotion would spend itself. But in that she was wrong: public and Parliament both demanded a victim and in the end Norfolk had to be sacrificed to save Mary. On June 2 the first of the English nobility gave up his foolish head with the same grace and dignity as his father, the poet Earl of Surrey, had done before him.

The other principal plotter had already been dealt with. The Queen summoned Don Guerau in December, told him what she thought of him in words that her own pirates would have envied, and ordered him to get out of the country within four days. He asked for a slight extension in order to put his affairs in order. When it was granted, he employed it in arranging for Burghley's assassination, meantime sending a courier to beg Alba to hurry over to his assistance. But Burghley proved as able to look after his own life as his Queen's, Alba answered with the impatient advice to take ship before Elizabeth became really angry, and Don Guerau found himself ruthlessly escorted to the coast by the same John Hawkins who had so heartlessly deceived him.

The Ridolfi conspiracy brought to light amongst other things facts and feelings that had previously been concealed by accepted tradition and the thickening fog of general strife. While the Florentine was holding his first conversations with Don Guerau and the Bishop of Ross, Elizabeth, despite growing friction, was still regarded as the friend of Spain, and Mary, in spite of Catherine de Médicis's coldness,

as

as the client of France. During the period of the plot, however, Elizabeth had been so deftly tampering with the European balance that Philip began to have the sickening sensation of moving slowly upward on those gigantic but sensitive scales, as his uneasy words to Alba with reference to the Anjou marriage and his meek acceptance of his ambassador's expulsion show. By the time that Norfolk was beheaded, the Queen of Scots had become the permanent, and not altogether welcome, dependent of Spain, Elizabeth the managing partner of an Anglo-French alliance.

The chances of such a *rapprochement* had seemed remote indeed in 1568. The French bill of complaints against England was quite as long as the Spanish and no easier of adjustment. The treatment of Mary, the assistance given the Huguenots, the raids on French shipping had all contributed to bring on in the dark days of 1569 the ultimatum from Paris already mentioned; only Philip's suspicion of French designs on the Netherlands and Catherine's jealous hatred of the Guises frustrated an attempt by the great Catholic family to draw the two nations into a league against their tormentor. Unable to retaliate alone, the French rulers gave as much underhand help as they could or dared to Elizabeth's rebels, and at awkward moments confronted the English Queen with demands for Mary Stuart's release. In the case of Norfolk and the Northerners, who were more or less Philip's protégés, France was merely fishing lazily in troubled waters, but Mary's imprisonment could be construed when convenient into an insult to the whole French people. As things were, no move towards an accord between the two countries held much promise while the vexed question of the captive Queen stood in the way.

Elizabeth's efforts to find a solution were many and ingenious: her Council's distress during those troubled years rose largely from the Queen's evident wish to undo the knots so cunningly fastened at York and Westminster. But every plan fell through because Mary was always her own worst enemy.

enemy. Time and again she got herself caught in criminal correspondence with Roman agents or Spanish cut-throats at the very moment that Elizabeth, in conjunction with the Scots and French, was on the verge of discovering the elusive formula. Mary's sufferings and her lust for revenge had apparently warped whatever judgment she may have once possessed; like many another spoiled high-spirited creature whose charm and beauty had spared her the need of clear thinking, she consistently underrated the intelligence of her opponents. When Elizabeth at the time of Norfolk's release relaxed the strictness of her captivity and restored to the deceitful Ross his ambassadorial privileges, Mary attributed her cousin's leniency to foolishness and fear and at once began a fresh attempt to rouse Alba through Don Guerau. She seemed utterly incapable of realizing that she was surrounded by all the resources of a great State, most of whose principal officers were itching to catch her out. It was no wonder that when Don Guerau's letter arrived in Brussels Mary's enclosures were missing, and easy to infer who had intercepted them. Nor was it hard to guess Elizabeth's feelings when Ross, summoned to Court to answer a few questions, affirmed under oath that his mistress was carrying on no communication whatever with Spain.

Over and over again Elizabeth wrote her such warnings as 'Madam, I am no fool to be deceived by your devices,' or 'Do you, if you please, remember that those who have two strings to one bow may shoot stronger but they rarely hit the mark.' It was all in vain: Mary was beyond teaching and in the end forfeited the consideration of France as well as of the Queen in whom her only salvation lay. Irritated, disheartened, and weary of the whole sorry mess, Elizabeth finally snapped at Fénelon that 'no sovereign in Europe would sit down under such provocation,' and that she 'would count herself unworthy of her realm, crown and name of Queen if she endured it.' Fénelon's apologies became feebler and less frequent:

frequent: his King openly marvelled that his sister-in-law had kept her head so long, admitting that in no other country would she have been so lucky.

Finally, in 1570, Mary made a will leaving to Philip her crown and her claim to England, to be disposed of at his pleasure with the advice of the Pope. It was one of the most significant acts of her life. It not only revealed once more her incurable belief that kingdoms and peoples could be handed back and forth by the stroke of a royal pen; it deliberately revoked the testament secretly drawn up on her first marriage years before, in which she had bequeathed her all to the rulers of France. When she made the earlier will she at least had no heir; by the new one she not only cut off the country she had once loved, but her own son, and in their stead bestowed her poor parcel of hopes on a distant king bound to her neither by blood nor affection. For Mary Stuart the past was erased — all the meaning of her birth, childhood, her French marriage, Darnley, her motherhood — and nothing was left but revenge. The hopelessness of her position and its exaggeration in her own mind may be gleaned from a letter she received from her new legatee at about this time: in answer to a fresh plea for help, Philip, disturbed by Elizabeth's success in putting down the rebellion and by information that reached him from no less a source than the Queen of England that Mary was secretly treating behind his back for a French marriage, wearily answered his petitioner through Don Guerau with the pious assurance that 'God will extricate her from all trouble and turn it into great happiness.' But on Spain's behalf he would promise nothing more substantial.

The Ridolfi conspiracy, by exposing Mary's large commitments to Spain, completed her estrangement from France and gave a strong forward impulse to the good understanding between that country and England. Elizabeth and the Queen-Mother, though they distrusted each other profoundly, with ample cause on both sides, yet had a shrewd respect for each other's other's abilities, and their tactics were often amusingly similar. In answer to one of Catherine's perfunctory clucks of concern over Mary's sad state, Elizabeth instructed her ambassador in Paris, Sir Henry Norris, to counter-attack with a reminder of various French misdemeanours, while promising on her own part to mitigate the rigours of Mary's captivity, and to mention casually that she was equipping an army of eighty thousand men — not, Heaven forfend, with any thought of France, but merely 'having regard to insurgents in her kingdom and the neighbouring kingdom of Scotland.' To which Catherine, after a sardonic acknowledgement of the English Queen's engagement to look after the captive's welfare, replied with an equally detached air that, if Elizabeth enlisted her eighty thousand, she herself would enlist a hundred and fifty thousand — but not from any fear of England, because 'the ditch which divided the two kingdoms was of such large dimensions that the ocean could pass through it.' Neither could have raised an army half that size, and both ladies knew it.

They had the good sense, however, to see the mutual advantage of an alliance if it could be achieved. The Spanish colossus was a growing menace to them both: Philip was tampering with the Guises as well as with the English Catholics, and if he managed to stamp out rebellion in the Netherlands he would be in a position to give such help to his friends in both England and France as would enable them to shake both thrones. It was Catherine's hope that she could reconcile her warring parties by uniting them in the conquest of the Netherlands from Spain, a project which Elizabeth, of course, could not for a moment tolerate, since French dominion of the Low Countries was even more dangerous to her than Spanish; both Queens, however, kept these thoughts for the future, each confident of her own power to outwit the other. In addition, each had a strong personal grievance against Philip, Elizabeth because he was trying to have her assassinated and Catherine because she

more

more than suspected that the Spanish King had got rid of his late wife, her daughter, by poison.

It was Elizabeth whose need at first was the greater and who therefore took the initiative. She was, she intimated, ready to get married to Catherine's second son, the Duke of Anjou. That trick was too threadbare: half the onlookers yawned, the other half laughed rudely. Courtiers and statesmen, under politely drooped eyelids, examined the deepening lines in the royal virgin's hollow cheeks, the increasing quantities of rouge used to hide their sallowness, the elaborately curled hair whose golden tints owed more to art than to nature, the robes cut low so as to attract the eye to charms which had suffered less from the ravages of time, and smiled into their neatly trimmed and perfumed beards. Too many men had frittered away their years in watching her beckoning smile turn gradually to amused indifference. No one could any longer take seriously anything the hardened middle-aged coquette had to say about her own marriage.

The French response to her advances would have damped any but the most indomitable ardour. Elizabeth summoned Fénelon to talk of Anjou and paid the Duke many pretty compliments for having 'changed his courtly life for brave and difficult enterprises.' Anjou was at the moment in nominal command of the Guise army and so taken with his own military prowess that he was boasting of his intention to rescue his fair sister-in-law from her English prison. Fénelon joined in the eulogy of the Duke, but said bluntly that if it was marriage Elizabeth was hinting at the offer must come from herself. She sadly objected that the time for that was past: she knew that she was old, her mirror told her so, and what could a handsome young prince want with an old woman like herself. The gallant Frenchman gracefully contradicted her: 'she had resisted the power of time, which had taken nothing from her beauty.' But there was a distinct flavour of irony in his words as in his report of the conversation to Catherine; the Queen-Mother decided to
wait

wait and see at least how Elizabeth would fare with her rebellion before considering her as a daughter-in-law.

Elizabeth put down her revolt despite French prognostications to the contrary; at the same time the Guises defeated the Huguenots so badly as to wreck Catherine's carefully weighted balance of parties. A new makeweight was needed, and the Queen-Mother gave further consideration to the English proposal. If only she dared believe that Elizabeth was sincere.... Nothing would have suited her better than to procure a crown for her favourite son and thereby also remove him from the influence of the Guises... but she could not bear the thought of submitting him to the same humiliations as the many others who had hearkened to the red-haired siren. The beaten Huguenots urged her forward, for her good as well as their own; even the *Politiques*, or moderates, were eager for the marriage as a means of restoring peace at home and ultimately ejecting Spain from the Low Countries. Catherine compromised by instructing Fénelon to listen attentively, but without committing her to anything.

The ambassador selected Leicester as the man most likely to know the state of Elizabeth's feelings. What he heard was extremely encouraging: the Queen was in such distress over public affairs that she would deeply appreciate a friendly hand from France; she had been outspoken in her praise of Anjou's beauty, as revealed by his portrait, and perturbed by the report that that formidable warrior of nineteen summers was coming in person to deliver and marry Mary. Leicester did everything but lead the Frenchman by the hand into the Queen's presence. Thus the lover: the Chief Minister when interviewed corroborated Robert's every word. But Fénelon, with the history of Elizabeth's wooings filed in his memory, still disbelieved. Too many of his fellow diplomats had fallen into the pit by giving heed to the English ministers' confident knowledge of their Queen's mind. There was as yet nothing to prove that this courtship differed in any way from a dozen similar manœuvres in the past.

Then

Then Guido Cavalcanti appeared on the scene. He was a Florentine chiefly but by no means exclusively in the pay of France, a man of mystery employed in every sort of secret and intricate business. He held no office, but he knew everybody and everything worth knowing, though how he made their acquaintance and obtained his facts only the Prince of Darkness could have told. He had passed like a shadow from the back door of the Louvre to the back door of Whitehall bearing Henry II's presents and offers to Elizabeth during the conference of Cateau-Cambrésis. He had also served the English Queen in various matters, and could, and did, tell Fénelon much of which the ambassador was ignorant concerning the final disappearance of the Archduke Charles from the list of Elizabeth's suitors. The Holy Roman Emperor had grown tired of playing a guessing game in which he was always the guesser, the King of Spain, for whom the entertainment had been primarily devised, had informed His Apostolic Majesty that he no longer found it either profitable or amusing, and the Archduke had at last got himself engaged to a plump and rich Bavarian Princess. Most of this Fénelon knew, but what Cavalcanti had to add was what Elizabeth had just said on hearing of her long-suffering suitor's infidelity. The Florentine had been on the spot when Elizabeth banged her fist down in rage and declared with a blasphemous oath that 'she would show the world that she could make a match as good as his.' She had even talked of sending an embassy to protest to the Holy Roman Emperor at this insulting rejection of herself.

Fénelon meditated thoughtfully on the old simile referring to hell's fury and a scorned woman. Here at last was a variation in the emotional key of Elizabeth's matrimonial symphony. Still wary but by no means wholly pessimistic, the ambassador was summoned to a private interview with the Queen. He found her 'more splendidly dressed than usual,' and in the evident expectation of hearing talk of her marriage. She herself delicately broached the subject in what may be
called

called the style of her middle period. If only the Duke were not so young, or she so old. She knew she was no longer a great catch.... She waited for Fénelon to answer and when he protested shook her head, smiled wistfully and heaved a gentle sigh. She spoke of Anjou's mistresses, mentioning two of them by name. How could she hope to compete with famous beauties? Yet 'she did not wish for a husband who would honour her as a Queen without loving her as a wife.'

The ambassador was impressed — who indeed could help being impressed by the sincerity of a lady who spoke so candidly of her own fading charms? — and answered that the Princes of Valois were noted for their conjugal fidelity, giving as an instance Charles IX, who had been living with his wife 'in such great love and privacy that I would recommend a Princess who wished for perfect happiness in marriage to take a husband from the House of France.' Charles's connubial bliss had already endured all of two months.

Elizabeth was still troubled: she was sure that her heart would break if she discovered that her husband did not love her.... On the other hand, she realized she would have to take the chance — it would be dangerous to wait until 'she became so old as to no longer have the chance of suitors or of heirs.' She seemed to be convinced; Fénelon was completely so, and wrote to Catherine that if she would empower him to proceed he would undertake to snare the butterfly which so many had pursued in vain.

Meantime, in France Elizabeth's new ambassador, Sir Francis Walsingham, and Lord Buckhurst, who had been sent over on a special mission to congratulate Charles IX on his marriage, were patiently explaining to the Queen-Mother the difference between Elizabeth as she had been and as she now was: her earlier suitors had been poor princes and at a distance from England, whilst Anjou was near and supported by a powerful king. Not only could Elizabeth love him more than his predecessors, but she realized that he could bring her a more substantial dowry. Catherine could not but accept

cept both premises: Anjou, the apple of her eye, was universally admitted to be his brothers' superior in looks and talents, yet, despite these advantages, no more depraved than they, while the still precarious state of England might well have brought Elizabeth round to a French marriage. The Queen-Mother read her ambassador's dispatches, weighed Walsingham and Buckhurst's words, and at length took upon herself the task of arousing Anjou's appreciation of the brilliant future in store for him.

That proved difficult. The Duke would at first have nothing to do with 'the old hag.' His favourites and mistresses laughed at him, the Guises scornfully upbraided him for deserting his faith and his knightly vows to rescue their unhappy niece. Catherine and her darling son alternately swore at each other and fell into each other's arms in tears. But momentarily the mother was stronger than the son's train of courtesans and pederasts: he gave in and chivalrously proclaimed his bride-to-be 'the rarest creature the earth has seen this five hundred years.'

The knowing smiles and headshakings ceased abruptly: the world gaped to behold the bride of thirty-eight and the groom of nineteen, firmly escorted by his mother, advancing to the very porch of the church. Elizabeth's transparent fantasy of courtship had amazingly materialized into solid preparation for a wedding. The extraordinary change in opinion during the course of a few months is mirrored in Don Guerau's confidential dispatches. On January 16, 1571, that malevolent watcher wrote that 'her matrimonial intentions are of no use any longer for deceiving people.' Six days later he hedged by adding that 'the fickleness of the Queen makes it impossible to say whether the marriage will go forward or not.' And on April 10 he announced categorically that 'This marriage will be effected....'

But at this point Elizabeth called Fénelon to her and complained of the unflattering descriptions of her person which Anjou was circulating in Paris. She had heard 'that a certain
person

person of high rank in France had said that Monsieur would do well to marry the old hag who had last year had an ulcer in her leg not cured and which probably would never be cured, under pretence of which he might administer her a French potion which would make him a widower six months after his marriage, and leave him free to marry the Queen of Scots, in whose right he could reign peacefully over the whole island.' Though she was not so young as she had been, there was no need to exaggerate her senility... it was a pity, she told Fénelon, that he had been unable to attend the Marchioness of Northampton's ball, for there he could have seen her dance and thus have been in a position to assure the Duke that he was in no danger of marrying a cripple.

Fénelon protested that the Duke had been foully mis-quoted — it was well known that Walsingham hated the match — and he grew hoarse with eloquence and flatteries. Elizabeth relented so far as to continue the negotiations, but now she must have security. If the Duke really loved her he would agree to the inclusion of a clause in the marriage contract forbidding him to practise the Catholic religion in England: only thus could she be certain that it was for her-self and not for ulterior reasons that he wanted to marry her. Until she was sure of the French proposal she had not seemed to care greatly about a Mass one way or the other; in fact she had told Fénelon 'that she had been crowned and conse-crated according to the rites of the Catholic Church... and that she would be sorry if Monsieur should abandon his religion; for if he had the heart to desert God, he might desert her.'

Catherine did not at first regard the reservation demanded by Elizabeth as of first importance between women of the world. She had few illusions about her son's piety and, though some pretences had to be kept up for the sake of the public in France, was sure that there would be no great difficulty in arriving at a formula. She was dumbfounded, therefore, to learn that the Duke had developed a violent attachment to his faith which would not permit him to forgo its

its ritual at the instance of a heretic. Suspecting that the Guises had been at him again, she once more subjected him to the whole répertoire of maternal tears and scoldings, in which the King and all the politicians at Court joined in. The marriage must not fail: the world now expected it, the Spaniards had been thoroughly frightened by it, and what were a silly boy's artificially cultivated scruples compared to a jointure in the throne of England? But Anjou continued to sulk inside his conscience and his mother desperately sent one aristocrat after another to aid Fénelon in arguing the Queen of England into a compromise. By some queer metamorphosis Elizabeth, who in 1570 had pulled every possible wire to get herself proposed to, was in 1571 in the position of being implored to marry.

She could not, she now maintained, enter into a marriage contract with the crucial clause left out. Even if her own inclinations permitted her to marry — and she frankly acknowledged that she felt her old preference for spinster-hood again creeping over her — she was very doubtful whether her people would allow her to take a husband who insisted on introducing Papist rites into the country.

Meantime, she took advantage of French eagerness for her good-will to send an army into Scotland, there to restore order and instal her own nominee, the Earl of Lennox, as Regent. When Fénelon protested that the entry of an English force into Scotland to the detriment of Mary's party would justify the French in protecting their interests there by a similar invasion, she answered sharply that if one Frenchman set foot in Scotland Mary would remain a prisoner for life and that if France wanted war she was ready for it. The rulers of France did not want war and did want the marriage, so Elizabeth without interference again made herself arbiter in Edinburgh — something no one would have believed possible six months before. She also used the prospects of the marriage to induce Parliament to vote her what she needed and go its way in peace.

All

All through the summer the statesmen and diplomats on both sides toiled to bring their respective principals into a more tractable mood. Anjou, tired of his elders' admonitions, ran away from Court. It was a privilege not available to Elizabeth, so she listened inscrutably to her minister's lamentations that if she now rejected Anjou she would make France her enemy for life and continued to admire the Duke's portrait in public.

In the autumn the affair took on a fresh lease of life. Burghley exposed the Ridolfi conspiracy, and Elizabeth, as yet ignorant of all its ramifications, unaware that the very threat of her marriage with Anjou had discouraged Spain from giving full ear to Ridolfi, at once indicated her willingness to discuss afresh the objectional clause in the marriage contract. Spain's victory over the Turks at Lepanto in October, which freed Philip's Mediterranean forces for action elsewhere, intensified for a short period the activity both in Paris and London. Charles IX and Elizabeth sent warm congratulations to the conqueror, messages of veiled dismay to each other, and the negotiations burst out furiously once more, with Elizabeth's ministers again begging her either to marry Anjou or call the whole thing off lest she offend the French irremediably and Catherine continuing to pursue the reluctant groom.

In January the courtship ended by mutual consent. France, far from being offended — how could she be when it was her own party to the marriage who had refused it? — discussed offering Elizabeth the Duke of Alençon, aged seventeen, in his brother's place. Fénelon hastily interposed, explaining to Catherine that the lad was too young and to other people that he was so ugly that Elizabeth would be insulted at the very suggestion. He was wrong, for Elizabeth was always ready to listen to a fresh proposal; but the project was swallowed up in the darkness of Saint Bartholomew's, not to be revived until six years later. It was enough for the present that out of the Anjou courtship grew the apparently hopeless

hopeless Anglo-French alliance. For three years Catherine had stubbornly refused a treaty which was not sealed by wedlock; Walsingham himself, who had striven so long and vainly for the alliance without the marriage, had finally withdrawn his opposition in despair. Yet, when the negotiators took an inventory of what they had accomplished, they found to their mutual gladness that Anjou was, after all, inessential — the work of those years could be completed without him. A few months more of chaffering and on April 29, 1572, the Treaty of Blois was signed, providing that if either nation were attacked the other would come to its assistance and that France would undertake to secure entry for English goods into the Continent. The French and Walsingham had wanted to add a clause binding both countries to an offensive against Spain, but this Elizabeth vetoed. She had what she wanted in security without forfeiting the vital balance of power, and an alternative to Antwerp or Hamburg as a Continental dépôt for her merchants. So long as the treaty was observed there was no chance of a combination between her two strongest rivals, while she stood in no way committed to helping the French instal themselves in Spain's place in the Netherlands. Had she written the document herself, it could not have conformed more closely to her wishes.

Four months later the new friendship was subjected to a test that nearly destroyed it. On the eighteenth of August the work of reconciliation in France culminated in the wedding of the young King of Navarre, titular head of the French Protestants, and Catherine's beautiful and vicious daughter Marguerite. On the twenty-second a tiff between the partisans of Anjou and Coligny resulted in a murderous assault on the admiral. Charles IX, roused from his habitual indolence, swore to bring the assailants to justice, but Catherine, frightened at her favourite son's peril and the growing power of Coligny's party, which she herself had done so much to foster, hurried to stuff the King's muddled head with

with fables of Huguenot plots. The effect of her tales on his imagination was the Massacre of Saint Bartholomew's.

As the horrible story of the slaughter in Paris and the provinces was borne across the Channel by the refugees, the sickening narratives of women and children, the old and the sick, butchered by the thousand, a wave of such hatred and fury passed over England that for a while it threatened to drive the Government into a war of vengeance against the new ally. Frenchmen who ventured out of their houses were beaten in the streets and the ambassador himself insulted whenever he appeared in public. Further details only added to the frenzy: the unconcealed jubilation of the Catholics, the Papal proclamation of thanksgiving printed in gold, the fervent ejaculation of Mary Stuart that she had not been so uplifted in spirit since her half-brother's assassination — everything indicated to the English people that the Bayonne Conference, where Catherine, Alba, and the Roman dignitaries had met in sinister concert seven years before, had sent forth at last its bloody shoots.

Fénelon in London waited feverishly for the official French account of the massacre to arrive. Catherine found some trouble in composing it, for though she was gratified at the impression her act had produced on Catholic Europe, she was terrified at the impression it would make on the Queen of England. Finally the *Mémoire justificative de la Barthélemy* was drawn up and hurried over to London. Fénelon, appalled alike at the stupidity of his own rulers and the hostility against him in London, rode swiftly after Elizabeth, who was on her customary summer progress.

He overtook her at Woodstock, where she had paused to review the terrible and delicate situation before her; it was the same house in which she had spent so much of her youth as her sister's prisoner. The possibility of the dreaded Catholic combination she had apparently avoided by the recent treaty seemed at last upon her; on the first receipt of the news she had ordered her fleet to sea, the musters to be

called

called out and transport to be provided for eight thousand men. Heart and soul she sympathized with her people's emotion, for no one on earth hated blood and anarchy more than she. Yet not for an instant did she confuse her responsibility as head of the State with her private feelings — one did not make war because one disapproved of one's neighbour's treatment of his subjects.

She kept Fénelon waiting in anterooms for three days listening to the unminced opinions of the Councillors. When finally he was allowed to enter the presence chamber, he found the Queen attended by several lords of the Council and the principal ladies of the Court, all dressed in black. Fénelon himself, one of the greatest reporters who ever practised diplomacy, describes the scene. In a dead hush Elizabeth advanced two or three paces to meet him 'with a sad and stern countenance, but still preserving her kindness of manner. She led me to a window apart and after having briefly apologized for the delay of my audience, she asked me if it were possible that such reports could be circulated as those which reached her of a Prince whom she had loved and honoured and in whom she had reposed more confidence than in all the rest of the world.'

The ambassador answered as he had been primed, explaining that he had come merely to obtain her condolences for the unhappy 'accident' — the word officially applied by the French to the massacre — to his King and country. The explanation fell flat; the ambassador himself felt it and humbly waited for the Queen's judgment. Elizabeth answered quietly that she hoped what Fénelon said regarding his King's innocence was true, but whether true or not he had committed a great wrong. Coligny had come to Paris under the mantle of a royal promise of safety; it had turned out to be a cloak for assassins. If there had been a Protestant conspiracy to avenge him, as the ambassador alleged, the law should have searched it out and punished it, for a sovereign had no business with private vendettas: there was a just King in Heaven

Heaven who would of a certainty avenge the slaughter of those thousands of innocent victims unless their own earthly protectors exacted full expiation for their death. How much Elizabeth believed in God is problematical, but her exposition of the law as between sovereign and subject came from her heart — and from England's.

Fénelon had known Elizabeth many years. He had observed and described her as flirt, fishwife, bluestocking, stateswoman, and many other things both more and less flattering. But in his narrative of that interview at Woodstock he presents another portrait of her, from which are omitted all those changing aspects of the woman Elizabeth. In lines bold and characteristic of himself the Frenchman drew the lineaments of a Queen — aloof, wise, fearlessly just — one of that rare race of beings born to rule.

The unhappy man, in inward agreement with her verdict, tried to extort some sign of concession, but Elizabeth was not in the mood to equivocate. She told him bluntly that a King whose word was worthless to his subjects might equally betray his allies. There had been a proposal to send the most distinguished mission that had ever left England, including Leicester and Burghley, to pick up the threads of the Alençon marriage, but she declared that she would not send her dearest subjects to a Court where men's lives were not safe: and the project was put to sleep for six years. Fénelon reminded her that she had promised to be godmother to Charles IX's expected heir and she intimated that she would keep the promise. That was all, and she dismissed him with the same reserved and gracious courtesy.

When Fénelon's account of that audience reached the Queen-Mother, it took all the gilt off the Papal proclamation. She saw that she had blundered miserably, for now her only security against the Guises were the Huguenots, whose brothers she had butchered, and their patroness the Queen of England. She had hoped for much from Philip — had he not smiled for the first time in his life when he heard of Saint Bartholomew's?

Bartholomew's? — but it now appeared that the smile had been at her expense, for she had torn France and rendered it harmless to himself. She implored Elizabeth to stand by her, abasing herself in the dust. The younger Queen did not say no, but she deftly exploited Catherine's isolation by patching up her differences with Philip and effecting a treaty that again opened the whole Continent to her merchants. Philip, delighted at the rift in the alliance against him, allowed a Huguenot garrison just captured at Mons to retire on most lenient terms, after they had resigned themselves to the inevitable massacre, in order to prove to his sister-in-law how much more merciful the Spaniard was than the Frenchman. The letter he wrote to Elizabeth on the occasion of the reconciliation was called by the disheartened Fénelon a 'quasi-submission, unworthy of so great a Prince and of the injuries he had received.' The King of Spain made further acknowledgment of England's improved position in the world by intervening at considerable personal embarrassment to save several English subjects from the clutches of the Inquisition.

Safe from both her Continental enemies for the time being, Elizabeth attended to a final piece of business nearer home. In 1571, Lennox, like Moray before him, was murdered by Mary's friends in Scotland. His successor, the Earl of Mar, who was also of Elizabeth's party, went the way of all Scottish regents in October, 1572, and again anarchy with its inevitable hurt to the English border counties broke loose. For a third time Elizabeth determined the choice of Regent, selecting the Earl of Morton, the strongest if the least scrupulous amongst the lairds. Morton put down the Marian opposition with an iron hand, but a nucleus fortified themselves in Edinburgh Castle under the leadership of the ablest of Scotch soldiers, Kirkcaldy of Grange, and defied all the efforts of the Regent to dislodge them. As long as the deposed Queen had a fighting force left, neither England nor Scotland was safe. Morton turned to Elizabeth. Various sordid bickerings followed, for his followers, more interested in her

money

money than in any abstract patriotism, wanted to be paid before they allowed her to deliver them from the common enemy. Elizabeth finally sent an army under Sir William Drury to take the citadel and after a month's siege it surrendered. Kirkcaldy was hanged by Morton, while Maitland forestalled a public execution by quiet suicide. It was his strange but characteristic fate to have deserted Mary in her need and to die in her service. Many Scots were to fight stoutly for other Stuarts, but in her own country Mary was no longer a cause, simply a memory.

Chapter IX

The Inventory of Peace

THE first great crisis of the reign ended with the fall of Edinburgh Castle and the renewal of friendly relations with Spain. In 1569, Cecil, after consultation with the Council, had laid before Elizabeth a memorandum stating that 'such decay of obedience and civil policy, as compared with the fearfulness and reverence in times past, would astonish any wise and considerate person... The Realm was so feeble that it was fearful to think what would happen if the enemies at hand were to assail... The case seemed so desperate as almost to take away all courage to seek a remedy.' By 1573, the country was again tranquil within, and every frontier, whether land or sea, free from foreign menace. Trade with the Continent had been reopened and was once more flourishing. For five years, while her neighbours were doing their best to annihilate themselves and one another, England peacefully recruited her strength for her next crucial test, which would decide her destiny and the future of the world.

Only half a generation had gone by since that raw November morning when Archbishop Heath, Queen Mary's Lord Chancellor, had announced to the assembled Lords and Commons the accession of their Sovereign Lady Elizabeth. The young had not yet grown middle-aged nor the middle-aged old, yet in those fourteen years had occurred a metamorphosis without parallel in history — a pouring of wealth undreamed of into a poverty-stricken little country, the conversion of a frightened, despised people into the most arrogant adventurers on earth.

Up to the time of Elizabeth's succession England's only venture into distant markets had been Chancellor's opening of the Muscovy trade. By 1573, Jenkinson and Bannister had

had successfully challenged Venice's age-old monopoly in the East, Hawkins and Drake had proved that neither Papal prohibitions nor Spanish arms could keep enterprising men from doing a profitable business in the West. English goods were on sale in Constantinople, Teheran, Tiflis, Samarkand, Cartagena, and San Domingo; from those places flowed in return great quantities of the bright-coloured stuffs with which the Elizabethans loved to deck their bodies, the spices and sweets and rich heavy wines that made up so large a part of their singular diet. Less and less, as time went on, were those exotic luxuries of dress and food and decoration exclusive to the rich: with every year their consumption spread more deeply and broadly amongst the middle classes, as one foreign visitor after another reported with incredulous astonishment.

With the change in the habits and the arts of living came another and even profounder change in the national psychology. Prices were soaring owing to the tremendous influx of precious metal from the Indies, the profits of established commerce were subject to the enormous insurance rates imposed by the activities of pirates and privateers, with the result that wealth became comparatively less a matter of capital and industry and more an affair of small investments with large risks. The world had suddenly become a storehouse of infinite treasure to be ransacked rather than a plot of earth to be painfully ploughed. One's neighbour might sail away in a crazy rented barque of fifty tons to reappear after two years able to buy out the local squire ten times over. The English, having nothing to lose by such a system of competition, developed within a decade into a race of gamblers.

The new wealth and the new outlook naturally had their effect on the country's economic and political as well as on its social life. There was money galore in the City for every sort of investment and speculation, far more than could be used in agricultural development or the new textile industries founded by the skilful artisans emigrating from persecution

in

in the Netherlands and France. The surplus flowed into the natural resources of the kingdom, into opening fresh coal seams in the north, tin and copper mines in the west. Many of these ventures were quite insane — sixteenth-century capitalists were as prone to listen to sorcerers as to engineers — but enough were sound to alter the whole complexion of England and permanently redistribute its labour.

The swift acquisition of wealth and its manipulation by the greedy and venturesome raised, as always, a mass of new problems. The sudden rise in prices brought its usual complement of hardships to the labouring classes; the drift from old occupations to new created unemployment in some places while providing fresh employment in others. No machinery had yet been devised for dealing with such a colossal readjustment and it devolved upon the Crown to guard against the ill effects of that teeming enterprise while encouraging it to the largest possible extent. It was the Government, as a study of the acts and ordinances of the middle and later years of the reign shows, who undertook to see that the worker received at least a minimum wage and that the necessities of life did not mount beyond his means; to regulate the relationship between master and servant and to compel each parish to provide for its poor, old, sick, and unemployed. Some of the ordinances for which Elizabeth and her Council were responsible have in one form or another survived over three hundred years of tremendous social evolution — and their underlying paternalism is not so anachronistic as it once was. Having no precedent to go by, the Queen was guided by her instinct that monarchy's function is to serve as the common man's shield against the excesses of wealth and power. The royal vessels which year after year patrolled with increasing effect her merchantmen's routes testified to her appreciation of her other duty, the protection of the sea-borne traffic which was England's life blood.

That period of incomparable expansion was created by the energy and genius of a whole people, but its preservation was the

the work of the woman into whose long white hands all the reins of government had passed during her years on the throne. In many things Elizabeth had changed, in others she was changeless. The slender body had grown harshly angular, the stately grace of her movement was marred by a limp resulting from an infection in her leg, the pale delicate skin was coarse and lined under its rouge, the finely modelled lips were habitually compressed, the aquiline nose stood out high and bony from the hollow cheeks, the alert blue eyes held a permanent irony, sometimes fierce, sometimes merely of amusement. On the whole, considering the stock from which she sprang, she had lasted well. She could still receive, standing for hours on end, the myriads of visitors who came on business or out of mere curiosity, examine and criticize all acts and instructions to her officials at home and abroad, ride to hounds with the best, and dance and flirt till early morning. She could always find time to interview distinguished foreigners or the young students whose education in foreign universities would be paid out of her own pocket, and to circulate amongst the great and the humble of her subjects. Her wit and vitality were if anything greater at forty than they had been at twenty-five: in tavern and at fireside her repartees and her eccentricities made unflagging gossip for her delighted people.

Men had said on her accession that the country would never tolerate a second female sovereign after its disastrous experience with her predecessor. All that sort of prophecy had long been forgotten. She was an autocrat such as England had never known before and would, in all probability, never know again. Parliament met once every four years or so, did her bidding after some grumbling, and dispersed. She was her own Prime Minister, Chancellor of the Exchequer, Foreign and Home Secretaries; the Privy Council was no more than a body of busy and capable executives to carry out her word. 'All things were moved and directed by a woman's nod in England.' The words were written by Francis Bacon, son of a Lord Chancellor, nephew of Burghley, cousin

of

of the Principal Secretary to be, Robert Cecil. If anyone had the opportunity and the wit to judge, it was he; and he committed his verdict to paper when Elizabeth had passed beyond the reach of flattery.

Yet, though England had changed, and she with it, in one vital respect she was the same. The old passions and opinions had been modified, the character of the parties had altered, their arena of strife shifted — but she was still in the centre, able to see all round, redress balances and discourage excess. As another who knew her, Sir Robert Naunton, an important minister of King James I and her first biographer, observed: 'The principal note of her reign will be that she ruled by faction and party, which herself hath made, upheld and weakened, as her own great judgment advised.' It was this determination of hers never to be owned or driven by a faction that gave England, amongst other things, those five precious years of peace — the years in which Francis Bacon, Christopher Marlowe, William Shakespeare, and the rest of that unbelievable generation were learning their letters and pondering on the brave new world that beckoned them to manhood.

At the beginning of her reign the conservative element in the country had been chiefly represented in the Council by the men inherited from Mary's day. Most of these, including their leader, the Duke of Norfolk, had disappeared after the rebellion, while the few that survived had adapted themselves to the new age. The Right, to use a modern term, was personified by the very men who had carried through the revolution in Church and State and their acknowledged leader was Burghley, now Lord Treasurer, whose flowing white hair and beard lent him the aspect of a Biblical patriarch. Its policy was essentially static: the severe coercion of Catholics and other 'dividers of religion' at home, in foreign affairs a more insular self-sufficiency, and the provision of an assured succession, preferably through the Queen's marriage. It was written of Burghley that 'as he has never been on the Continent
nent

nent he thinks England is the whole world,' and though the statement contains a trifling error of fact, since Cecil had paid a flying visit to Holland in 1557, it correctly represents his point of view.

The Left or progressive party had as its nominal leader the volatile Leicester, now grown somewhat fat, bald, and red in the face. But its best brains and force were supplied by Francis Walsingham, the swarthy Norfolk squire who had entered the Queen's service under Burghley's patronage and in 1574 succeeded him in the post of Principal Secretary. Walsingham was twelve years younger than the Lord Treasurer, only little less of a statesman and a great deal more of a crusader. He was a fighting Puritan, scornful of the diluted Reformation mixed by Luther and prescribed by Elizabeth, preferring the steaming highly seasoned potion brewed by Calvin to be served up later piping hot by Cromwell. His political dream was a vast Protestant league embracing France, Germany, the Netherlands, and Scotland, to be organized by English diplomacy and supported by English money, with the utter extermination of Papistry north of the Pyrenees and the Alps as its ultimate object.

Elizabeth agreed with neither entirely, though she was closer to Burghley, or rather Burghley was closer to her, for in his younger days he had been nearly as militant in his Protestantism as Walsingham. Perhaps age had cooled his temper; perhaps, being a wise man, long experience had taught him that his Queen's middle course was in part, at least, responsible for the confutation of the many dismal memoranda he had written for her enlightenment. On two matters, however, the sovereign and her First Minister could never agree, her marriage and the line to be taken with Spain. It is highly probable that she knew herself incapable of providing the heir that Cecil and the country so earnestly, and properly, craved, while his intimate letters show that he did not surrender his hopes until the Queen was beyond the age of childbearing. In due course she did arrange for a peaceable succession,

cession, though not in a manner that either Burghley or his opponents approved of. Meantime, being a woman who enjoyed the exercise of her wits, she continued to put her marriage to the uses of diplomacy; whilst he, being a cautious man, remained fearful that she would do so once too often. As for Spain, though Elizabeth no more than Burghley desired a war, she would not follow his advice to put her irrepressible seamen, the chief causes of Philip's grievances against her, under lock and key. She saw, as he did not, their value as auxiliaries to the floating white-sailed defences of Britain's long coastline. She had done much to control them, though to suppress them entirely would have been impossible in any event, since they were in the employ of some of the most powerful of her subjects, including the lord-lieutenants of the counties bordering the Channel; it was enough that she had to a remarkable extent converted them from outlaws into useful servants of the Crown. And even while she cursed them aloud she was in her heart proud of them. She appointed Sir John Hawkins, the slave trader, to supervise the building of the navy and to keep it fit for sea; she neglected to inform the Lord Treasurer of the commission that sent Drake on his immortal voyage round the world, and it was her idea to reward him with a knighthood on the deck of the *Golden Hind* after his return. The King of Spain pondered long on her bland thrust, in answer to his protests, that she was no more responsible for English piracy than he for the Spanish Inquisition.

Her differences with Walsingham went much deeper. She disliked his Puritanism, as she disliked all immoderation, and thought his scheme for making England sword and buckler for the European Reformation suicidal folly. When he tried to show her that the struggle in Europe was a simple issue between 'Christ and Belial,' she gave him such a browbeating, as a man 'fit to deal only with heretics,' that he went off to pour his sorrows into Leicester's understanding ears, while she exorcised her temper by boxing those of a lady-in-waiting who

who happened to be handy. She would not accept his thesis that England ought, for her own safety, to make common cause with Dutch and Huguenot in their battle for civil and religious toleration, nor did she see why she should spend her people's money for Continental quarrels. It was hard enough at best to squeeze the subsidies out of Parliament, and Walsingham made himself the advocate of every sponger who prefaced his application with the cry of 'Down with the Pope!' Great diplomat though he was, Walsingham had not the rudiments of financial sense, as his papers on the subject amply prove.

The principal danger to the peace during those years, and the concrete cause of division between her and her ministers, was the revolt in the Netherlands. The half of the Council led by Burghley wanted her to keep out of the struggle; Leicester and Walsingham wanted her to plunge in head first. She herself recognized that neither course was practicable: if the Dutch were crushed and Spain unquestioned master of the Low Countries, England would live under a perpetual threat; but if Spain were completely driven out the way would be open for France, who would attack and more easily hold the small provinces adjacent to her frontiers. Elizabeth's policy, though often blurred by her contradictions and vacillations, was simple and sensible: to give the rebels such help as would enable them to wring from Philip a recognition of the rights they had formerly enjoyed — it was all they were asking — while leaving Spain as acknowledged overlord to keep out the French. In pursuance of this policy she sent secret assistance in money to the Prince of Orange — despite her thrift and her critics' cries of parsimony she spent a third of the subsidies on the Netherlands — and tacitly allowed him to enlist volunteers in England under Sir Humphrey Gilbert and other free-lance captains; at the same time, by refusing a formal acknowledgment of Dutch belligerency, she refrained from offending Spain.

It was a tricky, underhand, unscrupulous game by its very

nature,

nature, and contributed more than anything else she ever did to tarnish her memory with accusations of dishonesty and vacillation. Its only justification is that it achieved its object of keeping England out of war, and came near to procuring a settlement in the Low Countries which might have spared Europe much of the seventy years of misery to follow.

Her methods were predestined, however — the usual fate of a neutral dealing actively, even if legally, with two belligerents — to gain her the vilification instead of the thanks of both sides. The Dutch navy existed largely as a result of her help and protection; by means of it Orange was able to keep up the struggle despite his almost unbroken series of defeats on land; yet when he attempted to blockade Antwerp he ran foul of England's important Flemish trade and found himself compelled either to withdraw the blockading fleet or embroil himself with Elizabeth. For the London merchants, though ready to drop large sums into the collection boxes on Sunday in aid of their co-religionists, shrieked to Heaven and to the Government on weekdays, if these same co-religionists interfered with business.

Elizabeth's treatment of the difficulties was typical of her attitude throughout. Her intention was consistent, her practice wildly confusing. She demanded that Orange return the seized vessels with compensation, taking special care that her stern language should be repeated to Philip and laid up to her credit. Orange was not to be moved: the blockade was his only offensive weapon against a superior enemy and he intended to make the most of it. Elizabeth replied with a threat to assist Spain unless her subjects' property were returned at once and not henceforth molested. The Protestant party in the Council argued to no avail: if Orange was fighting for Holland she was fighting for England, and if their interests clashed so much the worse for Orange. In the end the owners of the vessels got them back by paying a secret subsidy to the Prince, and Walsingham privately advised him to threaten Elizabeth that

that he would call in the French in order to frighten her into greater leniency and further assistance — a shady bit of work on the part of a leading minister of the Crown.

Orange took the advice, relations improved, and the Prince presently sent over his closest friend, Marnix de Saint-Aldegonde, to offer Elizabeth the sovereignty of the Dutch provinces if she would supply the means of liberating them from Spain. If she declined, Saint-Aldegonde was to propose an alliance and try to borrow one hundred thousand pounds.

Elizabeth had not the faintest wish for Continental dominions; they cost more to defend than they were worth, as Philip discovered after spending all the riches of Mexico and Peru in the vain attempt to reconquer his. Nor was she anxious for an alliance which would be the equivalent of a declaration of war against Spain. The very fact that Saint-Aldegonde was coming put her into a quandary: if she received him she offended Spain; if not, she offended Orange. When his coming was announced, she screamed 'very loudly that she was against sending forces openly to Holland and Zeeland,' flounced out of the room and 'entered a private chamber alone, slamming the door behind her and crying that they were ruining her over this business, and those who were there, her ladies-in-waiting and others, were much distressed, saying that if she did not open the door they would burst it open, as they could not bear her to be alone in such trouble.'

Saint-Aldegonde eventually received a more cordial reception than this little scene promised; but one of its spectators, the Spanish secretary of embassy, duly reported it to Champagny, the ambassador delegated by Requescens, Alba's successor as Governor, to protest against Elizabeth's dealings with Orange, and encouraged in him the belief that Elizabeth's objection to seeing Saint-Aldegonde was inspired by a salutary respect for Spanish power.

He was quickly disillusioned. Elizabeth told Champagny

pagny straight out that she had no intention of allowing the Dutch liberties to be extinguished. She did not want to interfere in what did not concern her, and triumphantly pointed to her refusal of the proffered crown as evidence of her disinterestedness, but she was resolved that Spain's pig-headed intolerance should not keep alight the fire of perpetual religious war under her window. When Champagny protested that her encouragement of the rebels was an unneighbourly act, she cut him short with 'Yes, I know all about that. Your master's intention is to draw a girdle around my realm, thinking he has only to do with a woman, and that the English are a nation of women. My father would never have allowed him to go so far as you have done, and I, although I am a woman, will also know how to look after myself.' A moment later she had relented, smiled most graciously on the Spaniard, and joined with him in damning the Dutch as rebels and pirates until he did not know, as he confessed in writing to Requescens, whether he was on his head or his heels. She earnestly pressed on Champagny, on Requescens, on Philip himself, the desirability of peace on a basis of mutual toleration — what did it matter to the King of Spain, she demanded, if his vassals 'went to the Devil in their own way'? Unluckily it mattered greatly to Philip, as it mattered to Walsingham and his fellows.

Yet events nearly forced a settlement along the lines she laid down. Requescens died in March of 1576, and seven months elapsed before the advent of his successor, Don John of Austria. During that interval the first genuine effort was made at Ghent to unite the entire Netherlands in a league against their foreign masters; previously religious differences and commercial jealousies had prevented the Protestant States of the north from meeting on common ground with the Catholics of the south. For months the representatives of the seventeen provinces haggled, in the traditional manner of Dutch and Flemish burghers, over

their

their respective contributions to the struggle and the eventual distribution of the fruits of a victory yet to be won. While they bargained, the garrison of Antwerp, whom the Spanish Government had quite forgotten to pay or even feed, broke into mutiny and set the city on fire. With the Flemish capital, then the richest city in Europe, in flames, the conference had no time to weigh the last florin. The Pacification of Ghent was quickly drawn up and signed on November 8. It provided for a union of the States until the Spanish army was removed and the ancient liberties, religious and civil, guaranteed by Charles V, restored. When, shortly thereafter, the victor of Lepanto arrived, he was not allowed to assume his duties as viceroy until he had submitted to the terms of the Pacification, which he did in the instrument known as the Perpetual Edict.

It was to Elizabeth that the Netherlands turned to maintain them in their victory. The money she had stinted earlier she now lent without hesitation to the new Council of the United Provinces, insisting, however, that Orange must be included in the terms of the Pacification. His compatriots' jealousies had excluded the illustrious Prince from the proceedings at Ghent, but Elizabeth, though she often and sharply differed with him, had the wisdom to realize that he was the one indispensable man in all the seventeen provinces. When Spain heard and complained about the loan, she smoothly explained that she was merely advancing the money to help to pay the Spanish troops so that they might be evacuated as promised in the Perpetual Edict; Don John, who had come to Holland with the romantic expectation of leading his army into England, for the purpose of freeing and marrying the Queen of Scots, was compelled to stand forlornly by as it marched away with English money in its pockets.

For the moment the cockpit of Europe was tranquil; Elizabeth had done her best to make it and meant to do
what

what she could to keep it so. She told the Dutch and Flemings that they need not expect another penny from her unless they could hold together, and to the new Spanish ambassador, Bernardino de Mendoza, who arrived early in 1578, she declared, 'By God, I will have the Treaty of Ghent allowed, or I will stand by the States as long as I have a man left in my realm to fight for them....' So saying she spat on the floor; whether by way of emphasis or to impress Mendoza, the bluest-blooded grandee in all Spain, is not clear.

Unfortunately, her vision if not her drawing-room manners were generations ahead of her time. The Perpetual Edict proved to be only too temporary, since neither Philip nor the sober-frocked members of his advisory circle were prepared to let the three million souls brought under their charge by prudent Hapsburg marriages burn in the heretics' hell without further effort to save them. Instead of allowing the Edict, Philip sent his nephew, the Prince of Parma, from Italy with a strong army to revoke it. In January, 1578, Orange's forces were decisively beaten at Gemblours, with the result that the southern provinces were torn from the northern and the Union of Ghent broken up. Elizabeth's great statesmanlike scheme for a permanent settlement between the Netherlands and their owners on the basis of union and toleration was swept away and with it all hope of present peace for Europe and England. The French, whose three civil conflicts in six years had rendered them innocuous to their neighbours, paused for a breathing space, during which the King and Queen-Mother tried to draw their warring parties together in the same common purpose, the conquest of Flanders, which had almost united Catherine and Coligny before Saint Bartholomew's; the Huguenots were willing, as before, but the Guises veered off in another direction, towards their cherished league with Rome and Spain for the invasion of England and the murder of its Queen.

Elizabeth,

Elizabeth, not to be behindhand, gave the word to Drake, who slipped off to the Spanish Main. The Dragon's departure was symbolic — in the spring of 1576 Elizabeth had lent Frobisher ships and money to search out a way to the Indies by the northwest which would not trespass on Spanish dominions, and waved him farewell from her window as he sailed by Greenwich Palace on the first of his three voyages. In December of 1577 she financed Drake, unknown to her pacific Minister-in-Chief, on a voyage to forbidden parts, during which he was to jettison a king's ransom in silver to keep the *Golden Hind* from capsizing under the weight of Spanish gold and precious stones aboard.

Chapter X

The Last Wooer

THE situation in 1578 resembled in most respects that of 1568, though its elements were somewhat altered in appearance and in their relation to one another. The Catholic Powers were stirring up a fresh insurrection in England, more through the activities of priests than, as in the earlier time, of political agents; the fire in the Netherlands was still burning, but with the ever gloomier prospect that Spain would stamp it out altogether; Scotland, after five years of order under the iron rule of Morton, was once more the playground of her political bandits; the French King was again taken with the dangerous idea of substituting himself for Philip as sovereign of Flanders; and instead of one cumbrous plot against Elizabeth's life there were hundreds of unknown assassins beginning to close in on her from every side.

The Queen herself was, as during the Anjou courtship, most immediately concerned with the French complication. The Spaniards had defeated the Dutch, Drake had preyed on Spanish commerce, and Scotland had exploded into disorder before now without dragging England into a Continental war; her servants had shown unquestionable ability to protect her life and she trusted them to do so again. But if France joined with the Dutch to eject Spain and claimed the southern provinces of the Low Countries as her reward, a thoroughly logical sequence of events, then England would have to fight until either she or the French were beaten into helplessness — a lesson that Louis XIV and Napoleon were to learn during the succeeding centuries.

The leader of French aspirations in Flanders was the Duke

Duke of Alençon, the suitor whose wooing had been cut short by Saint Bartholomew's. He was now heir to the throne, to which his brother Anjou had succeeded in 1574 as Henry III, and like most heirs in more or less chronic opposition to his sovereign. During the series of civil wars he had fought alternately on both sides, though principally on the Huguenots', to the gratification of Elizabeth, who occasionally rewarded him with sums of money, but to the annoyance of his mother, who tried solicitously to divert his mind from politics by corrupting it with the vice that flourished in such luxuriance at her Court; the young man was versatile enough, however, to indulge in the one without in any way forgoing the other. With the cessation of hostilities at home he found time hang heavy on his hands and at once turned to the Netherlands as a field for his talents and a possible means to a crown.

Henry III was not quite sure whether he approved of these ambitions or not. He was on good terms with Elizabeth, having renewed the Treaty of Blois soon after his accession. A war with Spain would be unwelcome for many reasons, particularly because it would be certain to set Huguenot and Guise to fighting again. On the other hand, he would be glad to be rid of his brother on almost any terms. If the Duke's restlessness got him killed, time, after all, cured all sorrows; while if he succeeded in conquering the Spaniards, the King was quite ready to annex his conquests and thank him for his services. Alençon approached the Dutch leaders without the definite authority of his brother, but with the prestige of the French Crown and permission to raise troops in France amongst his assets in the ensuing negotiations. At the same time he sent an agent, Bacqueville, to the Queen of England to say that he was prepared to do her great service and would be happy to marry her if she would help him in his enterprise.

The news of the impending alliance between the French heir and the Dutch was a blow to Elizabeth in more ways than

than one. It undermined her whole Continental policy, jeopardized her safety, and subjected her to the strident reproaches of the Protestants in council-chamber and pulpit. Her critics exclaimed that she had betrayed England: if she had sent the Dutch sufficient help in men and money there would have been no need for them to invite the French to their rescue. That she could not have foreseen the sudden ending of civil strife in France or Philip's unexpected activity in dispatching Parma with his army was beside the point. Her temporizing methods had failed and an avalanche of abuse fell on her head in consequence.

In order to avoid the impending catastrophe she sent Sir Francis Walsingham to the Netherlands in June of 1578 to see if he could prevail on Don John to come to terms with the Dutch and thus render French intervention unnecessary; at the same time he was to discover the conditions of the rebels' bargain with Alençon and what they would ask to call it off if she herself came to their assistance.

Walsingham found that Don John had no authority to conclude a peace except on impossible terms: Philip's blood was up and he would consider nothing short of unconditional surrender. In July, while the English ambassador was still treating with both sides, Alençon led his army into Flanders and captured Mons, and in August the States entered into a treaty with him whereby he was to furnish them with a stipulated number of troops at his own expense — or rather, at the expense of the French Crown, since the Duke had no money. Walsingham worked desperately to forestall and then to break off the treaty; he found the Dutch quite ready to discuss a substitution of deliverers, but only on conditions which would have put the whole cost of the war on England. They were the hardest traders in Europe, and had tried to buy Alençon with the promise of a bronze statue, a gold crown in the form of olive branches, and an annual public oration in tribute to his heroic efforts for their liberty. The Duke, who was no fool, had insisted

on

on more substantial emoluments; in the end he secured three towns as pledge for his expenditures, a promise of the crown if the Dutch decided eventually to change rulers, and the title of 'Defender of Belgian Liberty against Spanish Tyranny.'

Walsingham, who had neither hoped nor very seriously wished for concessions from Don John — his party considered Elizabeth's efforts to act as peacemaker between the combatants nothing but a sickening waste of time — recommended to Elizabeth that she should close with the Dutch offer. There seemed nothing else to do that was in the least likely to avert the French incursion into the Netherlands, and even Walsingham's opponents expected her to comply. To the intense consternation of everybody, Elizabeth refused. She would not, she said flatly, allow England to become a goose to be plucked by the Dutch for their own purposes; she would not throw away her money and sacrifice her soldiers for a pack of ungrateful tradesmen. If they persisted in treating her with such contempt, she would give her aid to Spain and defy rebels and French alike.

But this was spoken only in a moment of temper with the unthrifty Walsingham and his crowd of zealots. She was not one to fling money about nor to meet trouble halfway; nor was she convinced that her Secretary's extravagant expedients were as yet necessary. Through her conversations with Bacqueville and information from her ambassador Stafford in Paris, she had gleaned the impression that Alençon was by no means assured of his brother the King's whole-hearted support in his Flemish venture; the young man's eagerness to marry her only confirmed that impression. If that were so, she might hitch his wagon to her star instead of to France's.... Once more, and for the last time, she laid her hard-worked virginity at the service of England.

She wrote the Duke a letter of encouragement and he responded with a thousand apologies for the tepidity of his wooing hitherto and the assurance that his heart was Elizabeth's

Elizabeth's as much as, nay more than, ever. He called her his 'Perfect Goddess,' and described her perfections of mind, body, and heart in phrases modelled on the best masters. He vowed that he was seeking a crown only that he might make himself worthy of her, hoped that her hand would be the reward of his success unless indeed she would be so gracious as to give it as an inspiration to his efforts. He would do nothing in the Netherlands, he promised, without her consent and everything to win her approbation.

With knitted brows and slightly fluttering heart the spinster of forty-five read these burning protestations of her twenty-four-year-old lover. They might be nonsense, and they could not be altogether sincere, but it was safe at least to assume that the young man would be glad to have the Queen of England's support in his venture. It is also safe to assume that Elizabeth was anxious to have those flamboyant compliments paid her in person if it could be contrived without too much risk: the older she grew the more eagerly she listened to the words of adoration that issued from the mouths of young men. She responded to Alençon that her feelings had no more cooled with time than his, and suggested that since he had already proved his mettle by the capture of Mons, he should now retire temporarily from the field of glory and return to Paris to arrange the preliminaries of his coming to England.

The Duke obeyed. He left his affairs in the hands of a subordinate and hurried to enlist his mother and brother in his matrimonial cause. Elizabeth promptly demanded credit from the King of Spain for removing the French thorn from his flesh.

In January, 1579, Alençon sent over his personal emissary, a little brown man named Simier, bearing further proposals to his 'Perfect Goddess.' Elizabeth was disconcerted — an agent *ad hoc* gave more substance and speed to the business than she liked — but she could not very well rebuff Simier without rousing suspicion of her sincerity, so she welcomed him

him with cordial informality, promptly christened him her
'little monkey,' and admitted him to such familiarities as
to scandalize the respectable. He was a shrewd little fellow,
as distrustful of the Queen as of the rest of the human race,
but she soon had him literally at her feet. Together they
set about drawing up a marriage contract, and presently
even the French Court began to believe that this time
Elizabeth might conceivably be in earnest. Henry was
enthusiastic for the marriage, since he devoutly hoped to
get both his brother and his brother's expensive ambitions
saddled on the Queen of England; while Catherine allowed
her own current project for a match between Alençon and a
Spanish Infanta, with the Netherlands as joint dower, to
slip temporarily out of her mind.

The English Council were even more dismayed than
Elizabeth by Simier's arrival. They did not want the Duke,
suspecting him of being a secret agent of Papistry to rouse
the native Catholics, yet they shuddered at the thought
of the humiliating rejection he would receive if he favoured
the Queen with a sight of his unlovely face. Moreover, the
English people, hating both Alençon and the French, were
rabid against the marriage; never did Elizabeth's popularity
sink so low as during this courtship. If the Queen was not
serious, moaned the ministers to one another, there would
be an angry King of France and Queen-Mother to reckon
with; if she was, there would be an even angrier English
public. With might and main they laboured against inviting the Duke to London, taking what comfort they could
from the memory of the Austrian Archduke, Eric of Sweden,
and Anjou — and also from the fact that as late as May the
bookmakers in the City were offering two to one against
Alençon's coming and three to one against the marriage.

But after a few weeks it was known that Alençon's passport had been drawn up, and Simier was seen rubbing his
hands and grinning with pleasure. The quotation of three
to one against the marriage automatically became three

to

to one on it the moment Alençon set foot in England — on the authority of a leading professional descendant of the sporting gentlemen who laid the original odds.... Word arrived from France that splendid wedding garments were being ordered in Italy for the ceremony; Mendoza, whose every letter to Philip had expressed his complete disbelief in the whole business, now swung over and wrote that the Duke was coming, with the marriage certain to follow.

The Council, aghast, played their last card. As one man they turned to the colleague, once so despised, whom no other favourite or suitor had ever displaced in the Queen's heart. For twenty years and more, while time wrought its sad outward buffooneries on both, they had bickered and made each other jealous, but she still loved him devotedly and exclusively. That very summer, while war, rebellion, and conspiracy brought her to the edge of physical and nervous prostration, she had sat tending him night after night through an illness.... Leicester went to the Queen and on bended knee pleaded with all the fervour of his own and his fellows' conviction that the fatal passport should not be granted. Elizabeth was touched, wavered, and for a few days meditated whether there were not some other way of obtaining her end without giving hurt to Robert.

Simier, whose bright eyes and quick ears were never idle, put an abrupt stop to these emotional appeals. He went to the Queen privately and disclosed certain facts that everyone at Court had hitherto carefully concealed from her: Leicester, it appeared, had long been carrying on an affair with Lettice, Countess of Essex, Sir Francis Knollys's daughter, during her husband's official sojourn in Ireland; shortly after the Earl's death, which had occurred quite recently, Robert had married the widow in secret. To this bare outline the Frenchman added various embroideries of detail well calculated to drive an extremely jealous woman into a frenzy.

Elizabeth's rage was appalling. She drove Leicester out of

of her sight with a stinging slap on the face, expelled his wife from Court, and threatened to throw them both into prison. His frightened colleagues slunk from her sight as she furiously dashed her signature across the Duke's passport and ordered everything to be made ready for his reception.

In August he came, quietly, almost furtively. He had not the money to make a great show, and the cunning Elizabeth, realizing that the smaller the publicity given to his presence, the less offence there would be to her people, heartily encouraged him to dispense with the customary pomp and extravagance. With only a few intimate companions the heir to the throne of France and the aspirant to the crown of the Netherlands landed at the watergate of Greenwich Palace to lay his heart before the Queen of England.

A hundred pairs of anxious eyes watched that meeting, English, French, Spanish, and Dutch. What would Elizabeth say when she first set eyes on that spindly misshapen body, the scraggy yellow beard, the pimples and the discoloured pits left by the smallpox? Above all, what would she say when she beheld that incredible nose, that huge shapeless growth of flesh and bone which the facetious described as two noses imperfectly blended? It was the most notorious organ of its time; later, after Alençon's duplicity towards his Dutch allies, they celebrated that nose in the following doggerel:

> Good people of Flanders, pray do not suppose
> That 'tis monstrous this Frenchman should double his nose;
> Dame Nature her favours but rarely misplaces,
> She has given two noses to match his two faces.

Elizabeth said she was enchanted. She made an enormous fuss over him, fondled and kissed him before the onlookers, and brazenly invited him alone into her bedroom so that everybody should think the worst. All informality was dispensed with and he instantly became her dear little 'Frog,'

'Frog,' so joining the intimate company which included her Monkey Simier, her Spirit Burghley, her Moor Walsingham, her Mutton Sir Christopher Hatton, her Robin Leicester. Not the least part of the spell she wove round people was her fertility in inventing pet nicknames for them. Alençon was no fatuous boy, but a hard-headed young fortune-hunter, with plenty of ability and spirit, who was courting the middle-aged Queen for his own profit. Yet she succeeded in conveying to him that in her eyes he was the ideal of virile comeliness, and to the world that she was in the raptures of love.

How much of it was acting and how much genuine no one will ever know. Her contemporaries had to read her feelings in her inscrutable face, for her tongue told even the dearest of them nothing; posterity cannot read between the lines since she left no lines to read between. Yet there is an unmistakable atmosphere about this courtship which differentiates it from all the others. Since the departure of various lesser figures early in the reign, no suitor of importance save Leicester had stood before her in the flesh — and the very thought of Leicester was to make her heart angry and sore for several years to come. Because of him she felt herself cheated, betrayed, and lonely at the very moment that the lively little Frenchman turned up to soothe her vanity with his resounding polished flatteries. Whether they meant little or much, they must have rung sweetly in the ears of the unhappy ageing spinster. There would be no one after him, she well knew — long since she had half-mockingly, half-wistfully told Fénelon, while speaking of Anjou, that she could not much longer 'have the chance of suitors or heirs.' Surely there was something more than the usual pretences of her diplomacy in the haughty Queen's flinging of her dignity to the winds for the sake of the experienced compliments and caresses of that ugly youth.

At any rate, he obviously took that view of the matter, and

and he was a libertine not easily deceived by women. So did the spectators, and their opinions, circulated through London, drove the populace frantic with rage. The preachers fulminated in the churches against the impious union and crowds collected in the streets to hear inflammatory speeches denouncing it. A Puritan named Stubbs published a book entitled 'Discovery of a Gaping Gulf wherein England is like to be swallowed up by another French Marriage, etc.,' which had an enormous circulation until it was suppressed by the Government. On Elizabeth's order the author was tried and sentenced to have his right hand cut off. When the brutal ceremony was over, the crowd cheered the victim, who waved the bleeding stump and cried 'Long live the Queen!' It was horrible, but the time did not allow of too great niceties: nor was it permissible for the sovereign to justify herself for the sake of averting unpopularity.

With her advisers Elizabeth took another line. The pliant Burghley and Sussex, who for years had wanted the Queen to marry anyone who would be a begetter of children (in which respect Alençon was reputed to be notably proficient), were now inclined to support her; but the rest, though they lacked the courage to oppose her openly, declined to co-operate in the marriage with what she considered sufficient enthusiasm. She called them to her and wept copious tears in their presence. All these years, she complained, they had begged her to marry, and now that she had at last found a man who suited her they all turned against her. Had she not the right, like any other woman, to a peaceful domestic life and children to comfort her in her old age? Her audience, not sure whether she was in earnest or not — and it is quite probable that she herself was not altogether certain to what extent she meant what she said — heard her out more impressed by her anger than by her arguments, but after their dismissal sent her a memorandum offering to help in any way they could.

This did not please her either, for she had been busily
explaining

explaining to Simier that perhaps she could not after all follow her own inclination, since her ministers were so strongly against her. She turned to another avenue of escape, and complained that Alençon was opening his mouth far too wide: none of her previous suitors had demanded so much either in money or privileges. The conditions of the marriage must be considered further, the Duke must return to Paris in order to bring his family round to terms which she and her people could accept. Reluctantly he allowed himself to be shunted off with another kiss instead of the contract for which he had come. The public breathed a sigh of relief and poor Burghley tore his thinning hair in bewilderment and dismay. The memorandum he wrote after Alençon's departure displays vividly the fears Elizabeth's conduct aroused at the time:

> While Your Majesty desired the marriage I was in favour of it myself and so am I now persuaded that it would be your best security; but the matter being as it is, I am your servant, and will do my best for you in this and all conditions. You will find me more ready to defend you from the hurt when it comes than those of your Council who have been the occasion of its coming. Your marriage is now broken off, and no hope left of the good that was thereby expected. Alençon having been brought by your Majesty's means to be the author of the trouble in his own country, having by you been drawn from his late enterprise in the Low Countries, and by you hindered of his marriage with the King of Spain's daughter, having lately come hither to see you to be by you rejected, it may be taken as quite certain that he will now seek to be revenged upon you. You have no hope of an heir, sad eyes will be turned on your successor, Alençon will probably marry where we feared [i.e., the Infanta], France and Spain will then unite against us. Our trade will be destroyed. Foreign soldiers will be landed in Ireland, and in all likelihood there will be a rising at home, supported abroad in favour of the King and Queen of Scots....

Thus the wisest of living English statesmen. He was wrong on nearly every point. The only one of his prophecies that materialized was the landing in Ireland, a half-hearted affair

affair of a few hundred Italians and Spaniards paid by the Vatican, and they were easily ejected by a joint attack of Elizabeth's land and sea forces. The Lord Treasurer was in error because he did not know his Queen well enough: he assumed that the Alençon courtship was broken off when it had barely begun.

Year after year it went on. England and French statesmen continued to haggle over the conditions of Alençon's residence, financial settlements, religious observances, and a dozen other matters. Elizabeth insisted that Henry III must assume the liabilities for his brother's scheme in the Netherlands before she married him, while Henry naturally preferred not to spend his money until the slippery Englishwoman had been secured in bonds of matrimony, hoping that afterward his brother's liabilities would fall on his brother's wife. But the negotiations were carried on with extreme amiability on both sides, and with a crescendo of passionate avowals between the principals in their correspondence with each other. Meanwhile, Alençon became involved in another French civil war, carried on further desultory hostilities against the Spaniards on Elizabeth's money, made and broke a new treaty with the Dutch and in the end taught them to hate him. Elizabeth had his measure as completely as she had had Darnley's: there was not the remotest chance of his conquering Parma, the invincible soldier who had succeeded to the Governorship on Don John's death in 1578.

In November of 1581, the Duke, discouraged by his failures in Flanders and as usual short of money, returned to England determined that Elizabeth should not again escape him. Again the secrecy, the kisses, the compliments and the vows, and several magnificent entertainments paid for out of the loot taken by Drake from Spain. But this time the Duke meant business and so did his brother the King. Words would not do, nothing less than a marriage contract and hard cash if the French

were

were to continue playing second fiddle to England in the
Netherlands.

Elizabeth was nearly cornered, but not quite: her manner
of dealing with the persistent young man is described by
Mendoza in a letter to Philip. After mentioning that
'Alençon and all his company displayed, not discontent
alone, but entire disillusionment as to the marriage taking
place,' the interested ambassador tells how

> the Queen and Alençon were walking together in the gallery,
> Leicester and Walsingham being present, when the French am-
> bassador entered and said that he wished to write to his master,
> from whom he had received orders to give from the Queen's
> own lips her intention with regard to marrying his brother. She
> replied, 'You may write this to the King, that the Duke of
> Alençon shall be my husband,' and at the same moment she
> turned to Alençon and kissed him on the mouth drawing a ring
> from her own hand and giving it to him as a pledge. Alençon
> gave her a ring of his in return, and shortly afterwards the Queen
> summoned the ladies and gentlemen from the presence chamber
> in the gallery, repeating to them in a loud voice in Alençon's
> presence what she had previously said.

The suitor was soothed, France quieted, England momentarily secured from French action in the Netherlands either
independently or in alliance with Spain. The only drawback, so far as the Queen was concerned, was that she had
on her hands an unwanted wooer to whom she had publicly
promised herself. As a lover he had served his turn well
enough, and might even continue to do so, but he insisted
on becoming a husband, quite a different story. Never
before had she been committed so deeply or found the way
out so devious and difficult. She dallied, invented a thousand coy excuses for postponement, reminded Alençon that
duty called him to Flanders, where he had promised to
win great victories for her as her own true knight. Alençon
retorted that victories cost money. She admitted that he
was right in principle, but the exact sum was difficult to
arrive

arrive at; finally she compounded her breach of promise for sixty thousand pounds.

In February, 1582, he left, carrying Elizabeth's recommendation to the Dutch and the sixty thousand pounds in cash and notes, the Queen accompanying him to Canterbury weeping steadily at the prospect of the separation. Leicester escorted his rival and successor across the North Sea and returned to announce with a grin that he had left the Duke 'like an old hulk run ashore, high and dry... unable to get off a sandbank,' on the coast of the Netherlands. His surprising mistress wistfully answered that she wished she had her little Frog swimming in the Thames again.

Within a year the Defender of Belgian Liberty from Spanish Tyranny was involved in a hopeless quarrel with the Dutch and in a faithless bargain with Parma. Soon he was suspected on all sides. The mutinous French soldiers burned Antwerp for the second time, and their commander was thrown out of his promised kingdom to fuss and fret at home till he died in 1584. By then France, at the beginning of the longest and worst of her civil wars, was in no condition for foreign conquests.

The Alençon courtship was the masterpiece of Elizabeth's matrimonial diplomacy. A hundred assistants had been engaged in it, in England and in various parts of Europe, but she alone had conceived and alone understood the whole design. Her methods had been tortuous, dishonest, crablike in their progress, but they had succeeded in preventing Alençon from annexing Belgium to France by turning him instead into an English mercenary. The cost had been about one hundred thousand pounds instead of possible millions and the lives of thousands of English soldiers. However distasteful the Queen's personal intercourse with the Duke, she deserves to have it remembered in her favour that, though she postured like a giddy old coquette, and probably to some degree experienced the emotions of one, she carried it off so brilliantly as to achieve the indispensable

ble effect on her suitor's mind that she doted on him. Nor should it be forgotten that she managed the performance with cool wits and smiling lips well knowing all the while that death was in close and constant attendance upon her.

Chapter XI

The Silent Enemies

THE number of men who tried to assassinate Elizabeth in the decade preceding the Armada exceeded the number of those who wanted to marry her during the previous two. With each succeeding year her death took on an increasing importance in the great Catholic plan to recover England. The more ardent of her enemies would have preferred to settle the whole question once for all by an armed invasion, but for that the co-operation of Spain was essential, and Philip, burdened by many other troubles, was frankly reluctant to commit himself to an enterprise of such magnitude. Rome, the Guises, and the English exiles abroad undertook, therefore, to prepare the ground for the great day by a series of less heroic expedients: the murder of the Queen, a Catholic revival, and the conversion of Scotland from a dependent into an enemy.

The instruments for the first two tasks, and in part for the third, were supplied by the Society of Jesus, the militant apostles of the Counter-Reformation. After the rebellion of 1569, when the laws against Papists began to be enforced with greater severity, many of the English Catholics who clung in secret to their faith began to send their sons to be educated in the Jesuit seminaries of the Continent, at Douai (suppressed by Philip after the renewal of good relations with England in 1573), at Rheims, which was under the patronage of the Guises, and in Rome itself. By 1578 the graduates of those institutions were turning their faces homeward to put into practice the instruction they had been given.

With few exceptions they were a brave lot, the stuff of which martyrs are made. Their teachers had withheld nothing

nothing of what awaited them; they had been informed in detail, by word and picture, of the rack, the quartering-knife, the long-drawn-out torture, and death, yet unafraid they accepted their consecration and its penalties. By ones and twos they stole out of France to Flanders, were set down on the English coast at night by small rowing boats, and scattered to deliver their countrymen from the heretic gloom which encompassed them. From one manor house to another they stole under cover of darkness, the Government's agents and spies constantly on their tracks, traitors forever alert to denounce them for pay. For days on end they lived in black and airless priest-holes, hundreds of which still survive as the sole monuments of their labours, or in the forest caves of the sparsely settled land, stealing out at night to carry the Word to hall and farmhouse.

Amongst the earliest as well as the most famous of the English Jesuits were Edmund Campion and Robert Parsons, who landed in June, 1580. Between them they personified the two aspects of the brotherhood's campaign. Campion was a great-hearted soldier of Christ, Parsons a simple plotter of murder and treason. The one was caught after twelve months, the other escaped abroad to join Father Allen, as zealous an enemy as England ever bred from her own soil, in stimulating Europe's wrath against her. The alarm roused by the meaner priest recoiled on his companion; Campion was tortured to make him confess what he knew of the Jesuit schemes, and finally was put to death, the infernal sentence being carried out in all its refinements.

Many were to follow him. After twenty years of exemplary freedom from bloodshed, England had a taste of the official cruelty which amongst its neighbours had become a matter of daily routine. There was no help for it: the challenge had been issued by her enemies (unless one chooses to regard her determination to worship in her own way as a punishable provocation) and had to be met by any and all means if a State be granted the right to defend its existence. The

The priests were sent to preach not only religion but sedition, to assist in it, and to accomplish the death of the Queen if that would further their mission; the supreme reward of canonization was promised them by the Church if they themselves died in the attempt.

Without exception every plot for Elizabeth's assassination could be traced to one of the Jesuit missionaries. In the autumn of 1583, a young man named John Sommerville set out from Warwickshire for London to shoot her and set her head on a pole, 'for she was a serpent and a viper.' When arrested he confessed that a priest, disguised as a gardener in the employ of his father-in-law, the High Sheriff of Warwickshire, had persuaded him to the attempt. The foolish young man committed suicide in prison, his father-in-law was executed at Tyburn, and the priest became a Government spy. During the same period Walsingham was engaged in unravelling a conspiracy, known as the 'Throgmorton plot,' involving the Guises, Mary Stuart, and the Spanish ambassador Mendoza, for an invasion of England from the south and a simultaneous Catholic rising. The exposure of this 'main plot' was followed in the spring by the revelation of an ancillary 'bye plot,' for the murder of Elizabeth. There had been some hesitation amongst the higher conspirators over the selection of an assassin, the choice lying between Dr. George Gifford, an active, and William Parry, a renegade, priest as well as a criminal. Parry was chosen and given a hundred thousand francs for the job, but at the last minute his nerve failed — the reason he gave was that Elizabeth looked too much like Henry VIII — so he refunded the money and entered Parliament instead, where his too voluble defence of the Jesuits brought his past record to the attention of the Government and himself eventually to the scaffold. It is no wonder that priest, plot, and Pope became synonymous terms in the English mind during those years, or that the clamour for severity grew ever stronger; it would
have

have been strange law that allowed the agents of Rome to strike at England through the Queen's life, yet forbade England to retaliate merely because these agents happened to wear the garments of the Roman priesthood.

Yet the cruelty would have been infinitely worse, the executions many times their number, had not the Queen, against whom the forces of destruction were aimed, stood out against the prevailing hysteria; her imagination recoiled, as usual, from torture and bloodshed; it also instructed her that a martyred priest was more dangerous than a living one. Sentence after sentence she commuted or mitigated; in every capital case she required it to be made out to her satisfaction that the offender had threatened the security of the State, not merely by infringement, however aggravated, of the religious statutes, but by actual treason. There were unhappy instances, of course, of ordinary persecution, yet altogether, during the whole period of the Jesuit invasion, the executions averaged only seven a year, as contrasted with eighty under her predecessor and hundreds, even thousands, in Spain, France, and the Netherlands.

Her ministers, terrified of the invisible enemy filtering into the country from all sides, united in demanding the most drastic courses. With visions of the Queen's death, the anarchy of a disputed succession, revolution and counter-revolution before them, they implored Elizabeth to be more careful of herself and less indulgent to her frocked foes. She went her way as before, disdaining to show fear, recklessly exposing herself to all who sought audience. Walsingham, 'that most subtle searcher after hidden secrets,' and his minions toiled sleeplessly to make arrests and collect testimony, but he toiled even harder to make Elizabeth act upon his evidence and his fears. He would come to her with a sheaf of confessions and spies' reports, she would glance over them, laugh and tell him not to let his imagination run away with him. A man called Appletree (not a Jesuit) shot at her barge from the bank of the Thames, wounding

wounding one of the boatmen. He was tried, sentenced to death, and the Council, 'all most humbly on their knees, besought the Queen that this slave might suffer not this death, but a hundred thousand deaths (if it were possible in Nature so to do) for his vile and fearful offence.' Elizabeth, satisfied that either the shooting was an accident or the condemned man insane, ordered his release with the remark that she 'had rather suffered the wounds the bargeman now hath tenfold than the meanest of her subjects should be unjustly accused.' It was something few princes in any age would have done. The Paris correspondent of the great Austrian banking house of Fugger wrote to his principals that she was secretly giving money to various arrested Jesuits in order to enable them to cheat the gallows by escaping abroad.

Her behaviour wrung cries of admiration from her enemies as loud as the anxious protests of her friends. It was not mere foolhardiness, it was pure personal courage, and also perhaps the sort of faith in a personal destiny now and then granted to great leaders of men. She knew what her death would mean to the country, yet she could not bring herself to believe in it as a serious possibility for herself. When the State itself was threatened, she was not so calm. In the spring of 1584, after the exposure of the Throgmorton conspiracy, the air was full of rumours that the Spanish fleet was about to descend upon England. She consulted Walsingham, who, believing that the true battleground was the Netherlands, advised her to ignore the rumour, since there was not now nor ever likely to be an Armada. Just then a ship passed Greenwich Palace, where the Court was in residence, and fired a salute. Elizabeth heard the shot, inquired whence the ship came, and on learning that it had recently left Lisbon ordered the master to be sent to her. She examined him herself, in Walsingham's presence, and heard that the sailor had seen with his own eyes numerous galleys being prepared for the expedition against England.

England. Elizabeth turned on the Secretary, poured a torrent of sarcasm on his wisdom (the poor man happened on that occasion to be right), and looked about for something to throw at him. The handiest weapon was her slipper, and the startled minister caught it full in the face.

The fear aroused amongst her subjects by the hydra-headed menace to Elizabeth's life finally found expression in an extra-legal agreement, known as the Bond of Association, signed in 1584 by the leading nobility and gentry of the country. The subscribers,

> being natural-born subjects of this realm of England and having so gracious a lady, our sovereign Elizabeth by the ordinance of God, our most rightful Queen, reigning over us these many years with great felicity, to our inestimable comfort, [bound themselves] with our whole powers, bodies, lives and goods, and with our children and servants... to withstand, pursue and offend, as well by force of arms, as by all other means of revenge, all manner of persons... that shall attempt... anything that shall tend to the harm of Her Majesty's royal person; and will never desist from all manner of forcible pursuit against such persons, to the utter extermination of them, their aiders and abettors... [To any who] shall pretend title to come to this crown by the untimely death of Her Majesty so wickedly procured... was promised 'utter overthrow and extirpation.'

The document concluded with a vow on the part of the signatories never to separate from their association 'upon pain of being by the rest of us prosecuted and suppressed as perjured persons, and as public enemies to God, our Queen and our native country.'

In language of Biblical intensity the English people thus articulated their feelings towards Elizabeth, their determination to protect both her and the 'great benefit of peace, wealth and godly government we have more plentifully received these many years under Her Majesty's Government than any of our forefathers have done in any longer time of any of her progenitors, kings of this realm.' It was an outburst of national feeling almost without parallel, an

apparently

apparently unmistakable warning to enemies at home and abroad; yet the person to whom the warning was chiefly addressed, the woman on behalf of whose claims to the throne all the plots against Elizabeth's life were devised, lightly affixed her signature to the bond, so subscribing her own death.

But Mary Stuart had signed various other bonds in the past only to dishonour them when they no longer suited her convenience. Her aspirations, which Drury's artillery had seemingly interred beneath the toppling stones of Edinburgh Castle, had been exhumed and nourished into fresh life by her partisans in this new era of general uncertainty and disorder. In 1578 the last of her great Scottish enemies, Morton, was overthrown by his peers, who could no longer bear the unaccustomed tranquillity the Regent's iron rule had imposed on the country. They tried to reign in his stead through the medium of the young King, but his French relatives, the Guises, always on the alert to renew their lost dominion in Scotland, sent over, in 1579, Esmé Stuart, the Sieur d'Aubigny, to worm himself into James's favour. D'Aubigny, a man of unusual charm and talent, had no difficulty in gaining an immediate ascendancy over Mary's ugly and uncouth but precociously gifted son. Under his mentor's fond encouragement he declared himself ready to reign in his own right at the age of thirteen, turned away from his grim Presbyterian teachers and counsellors, pondered seriously upon the divine right of kings and found in himself a profound affinity for the Catholic mysteries. There remained only to join mother to son in a common purpose, and the Guises would have free entry for an invading force while the Jesuits were preparing their religious rising in England and the death of Elizabeth.

D'Aubigny, soon created Duke of Lennox, worked quietly and skilfully in his employers' interests. Like Mary of Guise he installed Frenchmen and francophile Scots in the important

important administrative posts, and himself gained control of Edinburgh and Dumbarton, the two vital spots for the landing of armies. He induced the foolish Lords to agree to Morton's trial before the Council for his part in the murder of Darnley, fourteen years earlier, and in 1581 the deposed Regent, the strongest man in the kingdom, was beheaded for a crime of which the majority of his judges had been equally guilty. While maintaining friendly relations with Elizabeth, Lennox prepared an agreement with Mary Stuart by which she and her son should share the throne of Scotland during her lifetime and he succeed her on the English throne after her death. Meantime, on the Continent the Guises were busily arranging a marriage between James and one of the King of Spain's daughters.

All these plans and proceedings were swiftly discovered to the English Court by the indefatigable resident in Edinburgh, Robert Bowes, and Walsingham's wideflung army of spies. The harassed Councillors, confronted on all sides with plots for murder, uprisings, and invasions, saw the work of twenty years undone, the Postern Gate once more flung open. They strongly urged Elizabeth to break off all friendly communication with d'Aubigny; immure or execute Mary and, above all, reunite the Congregation by a liberal distribution of bribes amongst the Scottish lairds. The extant letters and memoranda of the ministers indicate plainly their opinion that this year in which Scotland seemed lost and the Jesuit menace reached its height exposed England to the gravest danger since the beginning of the reign.

But again, as on countless similar occasions, Elizabeth refused to be frightened into parting with her money. Perhaps she was wrong — critics have judged her parsimony as hardly as her hesitations, and it may be that the policy of 1559 would have succeeded again in 1581. On the other hand, the Queen had little money to spare. It had been her guiding principle to keep the cost of government as low as
possible,

possible, and by following it she had contributed materially to her people's well-being and kept herself independent of a tight-fisted Parliament. She knew also that henceforth she would need her money as never before, with more and more claims on it from the Netherlands, from the German mercenaries she had to pay to keep the Huguenot cause alive in France, and with a navy to maintain against the day that Spain should be ready for the ultimate conflict.... Money, money, money — wherever she turned was an ally demanding it as the price of friendship or a courtier wheedling for it as the price of love. 'My servants and favourites,' she burst out in a moment of bitterness, 'profess to love me for my high qualities, Alençon for my beauty, the Scots for my crown; but at the bottom they are all after the same thing, my money, and they shall not have it!' Whether she was right or no in her thrift, there is something pathetic in that disillusioned and only too just complaint. The event at least proved that she was wiser to be stingy than to indulge in the easy popularity of a Lady Bountiful.

Again, as so often before, she set herself to use her wits instead of her people's money. She sagely suspected, and told her Council, that d'Aubigny's masters in France were not in a position to be as liberal with cash as with promises. If it was to be a contest of finances she could promise as much as they and, if the need arose, spend more.

Mechanical habit determined her first step. Instead of allowing or forbidding James to marry a Spanish Infanta, she submitted the outline of a proposal to marry him herself. James, aged sixteen, did not even raise his dark heavy brows at the suggestion, and answered that he was quite willing to entertain it, at a price. Elizabeth, aged forty-nine, who had not thought to be taken so seriously at once, and who fully realized that courtships were over even for her, hastened to lay before the Scottish King two other alternatives, either a suitable English girl or the daughter of the King of Denmark (who was in fact one day to be his consort). Thereupon

upon Leicester hopefully pushed forward his step-daughter, but Elizabeth answered with considerable profanity that she would rather give James her crown than let him marry the whelp of that she-wolf Lettice Knollys, and promised to proclaim throughout Christendom what a cuckold Robert's wife had already made of him unless he gave over the notion of being father-in-law to Mary Stuart's son. Leicester regretfully withdrew his candidate; and James was left prudently weighing the relative attractions of the Danish and Spanish princesses.

Meanwhile, unknown to all but a few intimate advisers, Elizabeth, while loudly declining to open her purse wide to the lairds whose appetites had always grown with eating, was quietly sending money to a small and purposeful group headed by Lord Ruthven, son of Rizzio's murderer. In August of 1582, Ruthven led his band to Court, kidnapped the King, and sent d'Aubigny flying for his life to France whence he came.

James soon freed himself and took revenge on his captors, but his enthusiasms for his mother's cause and his French relations began noticeably to abate. Elizabeth was now dangling before him the promise of something he wanted more than all the gold of the Indies, the succession to the Crown of England; not affirmatively, of course, for that would have made him independent of her, but negatively, by holding out hope of recognition if he conducted himself as she wished and a definite threat of exclusion if he misbehaved.

At the same time, disregarding the Council's warning that Mary and James were one enemy under two names, she shrewdly set out to increase and exploit the jealousy between the son who had displaced his mother and the mother who had disinherited her son. On a recent occasion Mary had asked permission to send a secretary to James, which Elizabeth had granted against her ministers' advice. A messenger was sent ahead to notify the King of Scots that

that the secretary was coming with a message for the
'Prince of Scotland,' whereat young James in a fury refused
to receive any communication from his mother addressed
to him under that title and swore to cut the man's head off
if he set foot in Scotland. Elizabeth saw that there was
little to fear in the way of collusion between those two
egoists, although even she did not fully realize how little
until the terrific moment of tension, a few years later, on
the eve of Mary's execution. Mary herself Elizabeth now
took so little seriously that in 1584 she offered to set her
free practically without restrictions. The captive, optimistic
that her deliverers were on the way, refused.

Only a little later, while Mary was weaving in preparation
for their arrival the most extensive of the plots for Elizabeth's assassination, the English Queen, after much haggling, signed a treaty of mutual defence with James, in which
she pledged herself to pay him a pension of four thousand
pounds a year and promised, more by implication than by
word, to do nothing to prejudice his succession. The clauses
in that treaty were what her Protestant extremists had
been asking her to buy at twenty times the price; the value
of the thrifty purchase was to be seen very soon, when the
Scottish army assembled for England's defence against the
invader in 1588.

Chapter XII

Reckoning Demanded and Given

THE treaty with Scotland, signed in 1586, was only the logical consequence of the general clearing of the air that had begun to take place two years earlier. Between 1568 and 1584 the pattern of European affairs was such a tangle of cross-currents and cross-purposes, of coalitions forming and dissolving, of states breaking temporarily into fragments and combining with other fragments across frontiers of land and water, that at no instant was it possible to trace a fixed design. But in April of the latter year the Duke of Alençon died, leaving Henry of Navarre heir to the throne of France, and three months later William of Orange was mortally wounded by an assassin in the pay of Spain. Alençon's death virtually ended the participation of the Guises, Elizabeth's most implacable enemies, in the Catholic offensive against England by plunging them into a long civil war to avert a Huguenot succession; while that of the Prince of Orange deprived England of the services of the man who had sustained almost single-handed the spirit of the Dutch rebellion. Even to contemporary eyes, bewildered though they were by the swift change of scene on all the many stages of the great conflict, Philip of Spain and Elizabeth of England henceforth stood revealed as the champions who would lead the two contending forces of Christendom into decisive battle.

Neither was eager to accept the rôles which ineluctable destiny had awarded them, Elizabeth because she had nothing to gain by fighting, Philip because he had everything to lose. Neither was possessed by nature with an itch for conquest; she would have been content to protect the growing prosperity of her kingdom, he to hold intact

what

what he had inherited. Though it had long been evident that the energy of her people and the integrity of his empire were incompatible, both had tried to avoid open offence by availing themselves of agents for whom they could disclaim responsibility, Dutch and Guises, sea-raiders and Jesuits. From now on, however, there would be little use in concealment or vicarious aggression: Elizabeth would have in her own person to fill the place left by William the Silent or allow Spain to mass her strength unopposed on England's most vulnerable flank, while Philip must himself subdue England before he could again enjoy in security the richest estate of his inheritance.

So much was plain and inevitable; and the result was that the two monarchs, Catholic King and English Queen, found themselves face to face in a struggle involving the passions and wants of uncounted millions, the growth and decay of whole races, the ultimate division of the earth's surface; a struggle affecting the relations of those yet unborn to one another, to the State, to their God — the whole future, in fact, of civilization. Issues such as these were to be decided, not by the transitory quarrels and scattered homicides of changing party groups in the Low Countries, France, and Scotland, but by nothing less than full-fronted combat between the mightiest Catholic Power and the one strong State the Reformation had yet produced.

Negotiations for an alliance between England and Holland were begun very shortly after the assassination of the Prince of Orange, but their progress was slow. The Dutch were hard and experienced traders; they knew that Elizabeth would have to come to their help whether she liked it or not and naturally tried to put as much of the burden of hostilities on her as possible. In Elizabeth, however, they found a bargainer every whit as stubborn and resourceful as themselves. She knew, as did everyone else, that the Dutch had grown rich out of their rebellion, since their blockade of Flanders had sent trade rolling into Amsterdam.

dam. When their commissioners attempted to depict for her a Holland starved through a decade and to obtain from her all the money and most of the troops and armaments required for its defence, she grew so annoyed that she threatened to call the whole thing off, and it took all the tact of the Dutchmen's friends amongst her ministers to bring about a renewal of the conversations. When the amount of the loan was agreed upon, there were differences over the security to be given for it, the command of the allied armies, the terms of the final peace, and so on for month after month. Moreover, it was not easy to decide how far the commissioners' authority extended — it is never easy to discover who speaks the genuine voice of a country in rebellion and possessing no recognized government. The greatest achievement of William the Silent had consisted, not so much in holding off Spain, as in inducing his countrymen to pull together and to part with their money for the support of their soldiers — the task that Elizabeth had now inherited. Some of the most influential of the late statesman's friends were busily treating with the French at the very moment that their colleagues were making promises to Elizabeth in London; if France had been in any position just then to take part in a foreign war, there would have been a veritable Donnybrook Fair all over the Low Countries. But Elizabeth had the resources, and also the strength to impose the conditions upon which she would employ them. On August 10, 1585, the treaty of alliance was signed. A first expeditionary force of five thousand infantry and a thousand cavalry was to be maintained at England's expense; Flushing, Brill, and a castle in the island of Walcheren were to be held as security for present and future loans; during the period of the war Elizabeth was to have a voice in the government of the Provinces, and neither party was to make peace without the consent of the other.

On dismissing the commissioners Elizabeth said: 'You
see,

see, gentlemen, that I have opened the door, that I am embarking once for all with you in a war against the King of Spain. Very well, I am not anxious about the matter; I hope God will aid us and that we shall strike a good blow in your cause.' The words expressed a fact, yet in a literal sense they were quite untrue. She never declared war against Spain, nor Philip against England; according to the curiously legalistic mind of the sixteenth century she was therefore no more at war now that she was committed to fight for the rebel Dutch than during the many years past when Englishmen and Spaniards had been killing each other in various parts of the world. Scarcely had the Dutch envoys taken ship for home than she engaged in negotiations for peace, not as a belligerent, but as a neutral with the interests of both Spain and the States at heart. These negotiations went on under that form to the end of her life; they were never more active than during the month before the Armada put out to sea.

The main body of her army embarked in December under the command of Leicester. The choice was not a lucky one, but it was not hers; the Dutch had specially asked for him, since his relation to the Queen and his position as leader of the war party in the country would give him a prestige in Holland that no other Englishman could expect. She parted with him sadly, and also distrustfully — for though she loved him she did not delude herself that he was a Cæsar.

Her doubts were amply justified. Leicester had not been a month in the Netherlands before he was being abused by high and low, while his men, first hailed as saviours, were soon cursed on all sides as insolent intruders. The fault was not altogether his: after a short experience of one another it is the rule that allies should hate one another more than either hates the enemy. The combination of circumstances that the favourite encountered was not dissimilar to those that later baffled even the genius of Marlborough. Many of the

the native politicians still preferred a French alliance and so did everything in their power to discredit the English. A considerable proportion of the people wanted peace, and the rest expected the newcomers to do all the fighting now that they were there. The Dutch leaders had explained frankly in London that what the discontented provinces most needed was a strong central authority, and soon after Leicester's arrival offered him the high-sounding but empty title of Governor of the Netherlands. The States gave titles with facility, but treated the holders with scant respect, a sour truth which Alençon and even the great Orange had had to swallow. Leicester tried to combine the functions of statesman and general to the best of his abilities, but they were insufficient; nor could he suppress his autocratic temper or his taste for grandeur any more than he could cultivate tact and simplicity at a moment's notice. On top of the difficulties created by circumstances of his own temperament was soon piled the angry suspicion of his imperious mistress.

When Elizabeth heard that Leicester had accepted the office of Governor, she flew into such a rage that he could count himself lucky to have a hundred miles of water between him and her. She herself had refused the crown of Holland, had recently given her pledge to Philip, in order to induce him to agree to a general pacification, under no conditions to interfere with its sovereignty. It was out of sheer vanity, she swore, that her lover had usurped a title which was only Spain's to give; he had broken his word, made her 'infamous to all princes,' infinitely complicated the problem of how to help the Dutch without tempting Spain to retaliate or France to intrude. She ordered him to surrender the title or return home. Meantime, she took her revenge on him by withholding financial supplies, thus leaving him to support his army as best he could out of his own resources, which he did to the serious detriment of the fortune she had lavished on him. When the Dutch protested

at

at the curtailment of her subsidies, she merely reminded them that it was their war as well as hers, adding that it was high time they repaid the various loans she had made to them during the previous fifteen years.

It was not an heroic performance, nor a very prudent one. Her annoyance with Leicester was justified, for his acceptance of the title conflicted with her own policy, but it was not unmingled with a vanity similar to his own, a resentment that he had dared to glorify himself without asking her permission. Since he was her representative on the spot, she might have left him some discretion of his own. And the neglect of her troops was unforgivable. But since she had never wanted to send a force to the Continent, she could not be brought to take any deep interest in it; she believed it was doing no good, that on the contrary it was doing much harm to her hopes of a peaceable settlement, and she heartily wished it home again. One cannot imagine a worse spirit in which to wage war. If she was English in her virtues, she was also English in the vice, prevalent for two hundred years amongst succeeding governments, of neglecting the armies they sent to the Continent.

Fear of the consequences of her trespass in the Netherlands made Elizabeth a sorry fighter on land, but there was quite another story to tell of her war by sea. There she was not afraid of what Spain might do in requital, there she had injured Philip again and again, yet each time, after protests and reproaches, he had been constrained to let bygones be bygones. As the vanguard of the little English army under Norris was crossing the North Sea, Drake and his seamen were heading southwestward across the Atlantic. They touched at Vigo on the Spanish coast and at the Cape Verde islands, collecting valuables and destroying sacred images with equal zest. They crossed the Atlantic and repeated the performance against the chief cities of the West Indies and the Spanish Main. When they returned in the summer of 1586, they had so devastated the enemy's trade

trade that Philip's Italian bankers refused him further credit and his merchants begged him to placate the terrible islanders at any cost in pride. There was no question of the Armada sailing that year, for the King could not even pay the contractors who were furnishing the vessels. The honours of the first campaign were undoubtedly with England.

Philip, as anxious for peace as Elizabeth, tried to please his merchants by treating for it on the one hand while pleasing Rome and his war party on the other by setting to work in his dogged way to repair his losses in anticipation of a fresh attempt the following year. His friends in England, who had waited eighteen years for his coming, would have to wait a little longer; Elizabeth, mistress of delay, might temporize for month after month, but Philip, its slave (for it was he whom it injured and she whom it served), acted as well as thought in terms of eternity. Meantime he perused with increasing interest the letters from his ambassador in Paris — the same high-born Mendoza who had been thrown out of England, breathing fire, for his part in the Throgmorton plot — describing a fresh and most promising conspiracy for getting rid of Elizabeth as his other chief tormentor, William of Orange, had been got rid of.

Anthony Babington, a well-to-do young English Catholic who had formerly been page to Mary Stuart, visited Paris in 1585 and as a matter of course was there drawn into the circle of English malcontents and exiles who, in every Catholic capital, were urging the invasion of England and serving as means of communication between their country's enemies abroad and their Queen's enemies at home. Amongst this group the traveller met Thomas Morgan, Mary Stuart's chief agent in Paris, and from him learned the outlines of a scheme for Elizabeth's assassination. On his return to England, Babington carried letters of introduction from Morgan to various of the Queen of Scots' active partisans, including

including a Jesuit priest named John Ballard who worked out the actual details of the plot. Babington and five friends who had access to the Court were to kill Elizabeth and her chief ministers, while another group was to seize Mary during the subsequent commotion, hurry her to London, and proclaim her succession to the vacant throne.

The plot was, in Mendoza's opinion, and he was an expert in such matters, by far the best yet devised for Elizabeth's undoing. Babington and his friends were unsuspected persons, the Queen of Scots was more laxly guarded than she had been for some time past, and Spanish arms were nearly ready to take advantage of the opportunity that success would create. On his ambassador's recommendation Philip sent the conspirators his grave approval of their efforts and a hundred thousand crowns to help defray their expenses, together with the interesting suggestion that Burghley should be exempted from the ministerial slaughter, since he was friendly to Spain and in any event too old (the Lord Treasurer was then sixty-six) to do much harm.

There was one serious flaw in the conspiracy, however. The one man who knew more about it than even Mendoza, Mary, Babington, or Ballard, the man who before it reached its climax became its most active member, was the Queen's Secretary, Sir Francis Walsingham.

The Babington plot had given the Secretary and his colleagues the chance for which they had yearned these many years. Time and again Mary had been caught in murderous intrigues, with Ridolfi, Throgmorton, Parry, and others; time and again Walsingham, broken in health and weary in spirit, complained that all his vigilance was in vain unless 'the bosom serpent' were removed; yet Elizabeth had persisted in shielding her from the punishment that the Council and public opinion strenuously demanded. On each previous occasion Elizabeth had given the excuse that the evidence of Mary's guilt was insufficient for the execution of the royal prisoner, or that there was

no

no law that covered her case, or else that the danger had not been sufficiently great to warrant a resort to extremities. This time, therefore, Walsingham, from the moment he obtained his first inkling of the conspiracy, made up his mind that the evidence both of Mary's guilt and of Elizabeth's danger should be so watertight that the Queen would no longer be able to overlook it, while he relied on the Bond of Association, signed by Mary and enacted into a statute by Parliament, to provide the legal machinery that had hitherto been lacking.

The strictness of Mary's captivity varied with the general state of affairs. In 1583, when Walsingham was on the scent of the Guises and the Throgmorton plot, she had been removed from the care of the kindly Shrewsbury to that of the less susceptible Sadler, and from pleasant Wingfield to gloomy Tutbury. The transfer was accompanied by a domestic scandal. Lady Shrewsbury, famous in her generation as the shrew Bess of Hardwick, was loudly accusing her husband and his captive of carrying on a love affair. There was probably nothing in the accusation — the termagant was never careful of her words — but in the precarious state of the time it was thought best to give Mary a sterner keeper. Mary retaliated by dashing off a furious letter to Elizabeth in which she repeated every lewd slander concerning Elizabeth that the coarse-tongued Bess had repeated to her during their long years under the same roof. The Queen had been accused, so Mary called God to witness, of indulging in the most disgusting familiarities with Leicester, Alençon, Simier, Hatton, and others not mentioned by name, all of whom were represented as sneering at her behind her back. It was also implied, still on the same authority, that she was suffering from a foul and incurable disease. As a specimen of feminine spite the letter could hardly have been bettered: it made one of the writer's enemies acutely uncomfortable and obtained the other's imprisonment while leaving the writer herself in the position

position of a disinterested conduit of information. On reading it Elizabeth ordered the Countess to be sent to the Tower, whereupon her amiable husband, just relieved of his royal captive, flung himself at the Queen's feet and fervently thanked her for having rid him of two devils simultaneously.

In June of 1586, Mary's jail and jailer were again changed. Her new keeper was the dour and incorruptible Puritan Sir Amyas Paulet, but her residence was as gracious as she could have wished, the Earl of Essex's country house, Chartley — indeed she had asked for it herself. Nearly all supervision of her visitors and correspondence was removed, and in general she was treated more as a guest than as a prisoner. She believed that her own cunning in dealing with Elizabeth had deluded the Queen into granting her these favours, never dreaming that it was Walsingham who had intervened to obtain them for her so that she might have full freedom to incriminate herself in the Babington conspiracy.

It was sheer stupidity that she did not see it. Previous experiences should have taught her the bitter lesson that her adversaries' resolution equalled and their resources greatly exceeded her own; they could still open her letters, search her rooms, arrest or bribe her servants at will. Yet she continued to pin her faith on her own ingenuity, to trust the vague promises of her powerful yet powerless friends abroad and the eager assurance of her little circle of enthusiasts in England. She took quite seriously the advances that various of Elizabeth's Council and courtiers had made to her, not realizing that those astute gentlemen were merely insuring themselves against an uncertain future and would be happy to diminish its uncertainty by having her permanently out of the way. After eighteen years of captivity she no longer understood anything of the world in which she lived, nothing of the difficulties in the way of her ambitions, nothing of the change in England or the spirit of the English people which had expressed itself

in

in that Bond which she had so lightly signed. She had become a living anachronism.

Whole-heartedly she entered into the Babington conspiracy and Chartley became the clearing-house for all the letters that passed between the various confederates in Paris, Flanders, and England. The Queen of Scots, with the aid of two secretaries, one French, the other English, read, dictated, coded all day and often until late at night. Immediately afterwards Walsingham read and deciphered the same correspondence. One of his spies, Gilbert Gifford, was amongst the most active of the conspirators. The brewer who supplied Mary's household with beer was in the Secretary's pay, and the letters which she thought were being craftily smuggled in and out by means of the brewer's barrels were always delivered first to Phillips, Walsingham's expert in codes, who opened and copied them before sending them on to their destination and deciphering the codes at his leisure. The brewer overcharged Mary for her beer on the ground that he was entitled to extra compensation for the risk he was running. Gifford demanded and received from her a pension for his services.

Throughout the summer of 1586 the game of cat and mouse went on. Dozens knew of the conspiracy from Mary's side; Walsingham told only Elizabeth and Leicester of his and his agents' discoveries. He had enough, and more than enough, to prove a guilty conspiracy, but he was not ready to spring until he was sure that the arch-plotter would not again be offered sanctuary by his Queen. At last he had what he wanted. On July 17, Mary, in answer to a letter from Babington describing the details of the actual assassination, wrote to her 'Trusty and well-Beloved' endorsing in all respects his plan for the Queen's murder. If that was not enough, reflected Walsingham, Elizabeth must positively desire a dagger between her ribs. Early in August he ordered the arrest of Babington and his fellow plotters.

It

It was nearly too late: the conspirators had already taken alarm and fled from out of the very hands of the Secretary's police come to fetch them in a London tavern. A few days later Babington and a few others were found hiding at Harrow. The rest were subsequently tracked down in other parts of the country, and only the priest Ballard got safely away to France. The prisoners were tried in September and, after confessing their own and one another's guilt, were condemned to death. The first batch were executed according to the terrible customary sentence, but the Queen, unable to bear the torture of her own imagination, ordered the remainder to be put to death by simple hanging.

Mary was removed, shrilly protesting, to the castle of Fotheringay in Northamptonshire, having vainly tried to destroy her letters and codes at Chartley — the immovable Paulet brusquely cleared her and her retinue out in order to leave the way free for Walsingham's search-party, who nearly dismantled the house in their search for the departing tenant's papers.

Not even yet did she realize the full extent of her danger; so often had she plotted against her cousin's life, and so often been let off, that she genuinely believed, with a conviction amounting almost to contempt for Elizabeth's weakness, in her own immunity. She was a sovereign, her friends were strong, her enemy frightened and indecisive: so she reasoned, and many of the English people feared that she was only too justified.

But this time she was wrong. Walsingham had foreseen her every excuse and explanation, had allowed for that illogical stubbornness of Elizabeth's where Mary Stuart was concerned. When he laid before his Queen her captive's cold-blooded approval of Babington's scheme to kill her by exploiting her trust in the people who surrounded her, she was less angry — though she was that, too, and fiercely — than resigned. She recognized that it would be mad to protect the 'bosom serpent,' the 'daughter of debate' any longer.

longer. Feeling was running so high against the Queen of Scots — Walsingham had seen to it that the public knew of her latest crime — that it would have been very difficult for Elizabeth to shield her at that moment, even if she had wanted to.

On October 11, 1586, Mary appeared before a jury of forty-six of the leading men of the realm to answer to the charge of high treason. She refused, as in 1568, to acknowledge the jurisdiction of the court on the ground that she was a foreign sovereign. With extraordinary ability she argued the complicated technical question of her liability to the law of England; gallantly and brilliantly she examined and attacked the fabric of evidence against her. The magnificence of her defence has largely obscured the fact that it was irrelevant and untrue. In law she had abdicated her sovereignty, and James was universally recognized as King of Scotland. It would indeed have been strange had she been able to plot murder and invasion on English soil, lay claim to the English Crown, yet hold herself above English law. She herself, by signing the Bond of Association, had voluntarily brought herself under its clear-cut provisions. She had a more plausible defence in the fact that she was allowed to see only the copies of the letters on which the prosecution was based; but the originals were of course unavailable, for they had been sent on by Walsingham to her friends. She herself openly withdrew her original statement that the Secretary had interpolated incriminating matter into the copies; and Mendoza's letters to Philip, which did not pass through Walsingham's hands, largely corroborated the story told by the Babington correspondence. It may be granted that the court was prejudiced against her, eager to secure a condemnation for reasons of State; but amongst the judges were friends like Montague and Croft, and they uttered no dissent when the majority found her guilty and passed sentence of death.

The last word, however, remained with Elizabeth, and the

the familiar paralysis of will came over her as she stood confronted by the fearful moment she had avoided for nearly nineteen years. If ever in her life Elizabeth stood alone, it was in those late autumn months of 1586. On the one side her ministers and the great majority of her people argued and implored that the implacable exile be put where she could no longer injure the State in the gravest hour of the reign; the Kings of France and Scotland on the other threatened revenge — at the moment that Spain was arming — if Mary's life were taken. As if unhearing, Elizabeth moved through her duties tight-lipped, non-committal, retiring into long periods of solitude from which she emerged with eyes red from weeping. Habit, principle, fear, an imagination terrified of death and the fearful responsibility of commanding it, all these plucked at her woman's heartstrings while her brain passed in cold review the consequences of signing the warrant that her ministers pressed upon her. A sentence in a letter from Leicester to Walsingham throws a vivid flash of light on those months during which Elizabeth fought out the greatest internal conflict of her life, with her advisers taking anxious note of each change in her mood: 'There is a letter from the Scottish Queen that hath wrought tears; but I trust shall do no further therein, albeit the delay is too dangerous.'

Parliament met at the end of October and sent a committee with a petition signed by every member of both houses that the Queen of Scots be executed immediately. The committee, kneeling, rehearsed the long list of Mary's 'wicked and detestable offences,' concluding with the plea that if the warrant 'be not put in present execution, we your most loving and dutiful subjects shall thereby (so far as man's reason can reach) be brought into utter despair of the continuance amongst us of the true religion of Almighty God and of Your Majesty's life, and the safety of all your faithful subjects and the good estate of this most flourishing commonweal.

Elizabeth

Elizabeth, 'with great majesty of countenance and voice,' answered candidly that if there were any way in which she yet could spare Mary's life she would gladly do so and begged her petitioners to retire to consider whether such a way could not be found. Her reply was drawn from the same well of speech that supplied the language for the Authorized Version of the Bible:

> And even yet, though the matter be come thus far, if she would truly repent, and no man would undertake her cause against me, and if my life alone depended hereupon, and not the safety and welfare of my whole people, I would (I protest unfeignedly) most willingly pardon her. Nay, if England might by my death attain a more flourishing estate, and a better prince, I would most gladly lay down my life. For, for your sakes it is, and for my people's, that I desire to live. As for me I see no such great cause why I should either be fond to live or fear to die. I have had good experience of this world, and I know what it is to be a subject, and what to be a sovereign. Good neighbours I have had, and I have met with bad; and in trust I have found treason. I have bestowed benefits upon ill deservers; and where I have done well, have been ill requited…

Parliament considered the matter further and in a long paper, filled with legal argument and historical precedent for a sovereign's execution, repeated its prayer —'as it were injustice to deny execution of law to any one of her subjects that should demand it, so much more, to her whole people of England, with one voice and mind making humble and instant suit for the same.'

Again Elizabeth put them off, not as she had dismissed the importunate Commons in 1566, but by a plea to them as fellow trustees of the State, to bear with her in this 'greater conflict with myself than ever in my life.... I pray you for this present to content yourselves with an answer that is no answer.' It was in this second speech that she uttered the defence of herself and her reign that no biographer will ever approach in eloquence — or essentially in truth:

When

... When first I took the sceptre I was not unmindful of God the giver, and therefore began my reign with His service and the religion I had been both born in, bred in, and I trust shall die in. And though I was not ignorant how many perils I should be beset withal at home for altering religion, and how many great princes abroad, of a contrary profession, would attempt all hostility against me, yet was I no whit dismayed, knowing that God, whom only I respected, would defend both me and my cause. Hence it is that so many treacheries and conspiracies have been attempted against me that I rather marvel that I am, than muse that I should not be, were it not that God's holy hand hath protected me beyond all expectation. Then to the end I might make the better progress in the art of swaying the sceptre I entered into long and serious cogitation what things were worthy and fitting for kings to do; and I found it most necessary that they should be abundantly furnished with those special virtues, justice, temperance, prudence, and magnanimity. As for the two latter I will not boast myself; my sex doth not permit it; but for the two former I dare say (and that without ostentation) I never made a difference of persons where right was one; I never preferred for favour whom I thought not fit for worth; I never bent my ear to credit a tale that was first told, nor was so rash to corrupt my judgment with prejudice, before I heard the cause. I will not say but many reports might haply be brought me in too much favour of the one side or the other; for we princes cannot hear all ourselves; yet this I dare say boldly, my judgment went ever with the truth according to my understanding. And as full well Alcibiades wished his friend not to give any answer till he had run over the letters of the alphabet; so have I not used rash and sudden resolutions in anything. And, therefore, as touching your counsels and consultations, I acknowledge them to be so careful, provident, and profitable for the preservation of my life, and to proceed from minds so sincere and to me most devoted, that I shall endeavour myself all I can, to give you cause to think your pains not ill-bestowed, and strive to make myself worthy of such subjects...

It was a pity for her own reputation that she did not on this occasion obey Parliament. In her torment and indecision she did shameful things: wrote lying and disingenuous letters to Henry III and James VI, which were perfectly futile to deceive even a child; listened to the sinister hint

hint of the Scottish ambassador, the Master of Gray, that there was a simpler way out than a public execution, and brooded over it until at length she had Walsingham write to Sir Amyas Paulet an intimation that he would earn her eternal gratitude if his prisoner happened to die suddenly. But honest Paulet, 'that precise and dainty fellow' as the distracted Queen called him, responded that 'my life and my goods are at my Queen's disposal,' but that 'God forbid I should make so foul a shipwreck of my conscience, or leave so great a blot to my poor posterity to shed blood without law or warrant.' He was right and she soon saw it, for she never held his refusal against him. But his uprightness did not help her in her dilemma.

Her final decision was hastened by a group of her ministers, led by Walsingham, who laid before her the details of a new plot on Mary's behalf involving several important Englishmen and the French ambassador. The plot was largely imaginary, but the fraud succeeded in frightening Elizabeth, as it was intended to do. On February 1, 1587, she asked for the warrant, which had been for two months lying drafted but unsigned, and wrote her name across it without a tremor. The document was then taken by one of the secretaries, Davison, to have the Great Seal stamped upon it. As she handed it over she told Davison, with a flash of sardonic humour, to call and inform Walsingham, who was lying ill at home, of what she had done: 'The grief thereof,' she remarked dryly, 'will go near to kill him outright.'

The Council finished the matter. While Elizabeth again hesitated and talked of recalling the warrant, the ministers hurried it off to Fotheringay, where on February 8, on the eve of the twentieth anniversary of Darnley's murder, the Queen of Scots made her glorious exit from life.

So she gained her eternal victory over her cousin. After nineteen years during which Elizabeth had protected Mary and Mary had repaid her by plotting to kill her, Elizabeth finally

finally issued from their contest as the mean victor and Mary as the sublime vanquished. Men are always magnanimous in awarding haloes to the defeated when the cause they fought for can do no further harm. Romantic sympathy goes out to Brutus rather than to Cæsar, to Lee rather than to Grant, to Cavalier rather than to Puritan; for the same reason posterity has dealt tenderly with Mary Stuart and harshly with the cousin who vanquished her. Yet Mary took from her cause far more than she gave to it, hurt it more than she helped it, and offered to betray it when she thought to benefit herself thereby. Her death made her an appealing figure of tragedy; nothing in her life justified her elevation to the high place she occupies in history.

To the harassed, desperate Queen who survived, alone with her appalling responsibilities, was left the task of writing the sordid finis to the story with the sacrifice of poor Davison, whom she flung into the Tower on the dishonest charge of having delivered the death-warrant without her consent. It was a last, vain, frantic effort to divert reproach for the Scottish Queen's execution from her own shoulders — and from the Crown of England.

For nearly a generation the hopes and efforts of Catholic Europe had centred in Mary Stuart, yet now that she was gone the friends on whom she had counted continued in their separate ways as if she had never been. Her brother-in-law, Henry III of France, and her son wrote the protests that were expected of them, whereafter the one returned to his three-cornered civil war and the other to winning the men who had been responsible for his mother's death to the support of his claim to the succession. Philip of Spain set his genealogists to work to prove that he had an equally good title to Elizabeth's crown, derived from distant John of Gaunt, and at length concluded his many months of bitter haggling with the Pope in a bargain whereby the Pontiff promised to contribute a million ducats in gold towards the

conquest

conquest of England, half on the landing, half by easy monthly instalments.

The reigning Pope was Sixtus V, who had succeeded in 1585. He was the first statesman to occupy the chair of Saint Peter for half a century, and the person he most admired on earth was the Queen of England. 'What a woman!' he exclaimed, 'she braves the greatest king by land and sea.' At another time he declared that 'if she had not been a heretic she would be worth a whole world,' and regretted that he and she were not free to marry, since they two would have bred progeny capable of ruling the whole earth. But circumstances forbade him to indulge his admiration and compelled him both to supply the million ducats for her destruction and renew her excommunication in 'a roaring hellish Papal Bull' — whereupon she, who in general reciprocated his sentiments, repaid the compliment by having the Holy Father excommunicated with full ceremony in Saint Paul's Cathedral.

Meantime, Elizabeth and Philip, through Parma, continued to discuss terms of peace, to the alarm and suspicion of the English ministers and the Dutch ally. She was sincere and he was not, for he was using the discussions as a blind for the undertaking to which he now stood irretrievably committed. But she was not deceived by his manœuvres into overlooking the shipbuilding going on in Spanish ports — there never was a better advertised expedition — and her preparations to meet her enemy were as efficient as and much quieter than his. In March of 1587, just as Mendoza was writing to his King that the English fleet was out of commission, Drake was making ready to sail to the very coast of Spain. So deep was the secrecy that only a few of the ministers knew what was afoot, and even they were not sure that Drake would be allowed to go. But go he did, on April 3, to be followed by an order forbidding him to do any damage to Philip's subjects. The order was sent by slow boat, so that it failed to overtake the English admiral, but it was preserved

to

to show to the King of Spain later in case he protested against Drake's ravages. The English vessels rode into Cadiz harbour, burnt thirty-one vessels of war and carried off four others loaded with supplies. Drake thought of going on to Lisbon, but after reconnoitring it decided that it was too well fortified and sailed for home, capturing a rich merchantman on the way. That ended the possibilities of an invasion during 1587. Philip, methodical and resigned, drew on the Papal loan for the replacement of his lost vessels.

The year 1587 passed with further parleyings and a few skirmishes in the Netherlands, including the action at Zutphen in August, where Leicester lost his brilliant, chivalrous nephew, Sir Philip Sidney; in December he surrendered his command and returned to England. All the Councillors were by then deep in peace negotiations, even the war party, who hoped as ardently as their opponents to find the successful policy and so win the Queen's favour. Elizabeth herself listened to and encouraged all, but committed herself to none. In the dockyards Sir John Hawkins was fitting out his new ships and repairing the old, with money largely derived from the profits the Queen had made out of her investments in his and his fellows' raids on Spanish property by sea and land. Otherwise there was in England little sign of warlike preparation except for the youths awkwardly drilling under their local captains on the village greens.

Winter turned to spring and over the whole of Europe there settled a tension as if the Day of Judgment were approaching. All other news sank into insignificance beside the reports, surmises, estimates that went forth from diplomatic and commercial agents regarding that legendary fleet nearing completion in the Tagus. Hostilities almost died out in France and Flanders; it was as if men had laid all else aside while watching in fascination the opening of the duel on which the success of their own affairs and the outcome of their own quarrels hung.

The Armada was expected with the first good weather. When

When it did not appear, Elizabeth's admirals impatiently asked permission to go and look for it. She refused; they as experienced fighting men took the line that the best defence is a strong offence, but she, with the morale of the country to consider, did not consider it prudent to leave the coast unprotected in case her fleet missed the Spaniards at sea. May passed without a sign of it, and in England and elsewhere it began to be said that perhaps the Colossus would not dare, after all, to send forth the Invincible Armada.

The reasons for the delay were the doubt and confusion in the mind of the larger adversary. Rumours came from Spain that Philip was so frightened of a catastrophe that he spoke openly of abdicating. His greatest subject, the Prince of Parma, wrote from the Netherlands in March that the expedition's prospects were dubious: 'It may be that God desires to punish us for our sins by some heavy disaster.' A common point of view amongst neutrals friendly to Spain was expressed by the Venetian ambassador in France:

> It is generally held that the King of Spain will not undertake so vast an enterprise… for he very well knows how much consideration ought to be paid to such a fleet as the English fleet, both on account of its size, and also because the English are men of another mettle from the Spaniards, and enjoy the reputation of being above all the Western nations expert and active in all naval operations, and great sea-dogs.

But Philip was only hesitating, as usual, over ways and means: there was no longer any question of his staying his hand. Long and laboriously he and his advisers worked over the plan of campaign. In the end his admiral was instructed, somewhat vaguely, to proceed up the Channel, effect a junction with Parma at the mouth of the Scheldt, and cover the transport of Parma's troops, together with the reinforcements carried from Spain, to the Thames estuary. It was confidently anticipated that the English Catholics

Catholics would rise to co-operate in the landing. The plan was much superior to the one originally considered, an invasion of the south coast by the fleet, for it concentrated all Spain's strength at England's weakest point and if it succeeded would be immediately decisive. In June the order was given and the Duke of Medina Sidonia, who had never sailed a ship, led out to sea his seven score of vessels, the lovely high-decked galleons for which Spain's future had been pawned.

England was ready. In that hour of its supreme trial every stone in the Elizabethan structure of State that had taken thirty years in the building was tested and found to be well and solidly laid. The Catholics, instead of rising to greet the deliverer, joined with the Protestants to repel him, for in the hour of danger they remembered only that they were Englishmen. In the rear stood the Scots, armed to defend their neighbour and ancient enemy; in France, Henry of Navarre and his German allies, both dependents on Elizabeth's treasury, kept the Guises desperately engaged. The Dutch ally roved the North Sea to threaten Parma if he came forth to assist the Armada by a sudden attack on England's eastern flank. Elizabeth, unlike her enemy, had no need of desperate last-minute borrowings from reluctant friends and extortions from disgruntled subjects, or the extravagant improvisation of a host of floating fortresses. She was the paymistress who by her disbursements had isolated her adversary; her small ships and her subjects' had evolved through the varied years into the most efficient fighting fleet that had ever ridden the ocean.

She has been accused of crippling her navy by starving it of ammunition during the action that followed. But this reproach, like so many levelled against her, is based on a complete misunderstanding of conditions. No such naval engagement had ever taken place in the world's history as that running fight of ten days up the Channel; Spanish veterans declared that Lepanto had been child's play
compared

compared with the fire they sustained in the single day of Gravelines. The English fleet was supplied according to the custom and experience of the time, and the supply replenished at sea as fast as possible, but no one had ever seen or anticipated such an expenditure of powder and shot as was poured into the enemy from the moment that Drake warped his vessels out of Plymouth Harbour until the great Spanish galleons were pushed through the Straits of Dover into the teeth of that immortal gale. 'God blew with His winds and they were scattered': the legend, at once humble and arrogant, that was engraved on the commemorative medal, was not intended to summarize the whole of the epic conflict that the south wind entered only in its last stage — certainly no one, least of all her sailors, would have read it as a criticism of Elizabeth's administration. Not twenty years ago the mightiest British fleet that ever breasted the ocean found its ammunition inadequate to the demands of an engagement which exceeded all expectation and experience....

The Council, anxious to keep the Queen from exposing herself to a bullet from a hired assassin or a fanatic unbalanced by that summer of broiling suspense, entreated her to retire from the capital until the decision was known. She complied, less from fear of being killed than because the only hope of resistance in the event of Parma's actual landing was her safe presence in some spot remote from London. But to remain in quiet seclusion at such a time was impossible for her: at the beginning of August she turned up at Tilbury, where Leicester was preparing the army for a defence by land in case the worst occurred, to hearten her soldiers by her presence and her words:

My loving People, we have been persuaded by some, that are careful of our safety, to take heed how we commit ourselves to armed multitudes, for fear of treachery. But I assure you I do not desire to live to distrust my faithful and loving people. Let tyrants fear; I have always so behaved myself that, under God,
                                                                    I have

I have placed chiefest strength and safeguard in the loyal hearts and good-will of my subjects... I know I have but the body of a weak and feeble woman; but I have the heart of a King, and of a King of England, too; and think scorn that Parma or Spain, or any Prince of Europe, should dare to invade the borders of my realms....

It is as well that she did not know at the time that the danger was already past, for that wonderful speech would have remained unuttered. Scarcely had the echo of her harsh, resonant voice died away than there flew in the dispatch scribbled by Drake in the heat and fury of combat, to announce that her confidence in herself and her people had been triumphantly justified:

We have the army of Spain before us and mind with the Grace of God to wrestle a pull with him. There was never anything pleased me better than seeing the enemy flying with a southerly wind to the Northward... I doubt it not but ere it be long so to handle the matter with the Duke of Medina Sidonia as he shall wish himself at Saint Mary Port among his orange trees...

— the exultant assurance from the commander of victory to his sovereign that the mightiest force her enemies could assemble against her had proved unavailing, and to the world that the unhappy little country which she had been called to rule had succeeded to its place amongst the great nations.

One cannot but wish that the young man of twenty-four, recently fled from Stratford to London, had chosen to record what passed before him during the day of November 17, 1588: the vast surging of the people between Whitehall and Ludgate; the joyous peal of the bells from the City's hundred church-towers; the gilded coach slowly driven through the narrow lane between the craning masses of humanity; the gaunt, grotesque figure in purple sitting upright within, her thin lips smiling their recognition of her subjects' frenzied cheers, her heart sad (for that this remarkable

able young man would have taken account of too) because the man she had so long loved had died but a few weeks before. The youth was not important enough to have been a spectator of the service in Saint Paul's Cathedral, where all the great of the land were joined in solemn thanksgiving both for the recent victory and for the blessings the realm had enjoyed in the thirty years, that day concluded, of the reign of its Sovereign Lady. He would more likely have strolled thoughtfully through the City to London Bridge and thence across to the low-ceilinged tavern he frequented on the other, less-crowded side of the river, there to hear his elders describe again, in their rich virile speech, the first coming of the handsome young Queen to her capital these many years since; exchange anew the anecdotes of her tempers and her graciousness, her courage and her wit, her hardiness and her extravagances; and count over once more with wealth of illustration and metaphor and wondering oath the marvels through which they had lived under her rule. It is a custom among poets to employ their eloquence upon times gone by rather than the time that is, and the listener deferred to that practice; or else he forsook his art too soon: so he cheated posterity of a last and the most splendid scene in the sequence of chronicles he composed to the glory of England's history.

THE END

BIBLIOGRAPHY

So FAR as possible I have tried to confine my studies to contemporary papers. The fundamentals for any historical knowledge of the period are contained in the various *Calendars of State Papers*. The series vary greatly, some stopping short of completion for the relevant years, some printing dispatches *in extenso*, while others contain bare *précis*. Hence I have filled in their gaps with such collections of documents, letters, etc., as are contained in Forbes, for instance, for the first five years, especially in foreign affairs; Fénelon and Sharp for the revolt in the North; *The Zürich Letters* for the Anglican Establishment; Kervyn de Lettenhove for relations with the Netherlands, etc. The title of the reference and the years that each covers will, I think, indicate which part of the book the various items in the bibliography have served.

As to the secondary sources, the grand historical framework is still best seen in Froude, though not many will now agree either with his views of the issues or the characters involved; nevertheless it will be long before any student will be able to dispense with the fruits of his scholarship, however much he may ignore his judgments. Mr. Conyers Read has provided the best and amplest study yet published of policy and its fluctuations between 1571 and 1590; while for a brief, lucid, and intelligent history of the reign, especially its earlier part, no single volume can compare with Professor Pollard's. I should like to add that, on the never-to-be-settled question of the Casket Letters, I have tried to read all the controversial literature on both sides, as well as the Letters in their surviving form and whatever relevant material came my way in the course of my reading on Elizabeth; I have not, of course, attempted to re-examine the whole matter from the beginning, as that would have been outside my province and is in itself a life-work; and I owe the view taken of the Letters themselves — not of Mary Stuart nor her relations with Elizabeth, however, in which I differ from him — to Andrew Lang's work on the subject, which seems on the whole to offer the most plausible solution.

A. CONTAINING CONTEMPORARY DOCUMENTS, LETTERS, DISPATCHES, ACTS, ETC.

Acts of the Privy Council, ed. by J. R. Dasent, 1893-1907.
Armada Papers, ed. by J. Laughton, Navy Records Society, 1898.
Ascham, Roger, *Scholemaster*, ed. 1904.

Birch, Thomas, *Memoirs of the Reign of Queen Elizabeth*, 1754.

Bruce, John, *Correspondence of James VI with Cecil and Others in England During the Reign of Elizabeth*, ed. 1861.

Calendar of State Papers, Domestic, of the reign of Elizabeth, with 2 vols. of *Addenda*, 1547-90.

Calendar of State Papers, Foreign, Elizabeth, 1558-88.

Calendar of State Papers, Foreign, of the reign of Mary.

Calendar of State Papers, Foreign and Domestic, of the reign of Henry VIII.

Calendar of State Papers, Roman, 1558-78.

Calendar of State Papers, Scottish, 1547-88.

Calendar of State Papers, Spanish, 1558-84.

Calendar of State Papers, Venetian, vols. VII-VIII.

Camden, William, *Annales*, 3d ed., by R.N. (Richard Norton), 1635.

Castelnau, Michel de, Sieur de Mauvissière, *Ambassade, etc.*, 1575-85, ed. 1856.

Cobbett, William, *State Trials*, 1809.

Corbett, Sir Julian, *Spanish War Papers*, 1585-87, Navy Records Society, 1898.

Cottonian Manuscripts.

D'Ewes, Sir Symonds, *Journal... of the House of Lords and Commons Throughout the Whole Reign of Elizabeth*, ed. 1693.

Digges, Dudley, *The Compleat Ambassador*, 1655.

Elizabeth — *Letters to James VI*, ed. 1849.

Ellis, Sir Henry, *Original Letters Illustrative of English History*, ed. 1825.

Fénelon, Bertrand de Salignac de la Mothe, *Dépêches et Correspondance Diplomatique*, 1568-75, ed. 1838-40.

Forbes, P., *A Full View of Public Transactions in the Reign of Queen Elizabeth*, 1558-63, ed. 1740-41.

Fugger News Letters, Series I and II, 1568-1605. Ed. by Victor von Klarwill, 1924-26.

Gonzalez, Tomás, *Documents from Simancas Relating to the Reign of Elizabeth* (1558-68), translated from the Spanish; ed. by Spencer Hall, 1865.

Green, Mary E., *Letters of Royal and Illustrious Ladies of Great Britain*, 3 vols., 1864.

Hakluyt, Richard, *Principal Navigations*, ed. by Sir Walter Raleigh, 1905.

Hardwicke State Papers, ed. 1778.

Harington, Henry, *Nugae Antiquae*, ed. 1779.

Harleian Miscellany, ed. 1809.

Haynes, Samuel, *Burghley Papers*; *A Collection of State Papers*, 1542-70; 1740.

Hentzner, Paul, *A Journey to England*, 1598, ed. 1757.

Historical MSS. Commission, *Calendar of the MSS. at Hatfield House.*

Holinshed, Ralph, *Chronicles of England, Scotland and Ireland*, 1587.

Jewell, Bullinger *et al.*, *Zürich Letters*, ed. 1845.

Kervyn de Lettenhove, *Relations Politiques des Pays-Bas et de l'Angleterre*, 1555-79, ed. 1882-1900.

Klarwill, Victor von, *Queen Elizabeth and Some Foreigners*, from Austrian archives chiefly, ed. 1928.

Leicester, Earl of, *Correspondence*, Camden Society, 1844.
Leti, Gregoria, *La Vie d'Elizabeth, Reine d'Angleterre*; Amsterdam, 1694.
Lodge, Edmund, *Illustrations of British History*, ed. 1838.
Maisse, André Hurault, *Sieur de*; translated by G. B. Harrison and R. A. Jones, 1931.
Manning, Canon C. R. (ed. by), 'Bedingfeld Papers'; *Norfolk Archæology*, vol. IV, 1855.
Melville, Sir James, *Memoirs*, 3d ed., 1752.
Mumby, Frank A., *The Girlhood of Queen Elizabeth*, London, 1909.
Navarrete, Fernandez de, *Colección de Documentos Inéditos para la Historia de España*, tomo 87, 1842.
Parker, Matthew, *Correspondence of Archbishop Parker*, ed. 1853
Pollard, A. F., *Tudor Tracts*, 1903.
Pollen, Father S., *Papal Negotiations with Mary Queen of Scots*, 1561-67 (Scot. Hist. Soc., 1901).
Ranke, Leopold von, *History of England*, 6 vols., 1875.
Raumer, Friedrich L. G. von, *Geschichte Europas*, vol. II.
Rymer, T., *Foedera....* etc. (for texts of treaties), ed. 1704-32.
Sharpe, Sir Cuthbert, *Memorials of the Rebellion of 1569*, ed. 1841.
Smith, Sir Thomas, *De Republica Anglarum*, 1583.
Somers, Lord, *Collection of Tracts*, 1809-15.
Statutes of the Realm, vol. IV, ed. 1819.
Stow, John, *Annales*, 1605.
Strype, John, *Annals of the Reformation*, ed. 1824.
Tawney, R. H., and Power, E., *Tudor Economic Documents*, 1924.
Vertot, René de, *Ambassades de Messieurs de Noailles en Angleterre*, Leyden, 1763.
Weiss, Cardinal de, *Papiers d'Etat du Cardinal Granvelle*, vol. IV, Paris, 1843.
Wiesener, Louis, *La Jeunesse d'Elisabeth d'Angleterre*, 1533-58, translated by C. M. Yonge.
Winwood, Sir Ralph, *Memorials of Affairs of State Collected from Pages of*, ed. 1725.
Wood, Anthony à, *Athenae Oxonienses*, 1820.
Wright, Thomas, *Queen Elizabeth and her Times*, 1838.

B. LATER AUTHORITIES CONSULTED

Aikin, Lucy, *Memoirs of the Court of Queen Elizabeth*.
Cambridge Modern History, vols. II-III, 1903-4.
Cheyney, E. P., *Social Changes in England in the Sixteenth Century*, 1895.
Child, Gilbert W., *Church and State Under the Tudors*, 1890.
Corbett, Sir Julian, *Drake and the Tudor Navy*, 1898.
Creighton, Mandell, *Queen Elizabeth*, 1899.
Dictionary of National Biography (Oxford University Press edition, 1921-22).
Edwards, Edward, *Life and Times of Sir Walter Raleigh*, 1868.
Fleming, D. H., *Mary Queen of Scots*, 1897.

Froude, James Anthony, *History of England from the Fall of Wolsey to the Armada*, 1856, vols. VI-XII.

Goodall, W., *Examination of Letters said to be Written by Mary Queen of Scots to Bothwell*, 2 vols., 1754.

Henderson, T. F., *Mary Queen of Scots*, 1905.

Lang, Andrew, *Mystery of Mary Stuart*, 1901.

Machiavelli, Nicolo, *The Prince*. Everyman Edition.

Mahon, Major-General Reginald Henry, *The Indictment of Mary Queen of Scots*, 1923. *Mary Queen of Scots: Lennox Narrative*, 1924. *The Tragedy of Kirk O' Field*, 1930.

Motley, J. L., *Rise of the Dutch Republic*, 1912.

Naunton, Sir Robert, *Fragmenta Regalia*, 1641.

Nichols, John, *Progresses and Public Processions of Queen Elizabeth*, 1805.

Oppenheim, Sir J., *History of the Administration of the Royal Navy*, 1896, vol. I.

Pollard, A. F., *Political History of England*, 1547-1603; 1910.

Pollen, Father J., *Mary Stuart and the Babington Plot*, 1922.

Read, Conyers, *Mr. Secretary Walsingham and the Policy of Queen Elizabeth*, 1925.

Shakespeare's England. By various authors, 1926 impression, Clarendon Press.

Skelton, Sir John, *Maitland of Lethington*, 1894.

Spedding, James, *Letters and Life of Francis Bacon*, 1874.

Steuart, A. Francis, *Trial of Mary Queen of Scots*, 1923.

Strickland, Agnes, *Lives of the Queens of England*, 1840-9, vol. III (*Mary and Elizabeth*).

Taylor, William Cooke, *Age of Elizabeth*, 1842.

Williamson, J. A., *Sir John Hawkins*, 1927.

INDEX